ECONOMICS 2.0

ECONOMICS 2.0

WHAT THE BEST MINDS IN ECONOMICS CAN TEACH YOU ABOUT BUSINESS AND LIFE

Norbert Häring and **Olaf Storbeck**

palgrave
macmillan

ECONOMICS 2.0
Copyright © Norbert Häring, Olaf Storbeck
Translated into English by Jutta Scherer (JS textworks, Munich,
Germany), 2009.

All rights reserved.

First published in 2009 by
PALGRAVE MACMILLAN®
in the United States—a division of St. Martin's Press LLC,
175 Fifth Avenue, New York, NY 10010.

Where this book is distributed in the UK, Europe and the rest of the world,
this is by Palgrave Macmillan, a division of Macmillan Publishers Limited,
registered in England, company number 785998, of Houndmills,
Basingstoke, Hampshire RG21 6XS.

Palgrave Macmillan is the global academic imprint of the above companies
and has companies and representatives throughout the world.

Palgrave® and Macmillan® are registered trademarks in the United States,
the United Kingdom, Europe and other countries.

ISBN-13: 978–0–230–61243–3
ISBN-10: 0–230–61243–1

Library of Congress Cataloging-in-Publication Data

Häring, Norbert.
    [Ökonomie 2.0. English]
    Economics 2.0 : what the best minds in economics can teach you
about business and life / Norbert Häring and Olaf Storbeck ;
translated into English by Jutta Scherer.
        p. cm.
    Includes bibliographical references and index.
    ISBN 0–230–61243–1
    1. Economics—Psychological aspects. I. Storbeck, Olaf. II. Title.

HB74.5.H36 2009
330—dc22   2008031804

A catalogue record of the book is available from the British Library.

Design by Newgen Imaging Systems (P) Ltd., Chennai, India.

First edition: January 2009

10 9 8 7 6 5 4 3 2 1

Printed in the United States of America.

Contents

Preface / ix

From Dogma to Data—An Introduction by Axel Ockenfels / xi

1 Man—An Economic Animal? / 1

The Economic Split Personality / 5
When Economists Go to Kindergarten / 7
Why You Shouldn't Trust Your Children / 8
Arrival at Reality / 10
Macroeconomics in the Absence of *Homo Oeconomicus* / 13
References / 15

2 The Pursuit of Happiness / 17

That Obscure Object of Desire / 22
Master of My Fate, Captain of My Soul / 27
References / 31

3 The Enigma of the Labor Market / 33

Longer Unemployment Can Be a Good Thing / 36
Why Employers Don't Like to Cut Wages / 38
Economists in Defense of Minimum Wages / 39
Undesirable Side-Effects of Minimum Wages / 44
Fighting Unemployment in Kindergarten / 46

How Bible Studies Can Make You Rich / 49
References / 52

4 The Almost-Forgotten Small Difference / 55

An Economic History of Women's Emancipation / 57
Family Economics and Its Limits / 60
It Pays to Pay Women Less / 61
Women Are Less Effective Negotiators / 62
Competing against Men Is No Bed of Roses / 65
The Fear of Competition Is an Acquired Trait / 67
References / 68

5 It's All about Culture / 71

The Economics of Religion / 74
Culture as the True Engine of Prosperity / 75
America's Misplaced Faith in a Just World / 76
Thou Shalt Trust in the Stock Market / 78
References / 80

6 Economics by Scales and Measures / 81

What Causes the Leading Power to Shrink? / 82
Short People in Dire Straits / 83
Chubby People Live Longer / 84
With Elevator Shoes to Higher Income / 86
The Economics of Beauty / 88
References / 90

7 The Logic of Globalization / 93

How Globalization Spoils Drug Dealers' Margins / 95
Globalization According to Crustaceans / 96
Trade without Comparative Cost Advantages / 98
No Reason to Fear "Made in China" / 100
Global Competition Can Be Crippling / 102
The World—A Village? / 105
Africa's Sad Secret / 106
What Happened to All the Money? / 108
References / 109

8   Financial Markets—Totally Efficient or Totally Crazy? / 111

There's No Fool Like a Stock Market Fool / 111
What the Eye Does Not See, the Heart Cannot Grieve Over / 113
The First Shall Be the Last / 115
Lemmings to the Sea—Many Analysts Just Follow the Crowd / 116
Why Analysts Speak in Two Tongues / 118
The Dirt on Coming Clean / 120
So Let Us Predict the Past / 121
Rational Bubbles Burst Rationally / 123
Of Black Swans and Black Days in the Market / 125
Returns on Stocks Are Lower Than You'd Think / 126
References / 127

9   Subprime Surprises—Or: The Anatomy of the Financial Crisis / 129

What Kind of a Monster? / 130
How Rating Agencies Fed the Monster / 134
Did the Fed Egg the Monster On? / 137
Regulation Matters / 139
How Bad Will It Get? / 142
References / 145

10   Managers Are People, Too / 147

Why Employees Run Away after Mergers / 149
How to Keep Cocky Managers in Check / 150
Why Good Managers Are Reluctant to Correct Their Own Mistakes / 152
Company Leaders Are Not Born That Way / 154
What Businesses Can Learn from Heart Surgeons / 156
What Bosses Can Learn from Monkeys / 158
Bosses, You Need to Talk More with Your People / 161
The Best CEOs Manage the Largest Firms / 163
Lots of Money, Lots of Anxiety / 165
References / 167

11   The High Art of Buying and Selling / 169

The Winner's Curse / 169
Snipers Buy Cheaper / 171
The Illusion of a Strong Will / 173
Tallying Is a Matter of Luck / 175

CONTENTS

The Customer as King—Ungrateful and Unforgiving / 177
Brand Image Pays Off Twice / 179
Join Christina Aguilera in the Winner's Circle / 181
Information Is Power / 183
References / 184

12 The Athlete as a Guinea Pig—Or: Why Economists Love Sports / 187
Football Teams Don't Play It Right / 188
Cricket Players Learn Very Slowly / 190
Game Theorists Playing at Wimbeldon / 192
Of Incentives and Their Side Effects / 193
New Brooms Don't Sweep Any Better / 194
Slowing Down Others Will Get You There, Too / 196
When Referees Are Taking Sides / 197
References / 199

13 In the Dark Recesses of the Market Economy / 201
Betting on Hitler / 202
Investors, Check the Obituaries / 205
The Power of Rating Agencies / 207
Why Banks Don't Like to Google / 208
How Investment Funds Buy Good Press / 210
How a TV Station Helped George W. Bush Win the Election / 212
When Wall Street Whistles, the IMF Jumps / 214
References / 216

14 A Final Warning / 217
When Listening to Advice from Economists, Keep the Saltshaker Handy / 218
Soldiers of Fortune Riding the Statistics / 220
The Economics of Erring / 225
References / 228

Acknowledgments / 229

About the Authors / 231

Index / 233

Preface

This book was written not only to entertain, but also to help expand the reader's horizons. Even those who have learned a proper profession should for once have a chance to see the world from the vantage point of an economist. It is an experience not unlike looking through a thermal imaging camera: Many things appear blurred and distorted, yet certain features come into view that the naked eye would never catch. And it is certainly interesting.

The book is also meant to educate. Readers studying economics, or who have done so in the past or intend to do so, will obtain an overview of the many directions the discipline has taken. Especially in recent years, economics and business studies have made huge strides. They have become more empirical, more realistic. It is this type of a contemporary economic science which we refer to as Economics Version 2.0.

Mathematical formulae and abstract graphs facilitate scientific analysis. Alas, they have limited entertainment value and so you will find none of them in this book. Those who cannot do without may read up on them in the original scientific texts this book draws from. All sources are listed. Exceptionally trustful or highly skeptical types may want to peruse the detailed pointers in the last chapter first.

—*Norbert Häring* and *Olaf Storbeck*,
December 2008

From Dogma to Data— An Introduction

Axel Ockenfels
Professor of Economics, University of Cologne, Germany

"How many economists does it take to change a light bulb? Answer: not a single one. If a new light bulb was needed, the market would have taken care of it." These kinds of hackneyed jokes about economists come by the dozen. The spectrum reaches from one-liners ("Economists predicted nine out of the last five recessions") to intellectually glib aphorisms ("Economics is the only discipline where two scientists are awarded the Nobel Prize because they came to diametrically opposite conclusions"). Yet all these jokes shine a spotlight on the public perception of what economics really stands for. Economists are frequently depicted as removed from reality and vague by design, enamored with the market as they obsess about models and charts. Criticism of economics is as old as the discipline itself. As early as the nineteenth century, Thomas Carlyle described the profession as "the dismal science," a characterization that has stuck to this day. Economists, as the saying goes, know the price of everything and the value of nothing. Scientists from outside of the profession even accuse our profession of "imperialism," because as economists, we are wont to stick our noses into matters supposedly alien to us, from family life and happiness to health. In the past, such criticism may have been partially deserved. Over the last two decades, though, economics has undergone an exciting shift: the profession has moved closer to people and their problems. With increasing frequency, the often-decried gap between science and "real life" is being bridged. Data instead of dogma is the common denominator for modern economics. The engine for such development was the discovery and use of two new scientific methods: game theory and its empirical counterpart, experimental economics. Both fields of research have jointly revolutionized economics and its exponents' view of human behavior. Concurrently, they furnished means to economists that enabled them, not unlike design engineers, to build more effective institutions and arrive at better decisions. Game theory is a mathematically rigorous tool for analysis of a given strategic interaction. Prior to its "invention" around the middle of the last century by John von Neumann, Oscar Morgenstern, and John F. Nash, economic theory had traditionally assumed that there were so many players active in a marketplace that the response of each of them to another's actions was essentially negligible to that other player. This may be an acceptable simplification for the purchase of, say, a carton of milk in the supermarket; however, when it comes to labor and environmental negotiations, the regulating of infrastructural markets, or oligopolistic competition and other forms of conflict and cooperation, such models are obviously of very little help. Game theory frees us of such methodological constraints. It affords us the analysis of economic, social and political interaction inside and outside of markets by use of transparent methods. It lets us detect interdependencies of economic and social behavior and helps us better understand the influence market rules and the rules governing other types of interaction have on decision making.

Game theory proves to be a highly effective advisor where incentives and behavioral strategies are concerned. Nevertheless, it has its limits. Players populating the virtual worlds of game theory generally act without any cultural or social backdrop, but with unlimited capacity for computation. While such simplistic assumptions may be useful at times, they can easily lead to conclusions that are fundamentally wrong. One example may illustrate this point: From the angle of game theory, chess is a totally boring game. Since there are no uncertainties about the opponent's strategic options, and all moves can be exactly observed and verified, a perfectly rational player knows precisely how the opponent will react to any possible move. In other words, both players know before the first move how the game will unfold and what its outcome will be. Using game-theoretical methods, it is fairly easy to prove that the victorious side is determined prior to the first move, assuming rational behavior on both parts. On the other hand, it is equally certain that no mathematical capability of either man or machine would be enough to play chess rationally. So, how do individuals act in complex situations?

The second novelty, experimental economic research, rang in a new era for economics science. As early as in the late 1950s, economists began testing economic phenomena in laboratory experiments. The leading pioneers at the time were the later Nobel laureates in economics, Vernon Smith and Reinhard Selten. Yet decades would pass before the new methods became widely accepted. The preconception that experiments are impracticable in economic research was thoroughly entrenched in experts' minds. Today, experimental economics research is one of the most successful sectors within the science of economics. Hardly any faculty worth its salt can afford to do without a test lab.

Experimental economic research can be considered complementary to game theory, in that it concerns itself with the behavior of flesh-and-blood humans. And—lo and behold!—humans will act totally differently from what traditional economics asserts.

Fairness in negotiations, for instance, can be a great motivator and play an important role; cognitive constraints will induce systematic errors in financial market dealings, and past experiences may well skew future behavior. (This book is a goldmine for anyone wishing to delve deeper into those phenomena.)

The systematic investigation of such phenomena in tightly controlled, experimental environments reveals that individuals do not act irrationally or even chaotically. Flesh-and-blood humans hew to their own rationales. This may not always be in agreement with those of the "homo oeconomicus," but they behave in a generally systematic and predictable fashion that can be described by economic models. This fact enables economists to leave well-trodden paths behind and develop new, descriptively relevant theories of behavior. Some of them turned out to be surprisingly robust and empirically productive. They represent the foundation of a new kind of economics we call "behavioral economics."

The renewed vigor that game theory and experimental economics has brought to the science is further enhanced by exciting developments in related fields. Psychology, in particular, has greatly enriched economics over the past decades. It is for good reason that Daniel Kahneman became the first psychologist to receive the Nobel Prize in economics for his Prospect Theory, developed in collaboration with Amos Tversky, as it provided the basis for the emergence and popularity of the discipline of "behavioral finance." Lately, economists have been attempting to pry even deeper into the workings of the mind, as it were. Neuro-economics combines the methods of neuroscience with those of economics. It especially seeks to identify and understand processes taking place inside the brain that go hand-in-hand with the formation of perceptions and decisions.

Innovations in mathematical methods are another factor that, over the past two decades, contributed to the advancement of the science of economics. Economic theory and statistics continue to develop ever more refined and complex models and methods of analysis. Concomitant with it, economics has profited from technological progress. Computing power has exploded since 1980. With the press of a button, simple personal computers are able to perform complex arithmetical operations, which would have required entire computer farms two decades ago, and a tremendous amount of money and time.

An increasing reliance on mathematics, though, is not universally welcomed, even within the profession. The American economist Alan Blinder speaks of a mathematics race and complains about economics having become more math-dependent than physics. Indeed, there has been a time when our profession was in thrall to mathematics. This time is over now—at least as far as applied economics are concerned. Though modern economics cannot function without mathematics, today its methods are in thrall to us, helping us get a better grip on the economic problems of real life. How should the electric-power market be structured to achieve optimal efficiency? What tools of economic policy can help solve the unemployment problem? What are the effects of a minimum wage policy? How do cooperation, trust, and competition interact in anonymous online markets? Which incentive systems motivate people, which might have the opposite effect? How should places at day care centers or organs for transplantation be allocated? How should UMTS frequency blocks be auctioned off?

Modern economics seeks to answer these and similar questions. Rather than continuing to derive answers from its fount of eternal truths, it now employs a variety of methods and a clear focus in developing and verifying its theories. Modern economists are no longer content with just having an understanding of the markets—they are eager to use their expertise to actually improve them. Based on the latest advances in terms of methods and substance, it is becoming increasingly feasible indeed to dissect and control behavior and institutions. Innovative testing technologies allow for a seamless transition from lab studies to the field. Even highly complex, genuine markets such as the electricity market or electronic auctions, can be made accessible and manageable in the wake, as it were, of a profound scientific investigation. The gap between basic research and reality disappears, with positive results for the economy and society at large.

With this book, Olaf Storbeck and Norbert Häring provide an overview of the exciting developments and insights of modern economic science, easy to understand even for the uninitiated reader. Not only do the authors analyze the relevant—and sometimes hardly digestible—scientific literature in great detail, they also challenge its claims and conclusions with an unfailing journalistic instinct for what is crucial. The result is an exceptionally competent and elegant review of state-of-the-art research. The book is perfectly suited to soften any prejudices held about economics, and to strengthen our intuitive comprehension of economic causality. With scientific journalism of this quality, we have reason to hope that soon those economist jokes mentioned earlier will no longer be understood.

1

Man—An Economic Animal?

The machine sits deep below ground, in a windowless room on the second basement level of the Zurich University hospital. The way there leads through long halls lit by cold fluorescent tubes. "Caution: Powerful magnetic field," a sign warns at the last hurdle, a four-inch-thick steel door. Before entering the visitor is asked to hand over all metallic objects. Located behind the door is an apparatus taller than a man that resembles a computer tomography machine. It enables you to watch people thinking—it is a brain scanner made by Philips.

One wouldn't expect to meet economists at a place like this. Yet the Zurich economist Ernst Fehr conducts his research here, deep underground together with brain researchers and psychologists. The research team works on unlocking fundamental questions of human behavior and social interaction: When do individuals trust one another? When do they cooperate? What causes them to act selfishly and when do they care for more than their own narrow benefits? What conditions prompt individuals to break social norms?

A scientific revolution, at least for traditional economists. Until recently economists have not asked these types of questions. True, economics is the science of economic decisions and of dealing with resource shortages, but man himself, his likes and dislikes and the motives governing his decisions, has traditionally been treated as a non-issue. Economists, an old paradigm commands, do not get to the bottom of preferences—they take them for granted.

This form of economics was rooted in the basic assumption that man is an economic animal, a *Homo oeconomicus*. In the economic arena of situational decision making, so the dictum went, we will always act rationally, selfishly, rigidly pursuing our own interests. In economists' well-worn models, flesh-and-blood people became "economic subjects" who will mercilessly seek to maximize their own benefit—with nothing else on their minds. Much like a robot, *Homo oeconomicus* will impartially and rationally weigh advantage against disadvantage. Moral considerations, scruples or thoughts of fairness are utterly alien to him—he will grab any chance he gets to gain an advantage over others. Even today, every economics freshman is confronted with this concept.

Not a particularly likable image of the human race, even economists are quick to concede. None of them would want his daughter married to a true *Homo oeconomicus*. But not to fear: The risk of running into someone that rational and selfish, and bent only on maximizing his own advantage, is rather small. Over the past years, economists have shown that in real life, individuals behave neither as selfishly nor as rationally as economists tended to assume in their models. As demonstrated in countless lab experiments and field tests, man is a far more social and less rational creature than is postulated by traditional economics. Phenomena like the desire to be fair and cooperative are not negligible side issues—they are core constituents of human nature. Without them, economic action cannot be fully understood or described.

One of the first experiments to call into question the thesis of *Homo oeconomicus* was the "ultimatum game." In it, two individuals—let's call them Peter and Paul—are to decide how to divide between them a given sum (say, $100). The rules are simple yet strict: Peter may put forward one proposal only, which Paul can only accept or reject. If Paul rejects Peter's offer, both will go home empty-handed. Now, if both acted like a true *Homo oeconomicus,* Peter would try to get the best possible deal for himself, which is $99.99. Paul would accept this offer, cheeky as it may be, because one cent is better than nothing. The fact that the other party would get away with so much more would not keep him from accepting—as a rational egoist, he would only have his possible best interests in mind.

Yet in reality, it does not work that way. Hundreds of experiments have demonstrated that, as a general rule, both players will divide up the money much more equitably. Offers below 20 percent are likely to be rejected, as the second player will judge them to be unfair. At the same time, other experiments show that pure altruism is just as alien to us as extreme selfishness. All in all, individuals will tend to be interested in how their own situation evolves compared to other people, rather than focusing solely on their absolute situation (i.e., regardless of the other person's)—as would be of supreme importance to a true *Homo oeconomicus.*

One of the golden rules of human behavior is to pay like with like. "Most people act in reciprocal fashion," explains Armin Falk, director of the Laboratory for Experimental Economics Research at Bonn University. "They will reward fair behavior and punish unfair behavior, even if it costs them."

Another key driver of how fairly or self-centeredly we act is the institutional framework within which we move: In a highly competitive environment we will become more selfish than in one that emphasizes cooperation. In variations of the ultimatum game where the ratio of division proposed by one player becomes valid as soon as one of several coplayers accepts, the proposing player will usually be able to keep most of the cake to himself. From that we can conclude that, in highly competitive situations of decision making, the selfishness theorem of economists may be a reasonable approximation.

When, why and precisely under what circumstances adults will act selfishly or cooperatively, how they arrive at a rational or a gut decision is still a matter of speculation for economists. The cooperation with brain researchers, so they hope, may provide better answers. "We explore the biological foundations of human social behavior," says Ernst Fehr, one of the pioneers in the still-young discipline of "neuro-economics."

Its basic hypothesis is that to understand human decision making, we need to understand how the brain arrives at those decisions. In the past, this was a "black box" to economists, as were individual preferences. "The foundations of economic theory were constructed assuming that details about the functioning of the brain's black box would not be known," write neuro-economists Colin Camerer, George Loewenstein and Drazen Prelec. Today, the technology of image processing enables scientists to pinpoint the regions of the brain that are actively involved in economic decisions. "The study of the brain and nervous system *is* beginning to allow direct measurement of thoughts and feelings," Camerer, Loewenstein and Prelec point out.

The research team around Fehr discovered that altruistic punishment has biological roots. When an individual decides to sanction unfair behavior, the brain activates an important region of the reward system—which the scientists interpret to mean that the individual derives satisfaction or self-confirmation from effecting punishment. Other experiments show that the same brain regions are active when we suffer pain and when we witness the pain of others; this may be another reason why people do not act in a purely selfish manner.

The inclination to trust others is also contingent on biological factors. Another finding of Fehr's team is that the hormone oxytocin plays an important part: Test persons who had the hormone administered displayed more trust in others than did those who were given a placebo. "Oxytocin specifically affects an individual's willingness to accept social risks arising through interpersonal interactions," the scientists conclude.

The Economic Split Personality

A key finding of neuro-economic research is that during decision processes, different regions of the brain compete with each other. Put in simple terms, the sector responsible for emotion is in conflict with the sector governing logic. "In many circumstances—including those familiar to humanity's evolutionary ancestors—these different types of mechanism function synergistically to achieve our goals. However, in the circumstances of modern life, these systems may prescribe different behaviors. In such cases, the outcome of competition between these mechanisms determines behavior," emphasizes Jonathan Cohen, professor of psychology at Princeton, in a survey article published in the *Journal of Economic Perspectives*.

The phenomenon may explain why people come to contradictory conclusions when facing inter-temporal problems. If an individual was offered the choice of either receiving $10 today or $11 tomorrow, he would most likely opt for the $10. Given the choice of receiving $10 in a year's time or $11 in a year and one day, he will settle for the longer waiting time to get the extra dollar.

A research team around Cohen and Harvard economist David Laibson found that for decisions with a short time horizon, the brain sector predominantly involved is the limbic system, which is assumed to govern emotions and urges. Decisions involving a longer time horizon are the domain of the prefrontal cortex, generally regarded as the locus of reason.

Increasingly, these findings are making their way into economic theory. For instance, a model developed by Harvard economists Drew Fudenberg and David Levine takes explicit account of the internal competition between the brain's two agencies for decision making. Man is modeled as having two kinds of personalities—a "series of short-run, impulsive selves" and a "long-run, patient self." Our short-run selves are exclusively concerned with maximizing the good times of the moment, the long-run selves think ahead to the day after tomorrow.

Fudenberg and Levine's model explains a series of phenomena that traditional economics have taken for irrational behavior—such as the observation that people engaged in low-stake bets tend to show a degree of risk aversion that seems absurd, considering the overall assets they have at their disposal. Or the fact that people that have unexpectedly come into cash money will exhibit different attitudes toward spending it than they do after receiving the same amount via their bank account.

When different regions of the brain are responsible for either significant or insignificant financial decisions, this phenomenon becomes much easier to explain: The hedonistic, short-run part of the personality in Fudenberg and Levine's model is only permitted to spend what pocket money it has been granted by the long-run self. Longer-term financial decisions take place in another sector, the "banking sphere." Here, the long-run self is calling the shots. In daily life, the hedonistic, short-run self will relate each expense to the daily budget available, while the total assets in the bank account (to which it has no access) are essentially a non-factor. Going to the bank takes too much time. For a *Homo oeconomicus,* on the other hand, the crucial yardstick will always be the total asset base.

However, credit cards and ATMs open new vistas for the hedonistic self. It is these problematic ancillary areas of the model that are particularly instructive. If the hedonistic self obtains instant access to the banking sphere, it will max out the checking account and stretch the credit card to its limit.

The latter phenomenon has preoccupied economists for quite a while. Although credit card interest rates are substantially higher than those on consumer loans, countless Americans have amassed credit card debt instead of taking out a loan. For the *Homo oeconomicus,* this would be nothing less than a waste of money. For subjective man, though, it is quite sensible behavior: The higher interest payments are debited to the initiator—the hedonistic self. Its everyday budget will be cut. Yet if the planning self were to reschedule its debts, it would give the other (hedonistic) part of the personality more latitude for piling up debt, which it would soon take advantage of. The credit card business thus benefits handsomely from a phenomenon that, according to traditional economic theory, shouldn't even exist.

When Economists Go to Kindergarten

People of flesh and blood will react to economic incentives in ways that are altogether different from what economists—beholden to their traditional models—would predict. One reason for this is the potential competition between intrinsic and extrinsic motivation.

This was demonstrated impressively by the U.S.-based economists Uri Gneezy and Aldo Rustichini. They investigated a relatively simple question: What will happen when a kindergarten charges parents a fee for being late picking up their children? According to prevailing economic theory, the number of late pickups should decline, since incentives rise for parents to be on time.

The two researchers put the theory to the test in several Israeli daycare centers and found the exact opposite to occur: Once a fee for late-arriving parents was introduced, tardiness increased significantly. Even following abolition of the late fee, tardiness persisted on the higher level. For an explanation of the results, Gneezy and Rustichini took a page out of psychology's and sociology's book: The late fee, from the viewpoint of parents, changed the unspoken covenants of social relations vis-à-vis the kindergarten. Originally, it had simply been a case of proper conduct to be punctual—or else a kindergarten aide would have to watch the kids on his/her own time. Parents would perceive this as a favor being granted rather than a market transaction. It was a matter of honor and decency to take advantage of the favor only if it was absolutely unavoidable. The late fee, though, put a price on the act of tardiness. The supervision of the children became a service, payable like any other offered by the kindergarten. Thus, tardiness from the parents' viewpoint became acceptable behavior. In the jargon of psychologists: A powerful, intrinsic motive was crowded out by a weaker, extrinsic one.

Why You Shouldn't Trust Your Children

Social behavior is something we must struggle to learn in our childhood and youth. Children behave much more like a *Homo oeconomicus* than adults do, as shown by economists Matthias Sutter (University of Innsbruck) and Martin Kocher (University of Munich). Children act selfishly and will not extend their trust to others, nor will they honor any trust extended to them. Sutter and Kocher conducted an experiment with 662 people from 6 age groups—8-year olds through retirees—that is generally known as the "trust game": Each test person gets $10 and may decide how much of it he or she wishes to share with an unknown test person. The amount transferred to that other person is tripled by the test coordinators. The beneficiary has a choice to return a portion of the money to the original donor. Both players fare better when cooperating—the first party, though, only if confident that the second party will go along and share the gain. In the actual experiment conducted by Sutter and Kocher, if the first player donated all the money and the second player returned half of his take, each earned $15.

As the two researchers established, trust and trustworthiness increase almost linearly with age. Eight-year-olds would part with no more than $2 and in return got only $.66 back, ending up with a loss of $1.34. Sixteen-year-olds on average gave up almost half their money, but still lost $0.30 in the bargain. Working adults gave away the highest amount—$6.58—and received $2.45 more than they spent. With retirees the numbers started to reverse a bit. "On average, trust is rewarded only among the adult population," the authors concluded.

Advocates of traditional economics tend to argue that all those findings stand on shaky ground, as they are derived from role plays conducted in artificial lab environments and do not properly reflect real-life behavior. If larger sums were at stake in a real-life context, they argue, most of the phenomena contradicting the assumption of rationality would vanish. However, their argument is refuted by the results of a poll among 21,000 participants in the *Socioeconomic Panel,* an annual poll representative of the German population. Participants in this poll were given certain statements regarding a propensity for positive or negative reciprocity, and asked to what degree these statements applied to them.

A research team around the Bonn economist Armin Falk evaluated their replies and concluded that in real life, individuals fall into three groups: A majority will return favors of equal value, reciprocating mainly in positive settings. A minority will mainly reciprocate negative actions. In a third group the two traits are equally present. A *Homo oeconomicus,* however, who would return neither favors nor disfavors by equal measures, seems to be virtually nonexistent.

Not all groups cope with life equally well, the researchers found. Those living by the Old Testament's avenger concept must reckon with substantial economic disadvantages—probably because they will have to overcome higher hurdles to enter into and maintain social relations, the researchers surmise. Another reason may be that this type of individual is predisposed to react to unreasonable demands by superiors or coworkers in ways that will reflect badly on him. One of those reactions seems to be to skip work—individuals with an inclination toward negative reciprocity also have above-average absenteeism rates. On the other hand, those with a strong tendency to return favors at equal value earn a higher income on average than those of a more egotistical bent—and find themselves in the unemployment line less often.

Arrival at Reality

For many years, only a small circle of experimental and behavioral economists was cognizant of these research findings; now these ideas are slowly making headway into more and more sectors of economic science. Financial market researchers, labor market specialists and human resource economists are coming to realize that traditional economics has been too simplistic in its assumptions on human motivation and behavior patterns.

To wit, portions of the current *labor market research* must be rewritten. Historically, neoclassical economists have maintained that the labor market is no different in its workings than the market in goods—and, for instance, higher performance incentives automatically lead workers to work harder.

More recent experiments and empirical investigations on the effectiveness of incentives indicate, however, that this is not always the case, since individuals do not exclusively think of themselves and intrinsic motives will sometimes be supplanted by extrinsic factors. This becomes especially evident from the analysis of so-called *relative compensation systems,* in which workers' earnings depend on their performance relative to their coworkers' performance. In theory, incentives under this system will be much higher than in a pure piece wage system, as only those giving greater effort will earn above-average wages. Therefore, until recently, this type of income system was thought to be particularly suitable to promote greater output.

In fact, it is a downright performance killer. Extra-strong effort would mean cutting into coworkers' piecework, and thus into their wages. Most individuals do consider this, and consequently prefer going at a slower rate. Evidence of this can be found not just under laboratory conditions but also in real life, as was demonstrated by three labor market researchers using harvest helpers at a large orchard in England as an example. "We find the change in incentive scheme had a significant and permanent impact on productivity. For the average worker, productivity increased by at least 50 percent moving from relative incentives to piece rates," Oriana Bandiera, Iwan Barankay and Imran Rasul concluded in their study, which was published in the *Quarterly Journal of Economics*.

What's more, employers will rarely be able to measure the performance of their employees as accurately as in the case of those harvest workers. Due to a lack of reliable information they are usually left to guessing, as far as the commitment of their charges is concerned. "Nearly always, an employer will be dependent on the voluntary cooperation and willingness of his employees," explains Armin Falk. "Employees generally have ample discretionary leeway with regard to the commitment they bring to their work."

From the basic tendency toward *reciprocal behavior* we can conclude: When employees feel they are treated unfairly by their supervisors, their willingness to put more effort into their work than absolutely necessary will decrease. This kind of attitude can have very unpleasant effects for companies. For instance, as demonstrated by the Princeton professor Alan Krueger and Alexandre Mas from Berkeley, the massive quality problems occurring at the tire manufacturer Firestone in the mid-nineties, which cost the lives of dozens of drivers in the United States, can probably be traced back to fierce labor unrest at one of the Firestone factories.

As a general rule, it is worthwhile for employers to take advantage of the human propensity to return benevolent treatment in kind. For instance, workers enjoying the trust of their superiors will exhibit a stronger commitment than those constantly under management's watchful eye. Evidence of this was established in a joint study by the Bonn researcher Falk and Michael Kosfeld of Frankfurt University. In a lab experiment, the two scientists simulated an intra-business labor market comprising 100 participants. One half acted as employees, the other as employers. Each employee received a salary and could decide for himself how much commitment to bring to his job. And just like in real life, doing work involved some degree of "negative utility," a cost. As salaries were decoupled from actual performance, the workers had an incentive to work as little as possible.

Employers had the option to set minimum standards of performance, or alternatively rely on employees to fully commit to the job without supervision. The noteworthy result of this study was: Employers waiving tight controls were rewarded with performance that was on average one-third higher. Those setting a minimum generally got just that much in return. Only a minority behaved as one would expect of *Homo oeconomicus*: A quarter abused the employer's trust and did no work at all. One out of five was not influenced one way or the other by how much trust or distrust he was shown, and exhibited relatively strong commitment. The majority, however, behaved in the reciprocal fashion explained before: In return for their salary, they voluntarily turned in an honest day's work. Once the employer instituted controls, employees' goodwill seemed to dissolve into thin air. They interpreted controls as a sign of distrust, and their productivity dropped.

Macroeconomics in the Absence of *Homo Oeconomicus*

Even neoclassical macroeconomics could receive a jolt from the findings of behavioral economists—possibly even enabling Keynesianism to stage a comeback. At least that is the thesis put forward by economics Nobel laureate George Akerlof: In his 2007 presidential address at the annual meeting of the American Economic Association (AEA), Akerlof called for a paradigm shift in macroeconomics.

According to Akerlof, the assumptions regarding human behavior on which current macroeconomic models are based are far too restrictive and removed from reality, in particular since they completely disregard the fact that individuals do not always behave selfishly and rationally. "There is a sense in which those preferences are very narrowly defined. They have important missing motivation—since they fail to incorporate the norms of the decision makers," Akerlof says. By taking account of such norms in the models, he argues, economists would arrive at a macroeconomic theory that heavily borrows from early Keynesian thinking. "Early Keynesians got a great deal of the working of the economic system right," said Akerlof.

Keynesianism lost its cachet in the seventies, chiefly because its methods were thought to be out of date: Keynesian models used to be based on ad hoc assumptions about the economic behavior of players, rather than deriving macroeconomic inter-connections from stringent assumptions about the behavior of individual consumers and entrepreneurs.

The *neoclassical economists*, by contrast, emphasized the so called "micro-foundation" of macroeconomics. Their basic conclusion was that government interventions in the economy are bound to be largely ineffective: Since individuals rationally striving to maximize their benefit in perfect markets will peg their consumption to their lifetime income rather than their

current income, any short-term tax relief or income raises will be neutral in their effect on private consumption.

The same is true for businesses, which in a neoclassical world will not let their investment decisions be influenced by their current cash flow. As the models do not make a long-term connection between the rate of inflation and the unemployment rate, neither monetary nor fiscal policies will exert a lasting influence on the real economy.

All these assertions are based on the assumption that the decision makers are intent on maximizing their monetary benefit. If, however, social norms were taken into account within the utility functions, all core insights of neoclassical macroeconomics would collapse, says Akerlof. For instance, the proposition denying a permanent link between inflation and unemployment is based on the assumption that people will generally focus on real instead of nominal values—which is not the case in the real world. Cuts in nominal compensation, for example, are exceedingly rare. "Employees have a *norm* for what wages *should* be," stresses Akerlof. Even in times of crisis, he points out, businessmen will recoil from cutting wages out of fear that work ethics and staff loyalty will suffer. Norms also play a vital role in consumption and savings decisions. An important determinant of consumption is people's idea of what they ought to consume, says Akerlof. In other words: Only if we deem an expenditure appropriate will we spend the money—even though we could afford to buy inappropriate things.

Why, then, have economists ignored social norms for decades? According to Akerlof, the late Milton Friedman (1912–2006) is to blame for that. In the late fifties, Friedman had conceptualized the postulate of "positive economics," under which economists must use only objective, mathematically verifiable arguments in their models. "Current economic methodology inherently has created a biased economics," says Akerlof, pointing out that the contemporary methods produced one-

dimensional economists blind to norms. To do away with those shortcomings, he demands a methodical reorientation of the discipline—in his view, the current "positive" economics should be replaced by a "naturalistic" one. The profession should put greater emphasis on case studies and closely monitor economic decision makers—rather than make abstract assumptions about the impulses of human behavior—in order to find out what motivates them.

References

Akerlof, George (2007): "The Missing Motivation in Macroeconomics," in: *American Economic Review*, Vol. 97, pp. 5–36.

Bandiera, Oriana, Iwan Barankay and Imran Rasul (2005): "Social Preferences and the Response to Incentives: Evidence from Personnel Data," in: *Quarterly Journal of Economics*, Vol. 120, pp. 917–962.

Camerer, Colin F., George Loewenstein and Drazen Prelec (2005): "Neuroeconomics: How Neuroscience Can Inform Economics," in: *Journal of Economic Literature*, Vol. 43, pp. 9–64.

Cohen, Jonathan D. (2005): "The Vulcanization of the Human Brain: A Neural Perspective on Interactions between Cognition and Emotion," in: *Journal of Economic Perspectives*, Vol. 19, pp. 3–24.

Dohmen, Thomas, Armin Falk, David Huffman and Uwe Sunde (2006): "Homo Reciprocans: Survey Evidence on Prevalence, Behavior and Success,"Institute for the Study of Labor (IZA) discussion paper no. 2205.

Falk, Armin and Michael Kosfeld (2006): "Distrust—The Hidden Cost of Control," in: *American Economic Review*, Vol. 96, pp. 1611–1630.

Fehr, Ernst, Urs Fischbacher and Michael Kosfeld (2005): "Neuroeconomic Foundations of Trust and Social Preferences," in: *American Economic Review, Papers & Proceedings*, Vol. 95, pp. 346–351.

Fehr, Ernst, Michael Kosfeld, Markus Heinrichs, Paul Zak and Urs Fischbacher (2005): "Oxytocin Increases Trust in Humans," in: *Nature*, Vol. 435, pp. 673–676.

Fehr, Ernst and Tania Singer (2005): "The Neuroeconomics of Mind Reading and Empathy," in: *American Economic Review, Papers & Proceedings,* Vol. 95, pp. 340–345.

Fudenberg Drew and David K. Levine (2006): "A Dual-Self Model of Impulse Control," in: *American Economic Review,* Vol. 96, pp. 1449–1476.

Gneezy, Uri and Aldo Rustichini (2000): "A Fine is a Price," in: *Journal of Legal Studies,* Vol. 29, pp. 1–17.

Krueger, Alan B. and Alexandre Mas (2004): "Strikes, Scabs, and Tread Separations: Labor Strife and the Production of Defective Bridgestone/Firestone Tires," in: *Journal of Political Economy,* Vol. 112, pp. 253–289.

Quervain, Dominique J.-F. de, Urs Fischbacher, Valerie Treyer, Melanie Schellhammer, Ulrich Schnyder, Alfred Buck and Ernst Fehr (2004): "The Neural Basis of Altruistic Punishment," in: *Science,* Vol. 305, pp. 1254–1258.

2
The Pursuit of Happiness

It seems paradoxical: Between 1975 and 1995, the average real per-capita income in the United States rose by nearly 40 percent—yet Americans did not become any happier during that time. Despite plasma TV, PlayStation and a third car in the driveway, people are not one iota more satisfied with their lives than they were three decades ago.

The U.S. economist Richard Easterlin drew attention to this phenomenon as early as 1974. Today his observation is known in economic circles as the Easterlin Paradox. Not only in the United States but also in other industrialized nations, Easterlin observed that although today's generation is much more affluent than that of their parents and grandparents, people are no happier with their lives than they used to be. What could be the reasons for that? Traditional economists have dodged the issue for quite some time, as it hits them to the core.

After all, traditional economists start from the assumptions that we all strive to maximize our utility and that our utility increases with the money we have at our disposal and the opportunities for consumption open to us. If this was so, a generation with twice the income and wealth that their parents had should be much more satisfied with their lives.

Well, they are not. According to Easterlin's and other researchers' findings, only in poor countries does general life satisfaction rises in line with average incomes. Once the minimum subsistence level is reached, the correlation quickly breaks down. Easterlin drew a line at $15,000 to $20,000 in today's dollars (purchasing power) above which earnings hardly contribute to people's happiness.

An ever-increasing number of economics researchers explore the reasons for these phenomena. Research into the determinants of life satisfaction is among the hottest sub-disciplines of recent years. Since 1994, economic journals have featured an average of 35 articles a year with "Happiness" or "life satisfaction" in their titles, the British "happiness economist" Andrew Clark found.

The *absolute income* traditional economics use as a benchmark is certainly not insignificant for a person's contentment with life, but pales in comparison with other factors, according to the happiness researchers' findings. Most people are concerned with their situation primarily in relation to others. Income and consumption determine status—and the cachet attached to a higher income is more important to many people than the added utility of things they can purchase with that money.

Scientists Sara Solnick and David Hemenway have provided evidence of this in an experiment that is now widely known: They questioned students in what kind of world they would rather live—one where they earned $50,000 and everyone else half as much, or alternatively, $100,000, while everybody else would make twice as much. The majority chose the first option, even though they would have clearly improved their lot by picking the second. With twice as high an income (at a price level that was assumed to be unchanged) they would have had many more opportunities for consumption.

Exploring this further with questionnaires filled out by the participants, Solnick and Hemenway found out that these concerns about one's position relative to others are greatest with regard to attractiveness and praise from superiors, and lowest for things like vacation time. If your peers are just as attractive as you are and if your co-workers get as much praise as you do, you are not likely to feel very good about it, according to these findings. However, if you get an extra week of vacation you perceive it as a very good thing, even if your peers get it too. Other studies have similarly found that people hardly worry about their relative standing when it comes to vacation and insurance, but are deeply concerned with regard to cars and housing. The technical term economists use for models dealing with such relative concerns is "catching up with the Joneses."

There is a second important factor to explain the Easterlin Paradox: An individual will get used to anything—including a higher standard of living. As incomes rise, perceived needs and demands grow accordingly. Easterlin suspected as much in 1974, but was unable to corroborate it at the time. Meanwhile, psychologists and happiness economists have ascertained that the positive impact of a higher income on personal satisfaction will dwindle to less than half of the initial impact over a few years.

At the end of the day, with "happiness economics" the economic science is going back to its roots. When classic figures like Jeremy Bentham, John Stuart Mill and Adam Smith spoke of "utility," they had a very broad definition in mind, covering more or less what contemporary happiness researchers refer to as happiness or life satisfaction. Bentham, the patriarch of utilitarianism, advocated the maxim that the goal of politics should be to maximize the aggregated utility for all individuals.

Yet in stride with the scientification of economics, utilitarianism continued to lose influence. The strive for happiness and contentment was no longer deemed a useful research subject among economists—after all, scientists could not quantify happiness in a valid manner, nor tally or compare levels of happiness of different people. Thus, economics reached into its bag of tricks to equate utility with income: Whoever manages to increase his income, the assumption goes, will increase the utility derived from it.

One of the tenets of the prevailing non-utilitarian thought holds that each individual will make the most of his income by consuming products and services matching his own, immutable preferences. The sea change came with further advances in psychology and increasingly reliable data on life satisfaction. Today, many psychologists and happiness economists are of the opinion that happiness can be quantified and compared among different individuals.

A most important source of data for happiness economists has been long-running panel surveys in which experts ask questions on employment, income, health and general contentment. Meanwhile, psychologists have shown people's answers about contentment to be closely correlated to objective benchmarks— for example, how frequently they smile or how happy their peers judge them to be. Brain research has determined that activity patterns in the brains of people describing themselves as happy diverge from those of people expressing unhappiness about their lives.

In fairness it must be said, though, that the methods employed by happiness economists are not entirely uncontroversial. The longer scientists have been delving into the subject matter, the clearer it becomes: Measuring or quantifying happiness is fraught with inconsistencies and contradictions. If individuals are questioned in general on the pleasantness or unpleasantness of certain activities, being with one's children is far up on the list. If asked about their momentary contentment while taking care of the offspring, the picture changes—being around one's children drops dramatically down the happiness scale, providing about as much satisfaction as housecleaning or shopping.

It was the psychologist and Nobel laureate in economics Daniel Kahneman who revealed these contradictions. Together with other researchers, Kahneman clearly proved that people are often not able to give conclusive recollections of their feelings. The researchers made the test persons dip one hand into cold water and keep it there, simultaneously indicating their relative degree of discomfort by working a lever. The result: If a very unpleasant experience is immediately followed by a somewhat less unpleasant one—in this case it was having one's hand immersed in water not quite so cold—people will remember the entire episode as somewhat less unpleasant. This is true even though the test persons would always prefer to pull their hands out of the water immediately if given the chance.

How pleasant or unpleasant we remember an experience to have been mainly depends on the experience's maximum intensity, and on what we felt shortly before the experience ended. The overall duration is almost inconsequential for our memory, the researchers found.

A similar experiment was conducted with colonoscopies at a time when sedation was not yet customary. With half of the patients, the doctor left the instrument inside the colon at the end of the examination for one extra minute, without moving it. This was unpleasant, but much less painful than the colonoscopy itself. It turned out that patients who had this done to them later recalled the overall examination as less unpleasant than other test subjects who had the instrument removed earlier. Also, they were more likely to show up for follow-up examinations.

Another inadequacy of evaluating states of satisfaction, which has frequently been documented by psychologists, is people's inability to correctly forecast how happy certain events or achievements will make them. They consistently underestimate by a wide margin the degree to which they will adapt their expectations and aspirations to changing situations. A new house or a lottery win will make people significantly happier only for a very limited time. Paraplegics have been shown to regain, after only a few years, nearly pre-accident levels of satisfaction in their lives. Hardly anybody is able to predict this strong ability to adapt.

That Obscure Object of Desire

Regardless of methodological problems, the question is: How serious should we take the findings of happiness economics? And what are the lessons to be learned for economic policies? A fierce debate has broken out among economists over these questions. On the one side there are happiness economists, like Richard Layard from the United Kingdom, who tie far-reaching politico-economic demands to the maxim of maximizing the happiness of people. Opposing them are, on the right end of the political spectrum, people like the Chicago Nobel laureate Gary Becker and, on the left, Nobel laureate Amartya Sen and adherents of his methodological school. Both sides doubt that happiness research is contributing any insights that could be of practical use to economic policy.

In his book *Happiness—Lessons from a New Science,* Layard argues that modern, performance-oriented society does not make people happy. Although more money does not really make us happier, we ordain it to be the centerpoint of our lives and in the bargain are being saddled with sorrows that diminish our happiness. We work too much, taking away time that could be spent with friends and family—high divorce rates are just one consequence of this phenomenon. In industrial countries, the negative side effects of the performance society have annihilated a good deal of what income growth could have contributed to additional contentment.

In Layard's view, it is for the state to counter the trend—for instance, by increasing the marginal tax rates on income. Traditional economists have always criticized high marginal tax rates because they diminish incentives to work and to take risks—from Layard's vantage point, they turn into a blessing, as a performance-impeding tax policy will set boundaries to the happiness-inhibiting rat race for social status through higher income and consumption: If the state keeps a major share of each additional dollar earned, the struggle for ever-higher incomes will slow down.

The shorter work hours negotiated by trade unions in Europe are condemned by liberal economists. In essence, their argument is that those who want to work less are free to negotiate that for themselves. Happiness economists of the Layard school counter: An individual may be able to increase his happiness by giving up vacation time and trading it in for more income—that is, status—but the workforce as a whole cannot. Other than income, vacations are exempt from the status contest, as surveys have revealed. From this perspective, the unions' push for shorter working hours resolves the problem resulting from the discrepancy between individual incentives for employees and the overall interests of the workforce. According to Layard, Europeans do not work too little but Americans work too much.

The standard demand of economists to increase employees' geographical mobility for the sake of higher overall productivity is rejected by Layard. Frequent uprooting and moving, he argues, is detrimental to family ties and social networks and promotes criminal behavior—all factors affecting people's contentment with life. A somewhat higher income does not make up for these losses.

Nobel laureate Amartya Sen warns, however, against giving too much weight to general questions about life satisfaction. People may not always be the best judges of what is good for them, he argues. With regard to poor people, for instance, who are content because they do not expect much out of life, Sen raises the question of whether we should really believe they are doing well only because they are happy and content: Should we—or should the government—not care if a child smart enough to be a rocket scientist never gets beyond being a subsistence farmer, just because he had no chance to find out how smart he is? Sen proposes a capabilities approach instead, according to which the goal is not to make people happier, but to maximize their opportunities to use and develop the potential they have.

Sometimes happiness economics can produce political recommendations that are downright mind-boggling, as developmental economist Angus Deaton of Princeton University demonstrated in an impressive study. Based on the Gallup surveys in 132 countries, Deaton (who can be counted among the methodological circle of Sen) showed that life satisfaction surveys can sketch a heavily distorted image of actual living conditions. According to these surveys, the degree to which a country is affected by the AIDS epidemic is only marginally important for how satisfied inhabitants are on average with the state of their health. By and large, people in Kenya, where the AIDS epidemic has affected a high proportion of the population, are even more satisfied with their health than the British are. "Using such a measure to guide or evaluate policy would lead to the unacceptable position that dealing with AIDS in Africa need not be an urgent priority," writes Deaton. People in India, Iran, Malawi and Sierra Leone are happier with their healthcare systems than U.S. citizens are—the United States ranks eighty-first on a list of 115 countries ranked according to their citizens' satisfaction with the national healthcare system. Still, a hypothetical global health institution should probably not infer from this that it should give the U.S. healthcare system priority. These are impressive examples of how the level of expectation adapts to circumstances and potential.

Chicago Nobel laureate Gary Becker and his coauthor Luis Rayo challenge happiness economics in a similarly fundamental fashion: They ask the seemingly innocuous question of how a human aspiration mechanism stressing relative income could have developed in the course of evolution. Nature, by selection, took care to have only individuals survive whose feelings of contentment depend on anything promoting survival and pro-creation. From this perspective, happiness would not be the ultimate goal of human action but a trick of nature impelling man to keep moving on the treadmill of life. Or, in other words: Nature would not care about the level of happiness but only about the result—evolutionary fitness. Philosopher Ludwig Wittgenstein probably had something similar in mind when he wrote, "I don't know why we are here, but I am pretty sure it is not in order to enjoy ourselves."

There is one problem nature had to overcome, though. According to Becker and Rayo's elaboration based on a brief excursion into neurosciences, man's potential of feeling hap-piness is limited. If we continued to become happier as we get wealthier, we would soon reach the limits of happiness. The feeling of happiness would no longer be an effective incentive; we would no longer feel like making an effort. Thus, there is a need for a reset mechanism.

It is for these reasons that natural selection will permit man to experience happiness only when he has achieved more than his neighbor, or more than he has achieved yesterday, according to Becker and Rayo's thesis. In addition, they argue, nature has made sure that man is not fully aware of this escalation of aspirations. This ensures that we will all make continuous efforts to improve our situation.

Natural selection plays a crucial role in their line of argu-ment: Of two hunter-gatherers, one of them a relaxed hedo-nist, the other ambitious, power-hungry and never satisfied, the hedonist will have had less of a chance to pass on his genes. He might have led a happier life if his competitors let him—but natural selection is likely to have taken care that there are not too many traces of people like him in our genes.

Rayo and Becker do not suggest that we operate under exactly the same conditions today. Rather, they contend that much of our genetic makeup stems from the times when our ancestors were hunters and gatherers. Seen from this angle, the Easterlin Paradox looks nothing like a paradox any more. If people had become consistently happier since the Stone Age, to the extent that they and their tribes became wealthier, they would have reached a state of bliss a long time ago. Happiness would long ago have lost its ability to guide people toward their better options. The strong desire of most people to constantly improve their situation and catch up with the Joneses is what makes them perform and their societies thrive, at least materially—a result that might fly in the face of those who want to make the greatest possible happiness a goal of public policy.

Of course, this does not mean that everything must remain the way nature arranged it back in the stone age to increase the chance of survival. We are not hunters and gatherers any more and—arguably—we have alternative and better ways to deal with conflict than fighting it out. Societies like the Scandinavian nations, which have a long tradition of social solidarity, high taxes and high benefits, all attenuating the race for material riches at the top of the social ladder, can prosper just like the Anglo-Saxon variant, which values and rewards individual effort and success much more highly. What Rayo, Becker, Sen and Deaton would say, though, is that happiness economics does not provide a yardstick for choosing the "right" system. It is ultimately a matter of personal philosophy and established societal values.

Leading happiness researchers like Daniel Kahneman and his research group have adopted some of the reservations about the importance of self-discipline and the difficulties in measuring and comparing states of happiness. "A measure of Gross National Happiness would seem to us to be an overly ambitious goal in view of the limitations to subjective measurement," the researchers point out. At the same time, they propose the so-called U-index as a less-assuming measure of immaterial well-being. Rather than condensing the various positive and negative feelings of people into a happiness barometer, the index measures the time people spend experiencing unpleasant feelings. The negative U-state envelops us whenever discomforting moods like anger, frustration or boredom crop up and submerge our strongest positive sentiments.

Kahneman's research team uses detailed questioning of individuals as a basis for the U-index. They encourage the test subjects to reflect on the past day and take notes on the duration and intensity of feelings each of their daily activities triggered. This "Daily Reconstruction Method" has been borrowed from an established procedure in psychology.

For 909 Texas women, the index has already been worked out. On average, these women spent nearly 18 percent of their waking hours in a U-state. For women with household incomes up to $35,000, the percentage was one point higher; in household incomes above $55,000, one point less. Come to think of it, it's quite astonishing what little influence money has on well-being—women in households almost twice as rich spend only 2 percent less of their time in an unpleasant mental state. Two factors in particular drove up the U-index: a depressive disposition and long commuting times to work.

It comes as no surprise, then, that psychologist Kahneman and economist Layard share the conviction that one of the most effective things governments can do to make their populace more content, or less unhappy, is to improve the availability and quality of treatment for psychiatric illness.

Master of My Fate, Captain of My Soul

If one accepts either Angus Deaton's critique or the notion of happiness being an incentive devised by evolution, rather than a gift from God, happiness research loses much of its scope for useful application. Not all of it, though.

Happiness researchers in both economics and psychology are unanimous: An intact family, friends, pleasant coworkers and a high degree of personal autonomy and recognition in the workplace have the same positive influence on contentment as do large differences or changes in income. On the darker side, psychiatric illness, divorce, lack of social interaction, and long commutes are foremost among the happiness killers. More money will hardly lessen their dispiriting effects. *Unemployment,* too, causes unhappiness—not merely because people without jobs have less money to spend. Quality of life plunges because the unemployed feel ostracized and their self-respect becomes damaged. To treat unemployment as a mere financial problem for those affected would be severely underestimating the cost to individuals and to society as a whole. Even people still holding a job become increasingly worried when faced with rising employment insecurity that may jeopardize their own job. The fear factor can be overwhelming, the British economist Andrew Oswald found. If the unemployment rate rises by 1.5 percent, each citizen—not just the unemployed—would need to get paid an extra $500 to compensate for the higher insecurity in the workplace. In Europe, people still in the labor force feel strong bonds with the unemployed. Social inequality thus diminishes the contentment of people there—not so in the United States.

At first glance, it may come as a surprise that out-of-work people are less dissatisfied in regions of high unemployment than those where the rates are lower. According to traditional economic theory, the reverse should be the case, as lower unemployment rates imply better chances to find a new job. When discarding the narrow assumptions of traditional economics, it will be less of a surprise. Where it is quite common to be unemployed because of a region's lack of jobs, unemployment ceases to have a stigma attached to it—and it is easier to find equally idle buddies with whom to while away the days.

Indolence poses a high hurdle for contentment and a fulfilling life. A research team around the Swiss economist Bruno Frey found that people who watch a lot of TV are unhappier than people in comparable life situations who spend less time in front of the tube. For neoclassical economists, it's a sobering thought. Their theories revolve around the assumption of people acting rationally and acting in their own best interest. According to this logic, each individual watches just as much TV as he is comfortable with.

The fact is that many people do not have their TV consumption under control, and spend more time watching than is good for them. The study was based on a poll among more than 42,000 people in 22 European countries, which included questions about TV habits and happiness. The scientists noted that people watching less than half an hour a day are—other things equal—happier with their lives than those choosing a higher level of TV consumption. Especially pronounced is the difference for people whose eyes are glued to the screen for more than 2.5 hours a day.

TV addicts with little time to spare—such as the self-employed, senior managers and politicians—are especially discontented and unhappy. For them, TV watching involves considerable opportunity cost. If they watch a lot nevertheless, their life satisfaction will deteriorate dramatically. The drop is comparable to that of someone abandoned by his life partner. In contrast, retirees and the unemployed—that is, people with time on their hands—reveal no correlation between TV consumption and contentment.

There is a plausible reason for the propensity to excessive TV watching: The reward—relaxation and entertainment—is immediate, the effort minimal at first glance. Much of the "costs," such as lack of sleep or neglected social contacts, become apparent only over time. As a consequence, we underestimate the costs of watching TV and commit a systemic error when deciding how often and for how long we should lounge in front of the tube.

Sometimes, though, we are not lazy enough. The same Bruno Frey, together with coauthor Alois Stutzer, found that for many people the disadvantages of long commutes are not offset by the advantages commuting has to offer. "For most people, commuting is stress that doesn't pay off," the Swiss researchers write. Apparently, many people overestimate their capacity to suffer when commuting is concerned—and they find it hard to correctly assess the loss of free time and quality of life commuting involves.

In evaluating panel data from Germany, Frey and Stutzer found: the longer a test person's commuting time, the less satisfied he is with his life. People taking less than ten minutes to get to work reach 7.24 points on average on the life satisfaction scale, where 0 means "completely dissatisfied" and 10 "completely satisfied"—those who are on the road more than 30 minutes daily manage only 7.0 points. When commuting time rises by 19 minutes, satisfaction goes down 0.12 on average. In comparison, when a single person finds a new life partner, his or her life satisfaction increases by about the same rate. A professional spending 45 minutes on the road to work each day would need to earn an additional $380 to achieve the same level of contentment as her coworker who doesn't commute—which is almost a fifth of an average monthly income. Whoever is considering accepting longer commutes in exchange for a higher income better think twice.

To be sure, not everybody commuting to faraway workplaces has an equivalent alternative closer by. However, often there is a choice between moderate difference in income and moderate differences in the length of the commute. If in doubt, shorten the commute, recommend the happiness researchers. If you choose more income you will quickly get used to the extra money and hardly notice it any more. But you will notice—and probably suffer from—the long commute every day.

In general, when deciding which job to accept, compensation should be less of a deciding factor, a study by John Helliwell and Haifang Huang reveals. Work conditions not related to the amount of compensation can have an enormous impact on happiness, both researchers concluded from a set of Canadian data. A trustful relationship with superiors and coworkers will kindle as much satisfaction as a massive rise in income would.

Even more generally, one could say that if you consider making your daily life harder, less enjoyable or less socially involved, in exchange for more money, make sure it will be a lot more money—or think again. Contrary to income, non-monetary things are much more difficult to get accustomed to. The higher salary will give enjoyment for a little while, whereas the detrimental conditions one accepts in return will remain a sore spot day in, day out. To accept a higher salary in exchange for inferior working conditions, which additionally may turn out to be stressful for family life, could well be a grievous mistake. Since research has found that people underestimate the habituation effect and hope in vain for the higher salary to make them permanently happier, such misjudgments are likely to be the rule rather than the exception.

References

Clark, Andrew, Paul Frijters and Michael Shields (2008): "Relative Income, Happiness, and Utility: An Explanation for the Easterlin Paradox and Other Puzzles," in *Journal of Economic Literature*, Vol. 46, pp. 95–144.

Deaton, Angus (2007): "Income, Aging, Health and Wellbeing Around the World: Evidence From the Gallup World Poll," National Bureau of Economic Research working paper no. 13317.

Di Tella, Rafael and Robert MacCulloch (2006): "Some Uses of Happiness Data in Economics," in: *Journal of Economic Perspectives*, Vol. 20, pp. 25–46.

Di Tella, Rafael, Richard MacCulloch and Andrew Oswald (2001): "Preference over Inflation and Unemployment: Evidence from

Surveys on Happiness," in: *American Economic Review*, Vol. 91, pp. 335–341.

Frey, Bruno, Christine Benesch and Alois Stutzer (2007): "Does Watching TV Make Us Happy?" in: *Journal of Economic Psychology*, Vol. 28, 2007, pp. 283–313.

Frey, Bruno S. and Alois Stutzer (2002): "The Economics of Happiness," in: *World Economics*, Vol. 3, pp. 25–41.

Frey, Bruno and Alois Stutzer (2002): *Happiness Economics*, Princeton, N.J.: Princeton University Press.

Frey, Bruno S. and Alois Stutzer (2002): "What Can Economists Learn from Happiness Research," in: *Journal of Economic Literature*, Vol. 40, pp. 401–435.

Frey, Bruno and Alois Stutzer (forthcoming): "Stress That Doesn't Pay: The Commuting Paradox," in: *Scandinavian Journal of Economics*.

Helliwell, John and Haifang Huang (2005): "How's the Job? Well-Being and Social Capital in the Workplace," National Bureau of Economic Research working paper no. 11759.

Layard, Richard (2005): *Happiness—Lessons from a New Science*, New York: Penguin Press.

Rayo, Luis and Gary S. Becker (2007): "Evolutionary Efficiency and Happiness," in: *Journal of Political Economy*, Vol. 115, pp. 302–337.

Solnick, Sara and David Hemenway (1998): "Is More Always Better?: A Survey on Positional Concerns," in: *Journal of Economic Behavior and Organization*, Vol. 37, pp. 373–383.

3

The Enigma of the Labor Market

"Are Europeans lazy—or Americans crazy?" When looking at the annual hours worked on both continents that question inevitably comes to mind. The average U.S. worker puts in more than 1,800 hours a year, his European counterpart only 1,400. Americans enjoy fewer paid vacations and work longer weeks. In addition, the share of those not having any kind of paid job at all is much smaller in Europe than on the other side of the Atlantic. This was not always so. Until deep into the first half of the twentieth century, Europeans worked many more hours than Americans. They only drew level in 1970.

What causes these conspicuous differences? The question has been stumping labor market researchers for years. It is more than a difference in the number of work hours—Americans and Europeans live in two entirely different worlds. Another example is unemployment rates: While in the United States full employment is practically the norm during times of a booming economy, nations like France and Germany have been struggling with unemployment rates of 8 to 9 percent for decades.

Quite remarkably, labor market researchers have not had much success in identifying the reasons for the dismal employment situation in Europe, or in finding out why in nations with so many cultural ties, people have such differing attitudes toward work. While science has made substantial strides since the seventies, it has failed to offer a comprehensive theory to satisfactorily explain the situation ailing European labor markets.

According to the economics Nobel laureate Edward Prescott, it is the very difference in deductions from earned income that determine how much work an individual will do. He believes the supposedly greater hankering for leisure time (aka, laziness) on the part of Europeans is not part of the equation.

Olivier Blanchard, a professor at MIT in Boston and the chief economist of the International Monetary Funds (IMF) since September 2008, questions Prescott's results on methodological grounds. He is convinced that diverging preferences for leisure and work are the main reason. "I read the evidence as suggesting an effect of taxes, but with the larger role left for preferences," Blanchard writes in a 2004 essay published in the *Journal of Economic Perspectives*. The dispute hasn't been resolved to this day.

If we follow the standard microeconomic textbooks portraying wages as a form of indemnification for having to go through the miseries of work—since people prefer to lay back rather than put their noses to the grindstone—then unemployment does loom prominently as *voluntary* unemployment. Exponents of this theory, though, have a hard time reconciling their convictions with the indisputable fact that unemployment makes people unhappy.

Economists have made great efforts to bring their models more in line with reality. Nevertheless: "Many theories have come and—partly—gone. Each has added a layer to our knowledge, but our knowledge remains very incomplete. To use a well worn formula, we have learned a lot, but we still have a lot to learn," Blanchard concedes.

As a telling example of economists' problems, he cites Spain and Portugal: Both countries underwent political revolutions in the seventies and an explosion in personal incomes thereafter;

both had similar labor market institutions and extensive workplace guarantees for jobholders. Yet despite the commonality, employment records of both nations vary widely: Spain has been suffering from an extremely high unemployment rate that peaked at 20 percent in the mid-nineties; Portugal's rate reached its top level of close to 9 percent in the mid-eighties and dropped after that. Why this is so remains a puzzle to scientists.

Over the past decades, their efforts at grasping the issue of unemployment have almost been like trying to pick up a bar of slippery soap inside a bathtub. More than once they believed they had gotten a handle on the problems, only to see them slip from their grip once again. "Many researchers, including myself, have tried to trace the differences to differences in shocks or institutions," writes Blanchard. But, "I am not sure that our explanations are much more than ex-post rationalizations." In the early eighties, for the first time, economists were certain they had come up with a theoretically well-supported answer. Employment problems were blamed on the two oil crises of the seventies and the concurrently slowing rise in productivity. For employment to remain constant, incomes would have had to rise slower than before. Indeed, the opposite occurred. Rising unemployment was the logical outcome, the scholars determined. As of the mid-eighties, however, labor market researchers increasingly found themselves at a loss to explain why unemployment kept rising inexorably, in spite of the shocks of the seventies becoming a distant memory.

Blanchard's paper leads up to a fundamental question: Do economists have enough insight into the problem to advise politicians, in good conscience, on the subject of unemployment? "I believe we do—with the proper degree of humility," Blanchard replies, pointing out that despite all its shortcomings concerning the optimal architecture of the labor market, economics has produced numerous proven insights on the effectiveness of individual measures. One of these incontestable findings, according to Blanchard, is that whenever unemployment benefits are paid, regardless of the individual's efforts to find a job, the duration of unemployment will increase. Those parts of the puzzle have melded into a well-founded consensus, by which the economic policies of many countries are abiding—rightfully so, Blanchard asserts.

At the same time he cautions against nurturing exaggerated hopes: Even if all insights of labor market researchers were fully implemented in Europe, the labor market problems would not automatically disappear. For instance, labor market institutions proven effective in one country may not show the same, consistently positive results in another. If France were to adopt Denmark's system of income determination, the French labor market would not necessarily come to resemble the Danish one—not only because many other labor market institutions are fundamentally different, but because the Danish simply are different from the French. Mutual trust between employees and businesses, for example, is much higher in Denmark than in France.

Longer Unemployment Can Be a Good Thing

Labor market researchers have known for years that there is an undeniable connection between the amount of unemployment benefits and the length of unemployment spells. The more generous transfer payments are, the longer people will be out of a job. Studies in the United States have revealed that when unemployment compensation rises by 10 percent, the duration of unemployment goes up by 4 to 8 percent.

Economists blame a skewed incentive system: Unemployment compensation cuts into the fruits of labor; people collecting too much money while being on the dole will feel no real urge to find a paid job at the earliest time possible. In economist lingo this represents a case of "moral hazard"—a situation leading people to abuse an insurance system.

Raj Chetty, an economist at the University of California, Berkeley, challenges this view in a comprehensive study. His conclusion is that the negative incentives of unemployment compensation on people's behavior are vastly overestimated. Chetty's study, which debunks a central tenet of neoclassical labor market theory, was published in the *Journal of Political Economy,* one of the world's most prestigious economics journals.

Chetty demonstrates both theoretically and empirically that "moral hazard" is neither the only nor the most important reason why higher unemployment compensation tends to stretch out the duration of unemployment. A large part of the effect is due to the fact that unemployment benefits do exactly what they are intended to do: They protect people losing their jobs from a drastic loss of income for a time, affording them the option of not having to grab the first job that comes along. Without government-sponsored unemployment money, they could only afford some patience in looking for a better job if private savings or loans would tide them over. However, the unemployed are typically with few or no assets, and their borrowing capacity is usually limited as well.

Thus, unemployment insurance offers those in dire financial straits some breathing space to find a fitting job. This benefits not only the jobseekers but society as a whole: It is inefficient, for instance, if a skilled worker losing his employment is forced to take a job as street sweeper, in the process losing his professional skills. His know-how is lost to society, along with any tax and social security contributions a better-paid job would entail.

With two empirical investigations based on U.S. data, Chetty shows the argument to be more than just theoretical ruminations. In the first he uses the data of over 4,500 unemployed to analyze their financial situations and the duration of their unemployment, taking advantage of the fact that in the different states, benefits have gone in different directions over the years. He found that when compensation is raised, only those with no or limited assets will take longer to find a new job. In this group, a rise by 10 percent will result in a 7 to 10 percent extension of the unemployment period. Financially more secure households show an entirely different picture, for they are not directly dependent on government assistance for their daily living expenses. Higher benefits have no direct bearing on the length of their unemployment.

The same pattern is seen when evaluating data of employees who were paid a lump-sum settlement with their layoffs: "Individuals who received severance pay (worth about $4,000 on average) have substantially longer durations," Chetty states. Again, primarily those with low or no private funds respond to the extra money available, as they are unable to soften the loss of income by drawing on savings. For those people, severance pay is a vital financial buffer, enabling them to take more time in searching for a position to match their skills and preferences.

Based on the data, Chetty estimates that unemployment compensation helps the unemployed to find the right jobs, and this could be responsible for about 60 percent of the increase in unemployment duration that comes with more payments.

Why Employers Don't Like to Cut Wages

Economists are unanimous in seeing a flexible labor market as a precondition for a low unemployment rate—while inordinate government regulations artificially hamper the free interplay of market forces. Many free-market economists therefore consider the ample job protection laws of many Western European countries—originally intended to guard employees against unlawful dismissal—a significant obstacle to higher employment. These protective laws impose costs on businesses, which they take into account in their hiring decisions.

Economists also frequently claim that this causes wages to be downwardly rigid: Employees knowing they cannot be fired very easily will be more reluctant to accept lower wages during downturns; as a result, companies facing a crisis are unable to reduce payroll costs promptly. Due to these restrictions, firms will not hire people unless absolutely necessary, even during upturns.

In America, companies face little regulation regarding hiring and firing. It is all the more surprising, then, that U.S. wages are hardly ever cut—companies in trouble will fire people rather than pay them less. Why? There must be another reason besides job protection.

Yale economist Truman Bewley has polled those at the source—managers responsible for compensation policies. The result: Executives fear that employees will view wage and salary cuts as an affront, which would harm their identification with the business and be detrimental to employee morale. In addition, across-the-board compensation cuts would probably encourage the best workers to leave first. Their higher productivity usually is not fully reflected in their income, which gives them a strong position in the labor market. Still more importantly: employees who had to suffer pay cuts would stay on the job, harboring some degree of dissatisfaction. By contrast, when businesses lower costs by the layoff route, the affected individuals leave the company, and so does their anger.

For these reasons and when in doubt, businesses prefer getting a cost break by letting people go; cutting wages is nothing but a last resort. It is not an ideal solution for those affected, nor is it for society as a whole.

Economists in Defense of Minimum Wages

Flexible though U.S. labor markets may be, there is one area where the state gets involved to coerce market forces: Contrary to the otherwise highly regulated German labor market, for instance, the United States has minimum wage laws. This is a thorn in the side of many free-market economists: The arbitrary setting of a price that is too high to reflect prevailing supply and demand, they argue, will throw the market out of kilter, and the inevitable outcome in the labor market is higher unemployment.

In the United States a fierce debate is going on as to whether a substantial increase in minimum wages is called for to mitigate the effects of long-term inflation; in Germany, politicians are fiercely arguing whether minimum wages should be introduced at all.

Until the nineties, it was pretty much a consensus among economists that minimum wages are detrimental to employment chances. But the debate has since taken a turn. An increasing number of well-recognized economists have begun to question the traditional paradigm. Their impetus is fed by scientific investigations conducted over the last 10 or 12 years that cast serious doubt on the thesis that minimum wages automatically reduce job opportunities for low-qualified candidates. In 1998, the Organization for Economic Co-operation and Development (OECD) recommended to their member states a "well thought-out package of economic measures including appropriate minimum wage and income subsidies." Only four years earlier, the organization had pleaded for a discontinuance of minimum wages.

The shedding of the old dogma began in 1994, with an article published in the prestigious *American Economic Review:* Two U.S. economists presented an empirical study with the surprising conclusion that a sizable raise in minimum wages can lead to more jobs.

David Card of Berkeley and Alan Krueger of Princeton investigated employment trends in the fast food industry in New Jersey and neighboring Pennsylvania, following New Jersey's raise of the minimum wage by almost 20 percent, to $5.05. In contrast, Pennsylvania held its minimum wage unchanged at $4.25. Even though menial work in New Jersey became significantly more expensive, hiring in fast food restaurants picked up quite a bit more than in Pennsylvania. For each fast food restaurant in New Jersey, 2.6 additional jobs were created—corresponding to a 13 percent increase. The new minimum wage did not come for free, though; it was the consumer who paid the bill. In comparison to Pennsylvania, fast food prices rose in New Jersey.

Card and Krueger had clearly stirred up a hornets' nest. Their study caused a very heated debate among labor market researchers—several economists launched counterstudies to invalidate Card and Krueger's findings. Six years into publication, a comprehensive critique by David Neumark (University of California) and William Wascher (Federal Reserve Board) appeared; yet Card and Krueger had the last word and the upper hand. In their reply, they managed to not only come up with evidence that their critics used ambiguous data, but were able to reproduce their own findings with an improved set of data relative to the original survey.

Still, some economists held on to their cherished beliefs well into the twenty-first century. They tried to ignore the new evidence as best they could. One example is the German Council of Economic Advisors, nicknamed the Five Wise Men. "The fear that a legally promulgated minimum wage will have a detrimental impact on employment is amply supported by economic theory as well as empirical studies," the Five Wise Men stated in their 2004 annual report. As empirical evidence of job annihilation caused by minimum wages they cited a study dating to 1999. Relating to France, its conclusion was that raises in the minimum wage noticeably impeded the job opportunities for marginally qualified young men. A one percent raise in the minimum wage, the study contended, leads to a 1.0 to 1.3 percent reduction in the probability for people working at this income level to find another job. Minimum wages should therefore be rejected as an "ineffective, even counterproductive instrument," the expert council wrote.

Following a report in the *Handelsblatt* daily, which suggested that the Advisory Council had misrepresented the state of knowledge as embodied in relevant literature and completely disregarded the renowned study by Card and Krueger, the Council again addressed the minimum wage in 2006. Now the conclusion was that "for the United States, no unequivocal effects on employment can be found"; however, the experts maintained that the situation could not be applied to Germany, on account of the U.S. labor market being more flexible and deductions from incomes being lower. A comparison with France would be more appropriate, they argued, since it had similar labor market institutions—and negative effects stemming from minimum wages. They failed to explain, however, how a more flexible labor market implied that minimum wages would do less damage.

Card and Krueger's results can be explained assuming a certain buyer power in the labor market. For labor markets that are fragmented both regionally and in terms of qualifications, there is no all-out competition—rather, large employers influence the overall wage levels through their hiring decisions and wage policies. Employment in these kinds of labor markets is lower than in highly competitive markets. A smartly set minimum wage can increase employment under certain circumstances.

Imagine there is a small town with only one fast food restaurant. If the operator were to open a second location, he might not find enough personnel at existing wages. He'd have to pay more—to the staff in both places. Even if the second location was profitable in itself, it may never get opened because the owner wishes to avoid pushing up wages at the original location. A minimum wage in the first restaurant would set an end to these negative repercussions.

Could Card and Krueger's results be more than an odd coincidence? Not likely, English studies suggest. "Although standard economic analysis implies that wage floors should have a negative impact on employment, most empirical studies struggle to find a negative impact on jobs," is the conclusion of a research team of the Centre for Economic Performance at the prestigious London School of Economics, one of the leading economic research institutes in Europe. Mirko Draca, Stephen Machin and John van Reenen investigated the impact that the minimum wages introduced in 1999 had on employment and profitability in the United Kingdom. They found negligible employment losses in the low-wage sector.

One hypothetical explanation is that businesses simply ignored the new minimum wages. If law is evaded it can do no damage. But the argument does not hold, according to the findings of David Metcalf, another economist at the Centre for Economic Performance at the London School of Economics. Now if the national minimum wage is indeed observed, pushing the earnings of some workers above the current market level, the usual laws of demand and supply would cause us to expect a decline in employment. One reason why such a decline did not materialize is that businesses, just like the New Jersey fast food chains, passed on rising wages through higher prices. That works wherever there is only limited competition from foreign sources or sundry sectors.

The second part of the answer is profits. Companies in industries most affected had to put up with lower earnings, at least for the time immediately following the introduction of minimum wages. Later on they were more successful in passing on the cost increase. Businesses paying very low wages were most severely impacted. However, economists could not find any evidence of higher insolvencies due to declining revenues—for instance, in nursing homes—in the wake of minimum wage introduction. Should these results be borne out over the long haul, it might be an indication that businesses achieved disproportionate earnings from low wage payments—that is, at the expense of low-qualified workers.

Another potential explanation is that higher wages for especially poorly paid work help alleviate the chronic labor shortage in those lines. Such additional employment can balance out, at least partially, the employment losses encountered in other professions. Even the two vehement critics of minimum wages, David Neumark and William Wascher, had to concede in a 2006 literary review that there no longer was a general consensus on the negative employment effects of minimum wages in the low-wage sector. "What may be most striking to the reader…is the wide range of estimates of the effects of the minimum wage on employment," Neumark and Wascher pointed out. Depending on country, research methods and duration, studies come up with negative, neutral or positive labor market changes.

Undesirable Side-Effects of Minimum Wages

The introduction or drastic increase of a minimum wage should be considered carefully. It's akin to toothpaste, according to a study by a German-Swiss research team: Once the tube is squeezed the process cannot be reversed. Even following the abolishment of a minimum wage, its aftereffects will continue to resonate, affecting not only low-wage earners but tilting the economy's entire compensation structure upward.

The economists Armin Falk (University of Bonn), Ernst Fehr and Christian Zehnder (University of Zurich) obtained these results by using a method fairly new to labor market researchers: In lab experiments they created artificial labor markets.

The study involved 240 Zurich students assuming the parts of businessmen and employees. Wages and profits were settled in artificial currency, which at the end was converted into Swiss francs. The model's economics operated on simple laws: Sales rose with the number of employees, as did personnel expenses. At the same time, the productivity of each additional employee decreased as the number of staff grew. In each round of the game, each company could decide how many employees to offer a job at which wage. Each worker could decide for him- or herself whether to accept the offer. If one refused, he'd be out of work over the next round and deprived of an income.

Without state intervention, wage rates settled at an average of 188 lab-dollars. A two-employee company earned a profit of 364 lab-dollars. After 15 rounds played, the state introduced a minimum wage of 220 lab-dollars—but market rates settled clearly above. Now, businesses began paying their employees an average of 238 lab-dollars. Firms with two employees suffered a profit decline of more than 25 percent, while 93 percent of all wages were north of 220 lab-dollars—before, it had been 8 percent.

The minimum wage appeared to skew employees' conception of what is fair. A pay offer of 220 lab-dollars was viewed as fair and generous while the firm had an option to pay less. Yet when businesses were compelled to pay no less than the 220 lab-dollars, the same offer came across as unfair or stingy. Since people resent being taken advantage of, many workers would rather decline the job offer altogether.

The minimum wage thus pushed up the so-called reservation wages below which no worker would accept a job. The effect persisted when the state abandoned meddling in the wage system: For a long time, market wages remained notably higher than before intervention. "The temporary introduction of the minimum wage has permanent effects on actual wages, i.e., even after the removal of the minimum wage, actual wages remain close to the previous minimum wage level," the authors write. Workers had evidently gotten used to a better pay and were later unwilling to work for less.

What's particularly remarkable is the employment effect of the minimum wage: Instead of falling, the number of jobs increased—by 14 percent per business. The reason was that in some cases, the minimum wage reduced the marginal costs of hiring another worker. The mechanisms that the researchers observed in their test lab were the same as David Card and Alan Krueger had seen in New Jersey: Absent a minimum wage, only workers willing to take a low-wage job would find employment. To expand its staff, a company would have had to lure additional employees with higher wage offers. The minimum wage changed it all: For workers already employed the wages rose regardless—while the marginal cost of hiring a new employee, in many cases, was the stipulated minimum rate.

The authors issue a warning, however, as they found minimum wages to cause substantial profit decreases. In real life a possible consequence could be that businesses cut back on their investment plans or drop out of the market completely. Long-term, both scenarios would be detrimental to the labor market.

Fighting Unemployment in Kindergarten

When people are unemployed, or unable to earn enough to make a living, or if they have resorted to criminal activities, the damage is done. Government can try to ameliorate the situation for individuals and society somewhat, but there is only so much it can do. This is not to say that the state is powerless—it just needs to take action at an early stage, that is, at the time of infancy. This proposition has been advanced by an interdisciplinary team headed by economics Nobel laureate James Heckman, who had compiled research results from psychologists, neurobiologists, behavioral specialists and economists. The core message is: In economic terms, it is worthwhile for society to pay special attention to children from disadvantaged backgrounds.

The first years in life are crucial for what abilities a person will develop in adulthood. Children at the lower end of the societal spectrum have extremely dim prospects: They are much more likely to have inferior schooling, and to have a difficult time finding a job. Often they have poor soft skills and an insufficient level of motivation. Little wonder they suffer in the labor market.

When the state intervenes early and resolutely, it may succeed in rectifying the shortcomings of a child's home environment. To effectively improve productivity and job chances of the under-qualified, early action is essential: Research in developmental psychology and neurosciences has found that the first years of life are the wellspring for the development of future abilities and skills.

Neurobiology has discovered a hierarchy of cognitive, linguistic, emotional and social functions. They build on basic abilities acquired early on, and cannot be fully acquired without them. Experiences gained during the formation of the neural networks required for a specific ability are particularly crucial: While these neural connections assigned to specific tasks can be revised to some degree later, the leeway for such modifications decreases with age. You can't teach an old dog new tricks, as the saying goes. Long-term studies have furnished empirical evidence of the effectiveness of intensive early-childhood intervention.

In one test, preschool children from dysfunctional families in the United States were enrolled in special education classes for six months. Scientists followed the lives of these children for several decades and compared them with a control group that did not participate in the program. What they found was that those having received special attention went further in their education, had higher incomes, more often owned their homes, and were less likely to go on welfare or to prison. Scientists determined these "social returns" of the preschool program to amount to an amazing 17 percent, that is, for every dollar invested in such a program for disadvantaged children the government, society at large or the children themselves gained 17 cents per year in extra income or saved expenses. For a government that pays less than 5 percent interest to borrow, this is not a bad dividend.

Programs beginning in babyhood appear to be even more effective, according to an ongoing evaluation of another guidance project for lower-class children in the age groups of four months through eight years. The first children benefiting from the program are in their early twenties today. They appear to possess a permanently higher IQ than their peers who grew up in the same environment but had not been in the program. Since the subjects are only starting their careers, the annual social returns of these much more elaborate programs cannot yet be determined in full.

If we take these scientific insights seriously, implications are evident: To fight unemployment, we need to do more for children coming from problematic environments. They should receive special guidance early on, thereby offsetting possible deficits in their home environment. Heckman stresses, though, that the positive evaluation of this type of intervention is limited to target-group specific and intensive special guidance programs. He is critical of perfunctory initiatives in the one-size-fits-all mold.

The findings of Heckman are corroborated by research into the determinants of intelligence, done by psychologists and economists. Since the Industrial Revolution, people's IQs have grown from one generation to the next. It does not show in common IQ tests, since the aspiration levels are constantly adjusted upward in lockstep with increasing intellectual capacities—10 percent for each new generation. In other words, if your IQ is not 10 percent higher than that of your son or daughter, you are dumber. This is pointed out by U.S. economist William Dickens of the Brookings Institution and the Australian psychologist James Flynn, who authored a study reviving the age-old debate about nature or nurture. Are differences in intelligence primarily due to our genes or to social environment? The question on the inalterability of differences in talent has tangible implications for educational policy, and for the extent of assistance to the socially disadvantaged. If the dictum "once a dummy, always a dummy" is valid, this would be a case for providing special support to the gifted. If, on the other hand, disparities in innate abilities were mainly due to environmental conditions, giving special guidance to the disadvantaged would be the right course to take.

Studies of adopted children and twins who grew up in diverse environments almost invariably showed different intelligence levels to be genetically conditioned. Yet the continuing rise of IQ levels over the generations contradicts that conclusion, as genes change only imperceptibly from one generation to the next.

William Dickens and James Flynn have developed a model that resolves this contradiction. In terms of methodology the model resembles a Keynesian multiplier model, except that a "social multiplier" is used instead of an economic one. The two researchers' conclusion is that an indivisible interaction between genes and environment is responsible for differences in intelligence and mental development.

How Bible Studies Can Make You Rich

Better education = greater wealth. This equation was just as valid in the nineteenth century as it is now. Economists Ludger

Woessmann (Ludwig Maximilians University at Munich, Germany) and Sascha Becker (University of Stirling, Scotland) have presented a fascinating economic-historical study using the example of Prussia during the Industrial Revolution.

Woessmann and Becker manage to show that the famous thesis by the German sociologist Max Weber, according to which Protestants are wealthier than Catholics by virtue of their superior work ethic, is flawed. While Weber was correct with regard to the differences in wealth between Protestants and Catholics, he erred when explaining the phenomenon: It was not their superior work ethic that made Protestants wealthier but their Bible studies. Because the Protestant church encouraged its flock to read the word of God in the Bible for themselves, they had noticeably better reading and writing skills than Catholics.

Becker and Woessmann used detailed data from Prussian statistics agencies for their study. For all 452 Prussian districts, their data show the demographic, religious and economic structures, including literacy rates and religious affiliation. And while it its true that there are no reliable district-level figures available for GDP around 1870, they do have information on how many people in each district worked in agriculture, industry and service industries. According to the authors, this permits drawing conclusions on a region's wealth at that time: The less importance agriculture held, the more abundant the area's wealth. Another indicator is the salaries of primary school teachers: They were financed almost exclusively through local taxes, thus giving some hints on the economic situation.

The more dominance the Protestant church had in a district, the more economically advanced that district was. In addition, Protestant areas had substantially fewer illiterates than did Catholic domains. The researchers find a clue for this in Martin Luther's admonition that every believer should experience God's word directly and read the Bible regularly. As a consequence, the Protestant church traditionally placed greater emphasis on a thorough school education, reflected in a higher literacy rate in Protestant regions.

"The results reveal that after conditioning on the effect of literacy, there is no difference whatsoever in economic outcomes between Protestant and Catholic counties," the authors point out. "Protestantism has no independent effect on economic outcomes beyond literacy. This leaves little room for substantive economic differences stemming solely from differences in work ethic, in that Protestants provided more effort, strived more for economic success, were thriftier, or had a more efficient approach to working life."

Becker and Woessmann also dismiss the argument that economic issues might have had a hand in whether a district had been preponderantly Protestant or Catholic. In that case, Protestantism would not have led to wealth, but conversely, economic development would have encouraged Protestantism. The authors show, however, that the factor most decisive for the dominant religion was the distance from Luther's place of activity, the town of Wittenberg.

Becker and Woessmann also delved into the possibility that Protestants, owing to their work ethic, had put a premium on education in hopes of achieving greater wealth this way. What they found here was that the Protestant church stressed reading and writing solely for religious, not economic, reasons.

The further the Industrial Revolution progressed, the more complex production processes became—with businesses being increasingly dependent on well-trained labor. This created a culture of converging interests between business and labor. "Due to capital-skill complementarity, the accumulation of physical capital by the capitalists increased the importance of human capital in sustaining the rate of return to physical capital," write the Israeli economists Oded Galor and Omer Moav in a study aptly titled "Das Human-Kapital" (the human capital) published in the *Review of Economic Studies*. According to Galor and Moav, this is the main reason why Marx's "lumpen-proletariat" (an underclass of non-class-conscious day laborers living in abject poverty) disappeared over time. As machines grew more complicated and work processes more refined, business in the late nineteenth and early twentieth centuries increasingly required better-trained employees and, in particular, workers that could read and write. This made it worthwhile for them to not only invest in fixed assets but in human capital as well.

The thesis is supported by the voting behavior in British Parliament in 1902, when decisions on possible school reforms—specifically, obligatory school attendance and the expansion of universities—were at issue. The larger the share of industry jobs in a parliamentarian's electoral district, the greater the probability that he would vote in favor of education reform—irrespective of whether he belonged to the Conservative party or Labor party. Politicians from rural electoral districts generally voted against the reform package: Their clientele, mainly farmers, had no use for better-educated workers.

References

Becker, Sascha O. and Ludger Woessman (forthcoming): "Was Weber Wrong? A Human Capital Theory of Protestant Economic History," in: *Quarterly Journal of Economics*.

Bewley, Truman (2004): "Fairness, Reciprocity and Wage Rigidity," Institute for the Study of Labor (IZA) discussion paper no. 1137.

Blanchard, Olivier (2004): "The Economic Future of Europe," in: *Journal of Economic Perspectives*, Vol. 18, pp. 3–26.

Blanchard, Olivier (2006): "European Unemployment: The Evolution of Facts and Ideas," in: *Economic Policy*, Vol. 21, pp. 5–59.

Chetty, Raj (2008): "Moral Hazard vs. Liquidity and Optimal Unemployment Insurance," in: *Journal of Political Economy*, Vol. 116, pp. 173–234.

Draca, Mirko, Stephen Machin and John Van Reenen (2006): "Minimum Wages and Firm Profitability," Institute for the Study of Labor (IZA) discussion paper no. 1913.

Falk Armin, Ernst Fehr and Christian Zehnder (2006): "Fairness Perceptions and Reservation Wages—The Behavioral Effects of Minimum Wages," in: *Quarterly Journal of Economics,* Vol. 121, pp. 1347–1381.

Galor, Oded and Omer Moav (2006): "Das Human-Kapital: A Theory of the Demise of the Class Structure," in: *Review of Economic Studies,* Vol. 73, pp. 85–117.

Knudsen, Eric, James Heckman, Judy Cameron and Jack Shonkoff (2006): "Economic, Neurobiological and Behavioral Perspectives on Building America's Future Workforce," in *Proceedings of the National Academy of Sciences,* Vol. 103, pp. 10155–10162.

Neumark, David and William Wascher (2007): "Minimum Wages and Employment: A Review of Evidence from the New Minimum Wage Research," in: *Foundations and Trends in Microeconomics,* Vol. 3, pp. 1–154.

Prescott, Edward (2004): "Why Do Americans Work So Much More Than Europeans?" in: *Federal Reserve Bank of Minneapolis Quarterly Review,* Vol. 28, July 2004, pp. 2–13

4

The Almost-Forgotten Small Difference

The prospect of finding a job as a lawyer was pretty grim for Sandra Day O'Connor. In 1952, she had passed the bar exam at Stanford University, where she was among the top three in her class. Still, no law office was willing to hire the young woman—all she would have been able to get, through connections, was a secretarial position in a law firm. By contrast, her male fellow graduates, sporting inferior grades, were in hot demand by the leading law firms. O'Connor finally joined the state attorney's office and worked her way up in public service—until in 1981 President Ronald Reagan nominated her as the first woman ever to serve on the Supreme Court.

As recently as the 1950s, typewriting speed was just as valuable for women as was a law degree. For decades to come, female academics would be asked in job interviews how fast they could type. Jobs matching their professional qualifications were hardly available to them, as employers took it for granted that they would soon get married and have children. Those days are over, even though women still earn less and hold a greater number of menial jobs today than do men. Pursuing careers and working a full lifetime is more of a rule now than an exception.

Nonetheless, the rise of women in the labor force had a momentous effect on the labor market and the entire economy. To understand the revolutionary changes shaping the labor market over the past five decades, we must look at the employment curve of women. And to influence or predict the labor market, we need to immerse ourselves in economic gender research. It should no longer be considered a marginal topic within the economic realm.

The steep rise in U.S. employment between 1970 and 2000 is largely owed to more women entering the labor market. And when an American worker puts in longer hours per week than his European counterpart, it is because of the fact that women in Europe are less integrated in the labor market and more frequently hold part-time jobs, say economists Richard Freeman (Harvard) and Ronald Schettkat (Wuppertal). "If Europe were to emulate the American job miracle, it would have to change the status of the sexes in the labor market quite dramatically," Freeman concludes. In his view, this point is of almost greater importance for the state of employment in Europe than are traditional labor-market reforms commonly recommended by economists. As a remedy countering demographic developments, for instance, economists usually recommend later retirement, lower pensions and higher immigration. A more equitable participation by women in the labor market, which would help resolve the future funding issues of social security, is almost entirely neglected by the profession. Especially Germany would benefit—the country is way behind when it comes to women in the labor force. Even the debate around labor market policies, such as the creation of so-called mini-jobs or the changing of limits to the extra income permitted to welfare recipients, has largely been carried on without reference to the genders. A gender-specific analysis of said policies, however, is indispensable to assess both their short-term impact on the labor market and their long-term effect on the allocation of roles between men and women.

The employment rate of married women in Europe has unquestionably risen in the last decades, due mostly to a substantial increase in part-time work. The shortfall in income for women is still relatively substantial. In the World Economic Forum's "Gender Gap Report 2006," Germany finds itself in thirty-second place in terms of opportunity for women and their participation in the economy, which puts it far behind the United States. In the leading positions of politics, administration and, above all, business enterprises, women are still a rarity in much of Europe.

With the tools at their disposal, economists can contribute greatly to a better understanding of the problem, as Harvard economist Claudia Goldin has proved: The fact that she was chosen in 2006 to deliver the American Economic Association's prestigious Ely lecture on the subject is solid evidence that at least in the United States, gender research has entered the mainstream of economics. At the same time, her analysis points out the limits to such an approach—for even today, it is not just economic, but also psychological, social and cultural aspects that impede women in their professional advancement.

An Economic History of Women's Emancipation

At the turn of the twentieth century, married women only sought employment outside the house if it was absolutely necessary and there was no other way to feed their families. There was stigma attached when husbands had to send their wives out to work— not the least because available jobs were dirty and unpleasant. Single women worked only until they found a husband. Rising incomes actually hampered female employment: As men were earning more, the necessity for a second income diminished.

Change came with the proliferation of office jobs—in place of physically strong workers, smart workers were in increasing demand. A huge expansion of the educational system helped to fill that need and afforded young women new avenues for education. These developments, however, did not proceed apace in the United States and Europe, emphasize economists Freeman and Schettkat. In the "Old world," World War II retarded the process: Due to its upheavals, followed by arduous reconstruction, the educational system was reformed and expanded much later—which is why American girls had access to a superior education much earlier than their European counterparts.

There were consequences. Since European women were less educated and earned less than those in the United States, the custom remained to stay at home and take care of the children and housework. By contrast, many American families found that it paid off for them to seek outside help with the cooking, cleaning and childcare.

Yet Sandra Day O'Connor's experience illustrates that, until deep into the second half of the century, college was mainly a preferred way for girls to find a suitable husband. Owing to a lack of decent opportunities, young women did not plan for professional careers, but envisioned just a few years of office work until they could get married, or until the house was paid off. Prospective employers' expectations with regard to the duration of women's commitment were correspondingly modest. Women did not make major investments in their own human capital, nor did the jobs available lend themselves to such purpose. Many of the skills needed for their work as clerks they would usually bring to the job on the first day, Claudia Goldin points out. A gain of economically valuable experience, as a basis for building a career was utterly unusual. In short: Typewriting skills trumped law school.

Toward the end of the sixties began what Goldin dubbed a "silent revolution": Within a handful of years, the self-image of women changed radically. Polling of young men and women revealed how much their goals and ambitions converged. Within a few years, recognition on the job became a major goal in life for women, just as it was for men. The importance of family ties declined among women and rose among men, until both sides met halfway. Likewise, the wide gap in the importance attributed to financial success narrowed markedly, though it did not disappear completely.

Young women pushed into high-profile education and professions that until then had almost exclusively been open to men. They enrolled in medical school and law school, and they studied business economics. For the last 15 years, girls have outnumbered boys in college attendance, and even more so in achieving a degree. With some delay, this development has reached Europe as well. For some years now, the majority of German high school students are girls, and they have also taken the lead in terms of performance.

An achievement of pharmacological research has contributed mightily to this revolution: the birth control pill. The extent of its influence was revealed by Martha Bailey of the University of Michigan in her study "More Power to the Pill," published in the *Quarterly Journal of Economics* in 2006. Prior to the pill's introduction, half of the 21-year-old American women were already married and 40 percent were either pregnant or had given birth. Soon after the pill became available, marriage quickly shifted to a later age, as did the point of the first pregnancy. To prove that this was a conscious choice by women that was enabled by the pill, Bailey cites the fact that in the different states, unmarried women under 21 had access to the pill at widely differing points in time—spanning from 1960 to 1974. For instance, the chief of gynecology at Yale Medical School was sent to prison in 1961 for having made birth control available to women. Only in 1965 did the Supreme Court overrule the states' prohibition of birth control for married woman and for women of legal age. It took many more years until unmarried women under 21 gained access to the pill.

Bailey's econometric analysis confirms: In states with early access to the pill, young women married later, had their children later and, until their mid-thirties, represented a higher share of the labor force than they did in other states.

Family Economics and Its Limits

The newly found self-assurance of women began to assert itself in the late seventies in labor market theory. A future Nobel laureate in economics, Gary Becker of the University of Chicago, popularized a proposition according to which marriage partners do not pursue a common goal, but negotiate from the strength of their relative positions: The spouse who is better qualified and makes more money will have an advantage in the marriage market, as well as in the familial struggle over power, resources and careers, with both sides using divorce as the ultimate threat.

Becker's economization of marriage, however, also reveals the limits of a purely economic viewpoint. For in about 30 percent of American households, the woman earns more than the man does, as an analysis by Richard Freeman reveals. If Becker's thesis were to hit the core of the problem—that is, if the decisions on who will do the cooking, cleaning and childcare were made primarily under economic considerations—the role assignments of man and woman in these families would have fundamentally changed. Yet this does not seem to be the case: In the United States, mothers still do the lion's share of childcare, even when they are holding full-time jobs and earn more than their partners. In childless households, we find that women earning more than their spouse work less around the house than do lesser situated females, but still more than their respective partners.

When we add up the working hours spent on the job, household and childcare, women with relatively high incomes compared to their spouses still work 10 percent more than their partners, finds Freeman. Surprisingly, the difference is narrower with women of lesser income. In the best of economic lingo, Freeman concludes: "Since there seems to be no obvious reason why men cannot perform more household chores, it cannot be ruled out that the elasticity of substitution between female and male time expenditures within the household is limited on historical and cultural grounds." Or, put in simple terms: When a woman wishes to hold a paid job besides her household work, she is welcome to do so from her spouse's standpoint—which does not mean, however, that he is prepared to shoulder a greater share of household chores, never mind economical incentives and contract theory.

It Pays to Pay Women Less

Why do females still earn lower incomes than males—despite the "silent revolution," despite several decades of the women's movement? Is it because the (predominantly male) bosses act out their prejudices against women? Do they resent women, or accept them only as housewives and companions? Economically speaking, it would be unreasonable to give preference to male associates for those reasons as this would be detrimental to the business's profitability. We would therefore expect competition to prevent such discrimination.

Three economists from the University of Erlangen-Nuremberg perused a large set of data and found an alternative explanation: Women make less money because it is not all that important to them. Important in this instance means: Their decisions as to whether and for whom they will work are less influenced by monetary considerations than is the case with men.

Translated into the language of economics, this means: Businesses are faced with a supply elasticity that differs between men and women. A company paying 10 percent less than a comparable competitor will lose its male employees first. To retain them, the company must pay higher salaries. And since its experience has been that women's decisions are less influenced by the rate of compensation, it fares better if it offers a higher pay to the men in particular.

This would mean that the pay discrimination against women is a strategy for profit maximization, rather than the acting out of prejudices to the economic disadvantage of the business. Women would be penalized with lower incomes for defining (or allowing to define) their professional role as a second earner. They will move when their husbands change jobs, but they have a hard time persuading their families to move when better job opportunities are available to them elsewhere. Businesses are aware of these facts and concentrate on men, who are easier to retain or recruit with attractive compensation packages.

Boris Hirsch, Thorsten Schank and Claus Schnabel have calculated the wage elasticity of labor supply of men and women. Their data were based on the figures that businesses report to Social Security. They contain information on salary levels and on how many men and women have left a company or have been newly hired.

As expected, the higher a business's pay rates, the fewer employees leave. Yet the elasticity factor of about one is relatively low. An increase in salary of 1 percent lowers the departure rate by only about 1 percent. With regard to gender-specific rates, the scientists noted that women's response to salary differences was only half that of men.

Women Are Less Effective Negotiators

In bargaining processes women often get the short end of the stick, a research team of (female) political scientists, economists and management experts from Harvard and Carnegie Mellon universities found—but it greatly depends on the circumstances.

The researchers' conclusion: Women achieve poor results in negotiations in particular when they are uncertain about the negotiation scope and there are no objective benchmarks.

The researchers investigated at which salary levels 525 men and women graduates from a business management college were hired, adjusting the figures from their data base by factors like assumed responsibilities, relevant experience and similar. The bottom line was that women received a 5 percent lower starting salary than comparably qualified men. However, in industries where the job applicant had a clear idea of what starting salaries were customary, the disadvantage on the women's part was hardly discernable. By contrast, in industries with opaque salary structures women would earn 10 percent less.

The researchers provided an explanation for this by use of a laboratory test: They simulated price negotiation between a manufacturer and its supplier. Men and women were facing one another in assigned roles of buyer and seller and had to bargain about the price of halogen headlights.

The sellers were given a minimum acceptable price, along with information as to what price would represent a very good deal for their principals. The buyers were given a maximum acceptable price. Half the buyers were also advised that their principal wished to pay no more than about half that maximum price, a supplementary piece of information that considerably eased the uncertainty they felt about their negotiating positions.

The test revealed: At a high uncertainty factor, the price targeted by female buyers was already higher than that accepted by male buyers; the gaps in actual transaction prices were even wider. By contrast, in negotiating situations with better information and lower uncertainty, female buyers would even go for somewhat lower purchase prices than male buyers. While they could not enforce these, they wound up paying only marginally more than the men.

The research group evaluated the result as follows: When both sides are mostly ignorant of the other side's negotiation latitude, male negotiating postures like dominance, obtrusiveness and selfishness will have a positive effect on the negotiation's outcome. Primarily female virtues like empathy, understanding and readiness for compromise, on the other hand, are inimical in this type of situation.

Negotiating success for women, however, is restricted not only by their personality makeup but also by the gender role behavior expected of them and inculcated in them from early childhood. This was one of the findings from the analysis of role plays that the researchers conducted with 176 managers in a training program: Here, men and women were called upon to conduct salary negotiations either for themselves or on behalf of a third party. On average, men obtained a salary of $146,000 for themselves or that third party, whereas women managed only $140,000 for themselves but $167,000 if they negotiated on behalf of others.

Yet the female gender is not unselfish or modest by nature. Lab tests have shown that society expects such behavior. Women asking for a pay raise were seen in a negative light by their male superiors; men were not. Female superiors, on the other hand, viewed male and female employees making demands as equally negative. The women participating in these tests were probably aware of this discrepancy: If the superior was male, their demeanor would be much more modest than that of men; with a female superior they would be just as aggressive as their male counterparts.

The experiment revealed again that greater transparency is an advantage to women. When female test subjects had a good conception of their work's worth, they defended their claims in negotiations just as doggedly as they did on behalf of third parties. They gained for themselves as much as men did.

To summarize, the expectations of men with regard to appropriate gender-specific behavior are highly influential on the behavior of women in negotiating situations. This may be an important reason why women are paid less than men and have fewer career opportunities. They are in a bind. Putting ambitions on display is important for climbing up the corporate ladder, but by doing so women risk the disapproval of their overwhelmingly male superiors.

As some conceptions deeply rooted in our culture and socialization, such as frowning on women who make demands, can only be eliminated over the long haul, the research results suggest that a certain degree of public intervention—for instance, through antidiscrimination laws and insisting on transparent procedures in personnel policies—seems justifiable from an economic standpoint.

Competing against Men Is No Bed of Roses

In a series of lab experiments, three American economists tackled the issue of why women are scarcely represented in top positions from a different viewpoint. In economics, the rise to the top is often modeled as a series of tournaments. Everyone fights to come in first, but only the winner gets a promotion and will be able to participate in the next competition, and so on. Only those who survive several rounds of this struggle will reach the very top.

For these reasons, Uri Gneezy, Muriel Niederle and Aldo Rustichini investigated the question as to whether women do less well in a strongly competitive environment: Students of an Israeli engineering college were invited to play maze games on the computer; each solved labyrinth was rewarded. When test persons were not in direct competition, only a statistically insignificant difference between men and women was noticeable.

Then the reward system was changed: The researchers divided the test subjects into mixed groups of six, and only the top performers in each group were paid. While the men were spurred on by the competition and solved more riddles, the women's performance remained unchanged—they solved the same number as when paid per game.

In same-sex groupings this was different. When women had to compete against women only, a similar competitive zeal took over, as was the case with men, and the performance difference between the genders almost disappeared. Gneezy, Niederle and Rustichini's conclusion was that it is not competitive pressure per se that lets women fade, but a reluctance to compete against men head on.

Psychologists have an explanation for such behavior, which is known as the stigma theory: People will shy away from activities in which they may encounter prejudices due to their group identities or other distinguishing features. Here, it would be the prejudice that women are not able to assert themselves vis-à-vis men.

The lab test results are all the more remarkable as the test subjects were students at an elite engineering college in Haifa. Participants were women who had opted for a professional education that was traditionally a domain of males, and in which they could be proud of being accepted. Nonetheless, it appears they still felt that they were not on an equal footing with their male cohorts.

Gneezy, Niederle and Rustichini carried out one more experiment with their subjects to determine whether it was indeed a lack of self-confidence that caused women's reluctance to compete against men. This time, participants were allowed to choose the degree of difficulty for which they were to be rewarded. The trickier the riddle, the higher the reward per task solved. Before the actual start they were allowed to solve a single labyrinth game at a lower degree of difficulty, in order to get a feel for the level of complexity. In this experiment, men were only marginally better in solving the riddles than women—but they showed much more confidence in picking the degree of difficulty.

Female reluctance to compete against men may well play a major role in filling senior executive positions, the researchers presume, and base their conjecture on the following: If the top 40 percent of all participants had been selected for a senior management position, the share of women would have been 24 percent in the competitive test situation among mixed-gender groups. In the experiments without competitive pressure, and in those conducted with same-gender groups, however, the women's share among the best would have been around 40 percent.

The Fear of Competition Is an Acquired Trait

Yet what could be the reason for the women's behavior? Is timidity part of the female genetic make-up? Or is it a result of upbringing? This question was followed up on by Uri Gneezy, who had been part of the Haifa experiments, together with two American colleagues. The researchers traveled to India and Tanzania and looked for women who had undergone a very different socialization.

In Tanzania they visited with the Masai tribe, which has a highly patriarchic order. If a Masai is asked the number of his children he will only name his sons, the economists report—daughters do not count. Girls are married off at a young age to older men who have several wives and see them as property rather than partners. The very opposite is the case, according to the researchers' findings, in the Indian tribe of the Khasi—here it is the women who hold sway. The line of descent in inheritances follows the female branch via the youngest daughter. She and her children stay at the mother's house, even when married. Her sisters, too, do not move in with their husbands but form a new household at their mother's home. The men work for the welfare of their wife's families and own no property, nor do they play any significant social role. A men's rights movement is attempting to challenge the evidently extreme inequity of the situation.

Uri Gneezy, Kenneth Leonhard and John List did several tests with men and women of these two tribes. They gave them a simple task that women and men could do equally well: tossing a ball into a bucket from three meters' distance. The test subjects had the choice of receiving $.50 per successful toss, a sum equivalent to a day's work. As an alternative, they could opt for a reward system that paid them $1.50 per successful toss, but only when they proved to be better than an anonymous opposing player whose gender was unknown to them. The second option was especially attractive to those who felt they could rise to the occasion by doing extra well.

Altogether, 156 individuals took part in the experiment, nearly 40 per tribe and gender—a sufficient number to lend credibility to the results by the usual statistical standards. Of the Khasi women in India, more than half chose the competition; of the Masai men, exactly half. By contrast, only about 25 percent of the Masai women and barely 40 percent of the Khasi men preferred to compete.

The researchers interpret these results as an indicator for the substantial influence of socialization on the individual's eagerness to compete. Gender-specific factors, it seemed, played only a secondary role relative to social factors in explaining the differences in behavior.

References

Bailey, Martha (2006): "More Power to the Pill: The Impact of Contraceptive Freedom on Women's Life Cycle Labor Supply," in: *Quarterly Journal of Economics,* Vol. 121, pp. 289–320.
Freeman, Richard (2002): "The Feminization of Work in the USA: A New Era for (Man)kind?" in: *Gender and the Labour Market:*

Econometric Evidence of Obstacles to Achieving Gender Equality, ed. Siv Gustafsson and Danièle Meulders, London: MacMillan, pp. 3–21.

Freeman, Richard and Ronald Schettkat (2005): "Marketization of Household Production and the EU-US-Gap in Work," in: *Economic Policy,* Vol. 20, pp. 6–50.

Gneezy, Uri, Kenneth Leonard and John List (2006): "Gender Differences in Competition: The Role of Socialization," working paper.

Gneezy, Uri, Muriel Niederle and Aldo Rustichini (2003): "Performance in Competitive Environments: Gender Differences," in: *Quarterly Journal of Economics,* Vol. 118, pp. 1049–1073.

Goldin, Claudia (2006): "The Quiet Revolution that Transformed Women's Employment, Education and Family," in: *American Economic Review,* Vol. 96, pp. 1–21.

Hausmann, Ricardo, Laura Tyson and Saadia Zahidi (2006): "The Global Gender Gap Report 2006," published by World Economic Forum.

Riley Bowles, Hannah, Linda Babcock and Kathleen McGinn (2005): "Constraints and Triggers: Situational Mechanics of Gender in Negotiation," in: *Journal of Personality and Social Psychology,* Vol. 89, pp. 951–965.

5

It's All about Culture

Looking for a parking space in Manhattan can drive you crazy. Up until 2002 foreign ambassadors to the United Nations did not have to worry about this. They could freely disregard traffic rules by virtue of diplomatic immunity. The police had no enforcement power against diplomats parking in restricted zones and failing to pay their traffic tickets. The foreign representatives took ample advantage of said privilege: Between 1997 and 2002, diplomats left 15,000 traffic tickets unpaid—causing the city to suffer a revenue loss of some $18 million.

This exploiting of diplomatic immunity for private purposes equals unfair gain and is therefore closely tied to corruption. Immunity was instituted to protect envoys of foreign countries from arbitrary prosecution, not as a free pass to break the traffic rules of a host country.

However, not all diplomats abused their immunity for cost-free parking. Two economists, Raymond Fisman (Columbia University) and Edward Miguel (Berkeley), noticed noteworthy differences, depending on the native country—descendants of some nations systematically took advantage of diplomatic immunity while others painstakingly observed the traffic regulations, even though they did not have to fear any sanctions.

Diplomats from Kuwait, for instance, ran up 246 parking violations per head between 1997 and 2002, their Egyptian colleagues accumulated 139 tickets and each U.N. envoy from Chad had on the average 124 tickets.

By contrast, German U.N. diplomats on average collected one single traffic ticket per head in those five years; the envoys of Switzerland, Holland and Scandinavian countries had not a single complaint filed against them.

In an environment without criminal prosecution, these behavioral patterns reveal people's tendency toward corruption, the economists write. Their conclusion is that the diplomats' attitude toward corruption is closely correlated with the extent of corruption in their native countries: The ten states with the most parking violations are all at the top of the corruption scale, while representatives of nations with negligible corruption problems are unlikely to abuse their privileges.

Even though living thousands of miles away from their native countries, diplomats act in the same manner as their colleagues back home, is the researchers' summary, from which they draw two conclusions: First, societal attitudes toward corruption are deeply embedded in people; second, the true extent of corruption depends on other factors besides the threat of prosecution.

Drawing on cultural factors rather than incentives and restrictions for explaining human behavior is a rather new thing for economists. In the seventies George Stigler and Gary Becker, both to become Nobel laureates, coined a very skeptical attitude toward such soft factors. According to their point of view, economists using cultural factors to buttress their arguments were simply trying to disguise the failure of their analyses. The conceptual model of *Homo oeconomicus,* eternally striving to maximize his advantages, dismisses the importance of the cultural and religious background of a society for its economy, growth and affluence. Furthermore, there was a long-standing consensus among economists to accept the preferences and behavior of people as a given fact and not to question them any further. Typically, economists attributed different behavioral patterns in various countries to disparate politics, institutions and technological standards. "In fact, until fairly recently, the role of culture in explaining economic phenomena has been largely ignored by modern economics," said New York University professor Raquel Fernández, who in 2006 held the prestigious Marshall Lecture at the annual meeting of the European Economic Association about Economics and Culture.

Economists are not making it any easier for themselves by accepting culture as an essential economic component. To scientifically verify the influence of culture, they must go to great lengths in terms of methodology—separating purely cultural factors from traditional economic issues is anything but easy.

Fernández, together with her NYU colleague Alessandra Fogli, managed the trick: Using an innovative and highly sophisticated method, the two scientists show that cultural factors are of major import as to whether women hold jobs or not. Fernández and Fogli analyzed what factors impact the labor supply of second-generation U.S. women. These women were born in the United States, while their parents grew up abroad and immigrated to the United States. The beauty of this method is: While the political and economic institutions are identical for all women, their parents' cultural background is not. Results are remarkable indeed: Fernández and Fogli show that the willingness of women aged between 30 and 40 to seek employment in 1970 correlates noticeably with the customs in the parents' native country: The higher the female labor force participation in those countries in 1950, the higher the share of daughters who, decades later, held jobs as U.S.-born citizens. The same relationship can be observed for the number of children a woman will have. The outcome is especially consistent in neighborhoods with a high concentration of immigrants from the same country.

The Economics of Religion

An affinity between religion and economics was noted as early as some 100 years ago by the sociologist Max Weber. In 1905, he postulated that there would have been no capitalism without Protestantism.

Meanwhile, economists have tackled the question of whether the religiousness of a country has a bearing on economic performance. Robert Barro of Harvard University and Rachel McCleary of the Weatherhead Center for International Affairs used data gleaned from six different transnational polls on the frequency of church service attendance, as well as the strength of certain religious convictions, in 59 countries. These data were analyzed for significant correlations with macroeconomic variables such as per capita income. The result: In countries where certain religious convictions—especially a belief in heaven and hell or an afterlife—run deep, growth rates are generally higher than in nations lacking these distinguishing features. The two economists' hypothesis is: Religion is crucial for economic performance because church and faith shape certain character traits, such as thriftiness, honesty, work ethic and open-mindedness vis-à-vis strangers.

Luigi Guiso, Paola Sapienza and Luigi Zingales have explored that point further. Based on a survey of 100,000 people in 55 countries, the researchers—all of them working at prestigious American business schools—investigated whether confessional ties and a positive attitude toward the market economy are intertwined—for instance, whether Catholics hold different views on private property or competition than do Hindus or Muslims.

Again, results are surprisingly unequivocal: According to Zingales and his coauthors, Muslims all over the world are much more skeptical toward economic institutions and mechanisms than are people of other religions. The study revealed Muslims to be more distrustful, less tolerant and more discriminatory toward women, and to view private property and competition negatively. These findings do have relevance in practice—for instance, religion could be a reason why the introduction of a market economy in Iraq turned out to be so much more difficult than the Bush administration had imagined.

The researchers did not find evidence for one hypothesis, though: Weber's claim that Protestants are better capitalists than Catholics holds no water. "Catholics support private ownership twice as much as Protestants," they assert. Additionally, Catholics turn out to be more thrifty and favor competition more than do Protestants.

Culture as the True Engine of Prosperity

The economic consequences of cultural differences can be substantial, says Guido Tabellini, an internationally renowned Italian economist at Milan's Bocconi University. In an elaborate study he furnishes evidence that in the more prosperous European regions, people have ethical values particularly beneficial for business life in an advanced economy. This also explains the great differences in stages of development among regions that, as in Italy, have been forming a nation state for over 150 years.

Tabellini bases his study on surveys measuring the ethical values of people in various European regions. He distinguishes between values that positively or negatively influence economic outcomes. Positive for prosperity would be people's confidence in their capability to shape their own destiny, and their trust in others. Negative for economic outcomes are characteristics of mainly hierarchical societies—such as when children are taught absolute obedience.

According to Tabellini's findings, a colored map overlay showing cultural differences strongly resembles a map showing economic vitality. And an analysis of the relevant figures revealed an indisputable and statistically significant correlation.

This raised the question of cause and effect: Does economic development influence culture or do things work the other way around? To resolve this issue, Tabellini did a crosscheck, bringing into the equation historical facts that may produce cultural differences, but have no direct bearing on recent economic developments. Among others, he researched the prevalence of analphabetism around 1880 and the quality of political institutions from 1600 through 1850. Both are directly related to today's cultural differences—combined, they explain much of the current regional differences in ethical values. These findings prove that better economic development cannot be the main impetus for ethical concepts favorable to economic outcomes.

Tabellini concludes from his study that economically backward regions like the Mezzogiorno can hardly be helped with subsidies and transfer payments alone. To turn a large part of a population into recipients of aid would only reinforce the prevailing negative culture in the regions concerned, he argues. Much more important would be improvements in education and job training—and more effective support for start-ups to strengthen the entrepreneurial spirit.

America's Misplaced Faith in a Just World

The culture of growth seems to be particularly strong in the United States. The proverbial American dish-washer, convinced that he can become a millionaire through hard work, will put in a greater effort than his European counterpart, who perceives himself as the eternal underdog in an unjust world. It should not come as a surprise, then, that Americans work harder and—on average—earn more. The paradox in all this is that according to studies, chances for the individual to climb the social ladder are almost the same in America and Europe—the difference is in people's perception. Two prominent French economists, Roland Benabou and Jean Tirole, scrutinized with mathematical precision the reasons for the different attitudes.

The scientists started from the observation that most people are anxious to believe in a fair world, where effort and ability are rewarded with social and economic upward mobility. Experiments show how deep this yearning goes: Even when "rewards" are handed out to test participants on an arbitrary basis, many of them will conjure up reasons why they "deserve" their good fortune or bad luck.

Benabou and Tirole show in their study that there are significant feedback loops between individual attitudes of people and societal conditions. Again, the United States serves as an example: In the proverbial "country of unlimited opportunities," people have for generations considered themselves masters of their own destiny, more so than in Europe. They are therefore generally less inclined to share their well-deserved fortunes with the less fortunate—resulting in a lesser degree of social security. This makes it all the more important for individuals to motivate themselves and their children for excellent performance—people are more inclined toward selective perception, seeing the world as a fair place, and are particularly susceptible to propaganda encouraging that view. Political support for redistribution continues to erode. In Europe, on the other hand, less successful individuals can more easily afford to doubt the justice of the world—after all, there is a more elaborate social security system and, along with it, more general support for redistribution.

As unrealistic as American optimism may appear to some (non-Americans), it has positive economic consequences for a large part of the population. Since Americans are more optimistic about the fruits of their labor—and since government takes a smaller portion of it over to the state—they work harder to attain a higher standard of living. Left out in the cold, though, are the socially vulnerable and people of limited skills. They are more severely stigmatized and suffer more from their failed lives than comparable Europeans; after all, they find it more difficult to blame their situation on circumstances beyond their control. Unable to maintain their self-esteem, the economically and socially unsuccessful might more easily resort to desperate and criminal measures to improve their situation. This may explain to some extent the high crime rates in the United States.

Based on their model, Benabou and Tirole are also able to demonstrate why in Europe a retrenchment of social safety is underway at the very moment when social chasms are widening due to globalization and technological change. The two economists work on the assumption that the fruits of success are becoming larger. As a consequence, people feel compelled to give greater effort and invest more in education; in addition, increasing rewards of success are a strong underpinning for self-motivation and belief in a fair world. Both these mindsets are inimical to any form of altruistic redistribution. A backlash of this sort of mentality, combined with practical politics, could turn a gradual development into a fundamental change of policies.

Thou Shalt Trust in the Stock Market

In economic transactions, trust in the integrity of market players and institutions is key. The three researchers Luigi Guiso, Paola Sapienza and Luigi Zingales, who also explored the role of religion, show this in yet another study: For the smooth functioning of financial markets, investors' trust in other individuals and especially in companies is of paramount importance.

People will only buy a company share if they feel sure they are not being defrauded. "The decision to invest in stocks requires not only an assessment of the risk-return trade-off given the existing data, but also an act of faith (trust) that the data in our possession are reliable, that the overall system is fair."

While this sounds almost trivial at first, it permits important conclusions that help us to understand financial markets. Up to now, economists were unable to fully explain why share ownership rates vary so widely among industrialized countries. Whereas two-thirds of Swedish citizens and every second American directly or indirectly own shares, only one in five Germans do so. In Italy and Austria, less than 10 percent of citizens are stock market investors.

In the past, financial market researchers used to explain away the differences with transaction costs, which vary widely from country to country. The argument has a flaw, though: In numerous countries, people with high incomes stay away from financial markets—even though custodian fees and broker commissions would be of no consequence to them.

In their study, the researchers show by numerous data that trust plays a major part for the differences in equity culture. For instance, only 7.2 percent of Americans and a mere 6 percent of Swedes do not trust major corporations at all—in Germany and Italy, the corresponding figures are over 17 percent. Discrepancies are even more extreme for highly affluent people: In Sweden, only 2 percent of the wealthy doubt the integrity of business—in Italy, the figure is 29 percent. Little wonder, then, that in Sweden only 4 percent of the wealthy stay away from the stock markets, while in Italy 35 percent do so. When analyzing detailed data on about 2,000 Dutch citizens, who in a survey by the Dutch central bank answered questions on their investments and trust in other people, the economists made another interesting discovery: People expressing the opinion that most of those around them can be trusted are 50 percent more likely to own shares. They will also invest a larger share of their assets in stocks—on the average, around 3.4 percentage points more.

An increasing level of education will diminish the significance of the trust effect: A better education about the stock market can reduce the negative effect of lack of trust, the study concludes. The importance of trust for investment decisions has (indirect) macroeconomic consequences as well: "That lack of trust—either generalized or personalized—reduces the demand for equity implies that companies will find it more difficult to float their stock in countries characterized by low levels of trust."

References

Barro, Robert and Rachel McCleary (2006): "Religion and Economy," in: *Journal of Economic Perspectives,* Vol. 20, pp. 49–72.

Benabou, Roland and Jean Tirole (2006): "Belief in a Just World and Redistributive Politics," in *Quarterly Journal of Economics,* Vol. 121, pp. 699–746.

Fernández, Raquel (2007): "Alfred Marshall Lecture: Women, Work and Culture," in: *Journal of the European Economic Association,* Vol. 5, pp. 305–332.

Fernández, Raquel and Alessandra Fogli (2005): "Culture: An Empirical Investigation of Beliefs, Work and Fertility," National Bureau of Economic Research working paper no. 11268.

Fisman, Raymond and Edward Miguel (2007): "Corruption, Norms, and Legal Enforcement: Evidence from Diplomatic Parking Tickets," in: *Journal of Political Economy,* Vol. 115, pp. 1020–1048.

Guiso, Luigi, Paola Sapienza, and Luigi Zingales (2003): "People's Opium? Religion and Economic Attitudes," in: *Journal of Monetary Economics,* Vol. 50, pp. 225–282.

Guiso, Luigi, Paola Sapienza, and Luigi Zingales (forthcoming): "Trusting the Stock Market," in: *Journal of Finance.*

Tabellini, Guido (2005): "Culture and Institutions: Economic Development in the Regions of Europe," CESifo working paper no. 1492.

6

Economics by Scales and Measures

The discipline's name sounds exotic enough, and its research goals stray from the well-trodden paths of economics: *Anthropometrics* conducts economics research with scales and tape measures. From historical records about the height and weight of people, it draws conclusions on the economic circumstances under which they lived. This is especially useful when probing economic development and quality of life in ages for which no usable economic data exist. Yet even for our own era, practitioners of anthropometrics can contribute many vital clues from their vantage point.

The average height of people is a reliable gauge for the quality of nutrition in childhood and how much disease they suffered. Individuals with poor nutrition or frequent illness cannot fully exploit their genetic potential. "Physical stature is a useful measure across society for biological wellbeing, and it allows inferences about societal deficiencies," says John Komlos, an American anthropometrist teaching economic history in Munich.

Anthropometric research has produced quite a few surprises. During the first half of the nineteenth century, American Indians of the Midwest used to be the tallest people in the world. An adult male measured 1.72 meters (5'7") on average and thus outranked the average white settler. In the view of anthropometrists, this suggests that the living standards of supposedly poor Indian tribes were higher than those of whites. Two reasons may chiefly be responsible for it: The huge herds of buffalo roaming the Great Plains gave Indians access to high-quality meat rich in protein. Since the tribes followed the herds instead of settling in one place, there were no hygiene problems from trash and human waste, as was the case in the cities where white people lived.

What Causes the Leading Power to Shrink?

Official economic statistics today leave no doubt: Per capita income in the United States is substantially higher than in Europe. Americans have reached a higher level of affluence, mainly because they work longer hours.

The question is, are the living standards of large parts of the population really higher than in Europe? Anthropometrists raise serious doubts. Judging by their statures alone, not all is well with Americans. They shrink in terms of height and only grow in girth. Even their northern neighbors, the Canadians, have bypassed them. Relative to Europeans, especially the Dutch, they have slid down the scale. This finding cannot be explained with the immigration of relatively shorter people from Asia and Latin America, as one might expect—rather, it remains valid when restricted to Caucasians of European ancestry.

In the first half of the twentieth century, Americans were the tallest people in the world. In the second half of the century, how-ever, they ceased to grow. The average height of males in the United States has been stagnating since 1960; women even grow shorter. At not quite 1.78 meters (5'8") on average, American men aged between 30 and 40 are not much taller than their grandparents.

Most astounding is a direct comparison with the current world champions in physical height, the Dutch: Only 140 years ago, the average Dutch was seven centimeters (2.75 inches) shorter than the average American—now, the average American is six centimeters (2.36 inches) shorter. During the same period that Americans dropped back in height, their body weight became increasingly problematic. Komlos and his associate, Marieluise Baur, quote army records, according to which young American men of the mid-nineteenth century were not only very tall, but also slightly underweight, with a body mass index of 19. Today the United States finds itself among the countries with the most overweight populations. Likewise, it has fallen far behind other countries in terms of life expectancy and infant mortality.

In the past, lack of hygiene was to blame when higher material living standards did not result in greater height and longer life. The cities, with their higher productivity and incomes compared to the countryside, were notorious for their dreadful sanitary conditions. Today, this can no longer be a reason for the physical shrinking of the U.S. population. Economic historians Richard Steckel and John Komlos explain the phenomenon with the large and increasing social inequality in America. Members of the lower classes are especially susceptible to being overweight and below average in height. In addition, the researchers assign a fair share of the blame to spotty health insurance coverage. While more than every seventh American is without health insurance, Europe has practically 100 percent coverage in force. And finally, stresses Komlos, the weight problem could also be related to the fast food culture, which grew by leaps and bounds in the second half of the last century—particularly in the United States.

Short People in Dire Straits

If people had continued to grow over the course of centuries, there wouldn't be much for anthropometrists to find out. But

Richard Steckel determined that Northern Europeans were shorter in the eighteenth century than their ancestors in the eleventh century. And after the Thirty Years' War, even a full century seemed not enough for Europeans to make a complete recovery. John Komlos and Francesco Cinnirella estimate the height of European men at the time to have been no more than 1.64 to 1.68 meters (5'4" to 5'6"). Their contemporaries in the American colonies, on the other hand, were well fed and much taller accordingly.

The seventeenth century had to be a catastrophic time for the Europeans, in many respects. During the period, the average height fell to 1.60 meters (5'3") for males, while the average female could muster no more than 1.52 meters (5'). During that time, just about everything came together to stunt people's physical development. The so-called Little Ice Age brought poor harvests, and the Thirty Years' War made it well nay impossible to decently feed a family. To top it all, the impending urbanization brought devastating epidemics in its wake. During the eleventh century, there appeared to be no problems with nutrition and epidemic diseases. According to Steckel, males at the time measured on the average more than 1.70 meters (5'7") in height.

Chubby People Live Longer

Anthropometry also aids in daily life. The discipline's findings allow us to keep a somewhat closer check on those demi-gods in white—which might be judicious, as it appears that doctors aren't too meticulous about the statistical and scientific evidence on which they base their medical advice.

For example, dire warnings about the high risks of being overweight or obese may well be exaggerated. To be a tad on the chubby side does no harm; it may even prolong your life: This is the result of a study by Marco Sunder, a Munich-based economic historian. Sunder analyzed a large database in the

United States of over 14,000 individuals between the ages of 25 and 75 who had been questioned on their daily habits and had been weighed and measured. Their lives and deaths were followed up to 1992.

His surprising finding: Life expectancy is highest among people with a body mass index (BMI) of somewhat more than 25 through close to 29—whereas physicians categorize people with a BMI of 25+ as overweight. A person's BMI is determined by dividing his/her weight in kilograms by the square of his/her body height in meters. For someone 1.80 meters (or some 5'11") tall, a BMI of 25 through 29 would translate into a weight between 81 and 94 kilograms, or between 178 and 207 American pounds.

In recent years, medical research has also found that being moderately "overweight" increases life expectancy. Yet the powers-that-be apparently cannot decide what to do with these findings, faced with an epidemic increase of obesity. Out of worry that a partial discounting of the problem may actually worsen it, they idly stand by while a great many people may decrease their overall health or even shorten their life expectancy with excessive diets.

"In recent years, and much to the alarm of adipositas researchers, studies have indicated a rising mortality in persons who were bringing down their weight," the German journal *Ärzte-Woche* (Physicians' Weekly) reported back in 2001. The journal quoted Aila Rissanen, professor at the University Clinic Helsinki. At a congress on obesity, Rissanen pointed out that such study results may be statistically distorted. All the more remarkable, then, that the same Aila Rissanen, in a later exhaustive, coauthored study with Thorkild Sørensen, had to concede that the same alarming results were found even after eliminating such alleged distorting factors. Overweight people (BMI greater than 25) who successfully reduce their weight shorten their life expectancy.

Women may benefit less from these results since they are more exposed to the pressures of being fashionably slim. It may be comforting for them to know, however, that beyond a BMI of 29 their life expectancy decreases much more slowly than is the case with men. As far as health goes, women can afford to be much more overweight.

There isn't much reason to be frustrated for those shooting past the upper limits of an ideal weight. As long as they don't smoke, they still have the prospect of a long life, according to Sunder's study. A 40-year-old male with a BMI of 35 shortens his life expectancy by close to 30 months, from nearly 74 to a bit over 71, a woman of the same age by less than a year, to 80. Nonsmokers, however, live six years longer than smokers.

Yet Sunder's results also show that you've got to make an effort to live a long life. Physically active people live two years longer on the average than others. Individuals with a daily routine only of walking from their bed to the garage, from the garage to the elevator, to the lunchroom, to the elevator and back to the couch, will shorten their life by almost as much as a smoker.

With Elevator Shoes to Higher Income

The finding that heavy people live longer is relatively new. Another insight from the science of tape measures and scales, which is almost standard wisdom today, is that taller people on average make more money. The rule of thumb here is: Two and a half centimeters (about one inch) more in height = 2.5 percent more income. Many an explanation has been trotted out, hinting at sometimes rather subtle backlash effects. The essence of all of them is that shorter people are discriminated against in their social lives—possibly because in evolution theory, size also stands for strength, health and self-assertiveness.

In all likelihood, tall adults have already towered over their peers as children or adolescents. This leads to the assumption that tall people, by virtue of long-term socialization, become more self-assertive and dominant and these characteristics are being rewarded later with higher incomes in their professional lives.

Two scientists from Yale University have submitted research results that back a much more mundane explanation: "Tall people earn more on average because they are smarter," is the hypothesis of Anne Case and Christina Paxson. The scientists evaluated two British cohort studies in which all children born during a certain week of both 1958 and 1970 were statistically accompanied throughout their lives. Regular medical checkups kept a close tab on the children's physical height. During adulthood, their professional status and incomes were captured.

Case and Paxson found that, in the age groups between five and eleven years, there was a close and statistically significant correlation between children's body height and their performance in intelligence tests. The taller the children were, the better their performances in cognitive tests. The impact of height was even more pronounced than that of their parents' income. Statistically, the tallest 20 percent outperformed the average by the same measure as children whose parents belonged to the top 5 percent in terms of income.

One possible interpretation of this is teachers will direct more of their attention to taller students and teach them better. It is refuted by the fact that some medical studies have revealed correlations between height and cognitive abilities at even earlier ages. For instance, a British-Finnish group of doctors around David Barker from the University of Southampton found that body growth in the first year of infancy has a strong statistical influence on income during adulthood. An extra 2.5 centimeters (one inch) will result in about 4 percent more income later on.

To decide whether the income advantage of tall people is attributable to greater intelligence, Case and Paxson incorporated the results of the childhood intelligence tests into their econometric calculations. Without the data, regression analysis had suggested an income lead of 1 to 2 percent for each centimeter in height. With the childhood test results included, the impact was only half and became statistically insignificant. When throwing the income and educational status of parents into the mix, the correlation between tallness and income contracted even more. Thus, a personnel manager who believed it was wise to prefer taller people, as they may have a bit more innate ability, would commit a grievous error. Once she has unbiased information at her disposal about the qualifications, personality and background of the applicant, his tallness will not provide any meaningful extra insight about his productive potential, according to the study. Height and intelligence are evidently connected—if one takes intelligence out of the equation during analysis, the higher income is falsely ascribed to body height.

Quite remarkably, height during puberty is more important for later income than height in adulthood, Case and Paxson point out, reasoning that at this age the importance of one's social background and other ambient factors probably have the strongest influences on physical height. The typical growth spurt during teenage years sets in much earlier for juveniles raised in highly favorable surroundings. Part of the height difference will level out later on, as latecomers grow slower, but will eventually catch up.

The Economics of Beauty

If height affects a person's professional success, so do his or her looks. The U.S. economists Daniel Hamermesh and Jeff Biddle noticed this back in the nineties: Americans with above-average looks earn 10 to 15 percent more than those who are unattractive. Less-attractive women are less inclined to seek employment, and get married to less educated men, than prettier women.

What is the reason for the labor market's beauty premium? Two American economists got to the bottom of things with a complex laboratory test. Markus Mobius (Harvard) and Tanya Rosenblat (Wesleyan University) simulated a labor market in which the "job" was to solve mazes on a Yahoo web page. The time needed for a player to find his way depended entirely on his skills and quick wits—which proved to be independent of his looks.

In their experiment, the researchers divided 330 Argentine students into "employees" and "employers." The "employees'" job was to solve as many maze riddles as possible within a 15-minute time limit. For each maze solved, they were paid a fixed sum. To obtain a manageable standard of attractiveness, the economists had the looks of "employees" graded by 50 external experts. They rated each test person through photographs on a scale of 1 (nondescript) to 5 (very attractive).

The "employers" were asked to estimate the productive capabilities of each player beforehand. The more accurately they foretold actual performance, the higher their own compensation would be. Some of them were only given written information about the applicants—besides basic data like age, gender and line of study it included details on how long it had taken the applicant to solve a test game. Other "employers" were shown photos of the players. Still others were allowed to have phone conversations or face-to-face interviews with the "employees."

Something remarkable happened: After seeing someone's photo, "employers" attached markedly higher expectations to people of attractive appearance, overestimating their productive capabilities by 12 percent. In cases where additional phone conversations or face-to-face meetings took place, good looks were rewarded with an even higher bonus of up to 17 percent. This magnitude of the beauty bonus is quite significant: The authors note that it is in the same order of magnitude as the wage disadvantage of women or people of color. What was most noteworthy: Even if "employers" did not know about test persons' looks but had phone conversations with them, they accorded good-looking people greater potential.

Mobius and Rosenblat depict the beauty premium as being composed of three different factors. For one, attractive-looking test persons act with greater self-assurance—the number of riddles they believe they are able to handle is 10 percent higher than that of average-looking test persons. This self-confidence carries over to "employers." The study's results assign roughly 20 percent of the beauty premium to this factor.

Second, regardless of how self-assuredly attractive people act, employers expect them to be more productive as employees than physically less appealing candidates. This direct confidence effect takes care of an additional 40 percent of the premium. The remaining 40 percent are occasioned by better communication skills attractive "employees" have, apart from their looks.

What this study shows is that the largest portion of the beauty premium is due to an indirect effect: People with good looks are better at marketing themselves and have better social skills. Thus, people wishing to improve their career prospects have options other than cosmetic surgery—such as enrolling in an interpersonal communications training.

References

Case, Anne and Christina Paxson (forthcoming): "Stature and Status: Height, Ability and Labor Market Outcomes," in: *Journal of Political Economy*.

Hamermesh, Daniel and Jeff Biddle (1994): "Beauty and the Labor Market," in: *American Economic Review*, Vol. 84, pp. 1174–1194.

Komlos, John and Marieluise Baur (2004): "From the Tallest in the World to (One of) the Fattest—The Enigmatic Fate of the Size of the American Population in the Twentieth Century," in: *Journal of Economics and Human Biology,* Vol 2, pp. 57–74.

Komlos, John and Francesco Cinnirella (2007): "European Heights in the Early 18th Century," in: *Vierteljahrschrift für Sozial—und Wirtschaftsgeschichte,* Vol. 94, p. 271.

Mobius, Markus and Tanya Rosenblat (2006): "Why Beauty Matters," in: *American Economic Review,* Vol. 96, pp. 222–235.

Sørensen, Thorkild, Aila Rissanen, Maarit Korkeila and Jaakko Kaprio (2005): "Intention to Loose Weight, Weight Changes and 18-y Mortality in Overweight Individuals Without Co-Morbidities," in: *PLoS Medicine,* Vol. 2, e171 doi.

Steckel, Richard (2004): "New Light on the Dark Ages: The Remarkably Tall Stature of European Men during the Medieval Era," in: *Social Science History,* Vol. 28, pp. 211–29.

Steckel, Richard (2005): "Health and Nutrition in the Pre-Industrial Era: Insights from a Millennium of Average Heights in Northern Europe," in: *Living Standards in the Past: New Perspectives on Well-Being in Asia and Europe,* ed. Robert C. Allen, Tommy Bengstsson and Martin Dribe, Oxford: Oxford University Press.

Steckel, Richard, Clark Spencer Larsen, Paul W. Sciulli, and Phillip L. Walker (forthcoming): "The History of European Health Project: A History of Health in Europe from the Late Paleolithic Era to the Present," in: *Acta Universitatis Carolinae Medica.*

Sunder, Marco (2005): "Toward Generation XL: Anthropometrics of Longevity in Late 20th-Century US," in: *Economics and Human Biology,* Vol. 3, pp. 271–295.

7

The Logic of Globalization

The journey was long and arduous. It took the 170 men over two years, from the middle of 1497 to late summer 1499. Fewer than one out of three returned alive, and two of the flotilla's four ships were lost. Economically, the adventure was a complete failure.

And yet, when seafarer Vasco da Gama disembarked on September 9, 1499, at the Port of Lisbon he was given a triumphal reception. He had accomplished what Christopher Columbus had failed to achieve seven years earlier: The sea route to India had been discovered. Three years hence, the discoverer once again embarked on a sea journey to India. This expedition, accomplished in 1503, brought commercial success. On his return, da Gama had 1,700 tons of spices aboard. He sold them throughout Europe at a 400 percent profit.

Vasco da Gama probably was the first global player in the history of mankind. He and his discovery of the passage to India set the stage for what today is called globalization—the growing together of the world economy across continents. "[T]here was a single global world economy with a worldwide division of labor and multilateral trade from 1500 onward," the late economist André Gunder Frank wrote.

Five hundred years ago, globalization had basically the same effects on the economy as today, economics historian Kevin

O'Rourke of Trinity College in Dublin and Jeffrey Williamson of Harvard University show. The discovery of a sea route to India invigorated market competition for spices from the subcontinent. Prior to that, the trade of Asian spices in Europe had firmly been in the hands of Venetian merchants. Pepper at one time was worth its weight in gold.

The Venetians acted very much as modern economic theories predict: They exploited their monopoly power to the hilt. It all ended with da Gama's discoveries. The Portuguese cargo vessels carrying spices, which would regularly cruise between Europe and India from the early sixteenth century, had a similar economic impact as today's broadband data networks, importing software and financial services from India to the West. "The Voyages of Discovery permanently altered the structure of trade between Europe and Asia," write O'Rourke and Williamson. In the decades following the sea route's discovery, real pepper prices continued to fall in almost all European trading centers—on the average, by about 10 percent each decade. Prices of nobler spices such as cinnamon, ginger and clove declined even more.

Put in economic terms, this means that the increase in wealth enabled by trading rubbed off on the consumer, at least partially. Market forces compelled the merchants to pass on some of their gains to the buyers. Yet it would take another 300 years until the general population actually felt the effects of world trade: Until the Industrial Revolution, the high cost of transportation limited intercontinental trade to luxury goods that could not be produced in the importing nations. Europe traded for spices, silk, sugar and gold; Asia for silver, linen and wool. These imports were not in competition with domestic products; da Gama's globalization had no repercussions on local labor markets and production structures.

Since only the superrich could afford imported luxury goods, there were no consequences for the living standards of the masses—until 1820, when a new era of globalization set in. Technical progress caused transportation costs to plummet within decades. "Steamships and the Suez Canal linked continents, and railroads penetrated their interiors," write O'Rourke and Williamson about what they dub the "Big Bang of globalization." Suddenly, long-distance trade in commodities like wheat, meat and oils became economically feasible, as did the import and export of raw materials like copper, coal and ore—all goods that had long been produced in the countries now becoming trading partners.

Trade caused prices to become increasingly uniform in widely separated countries. For example, in 1870 wheat prices in Liverpool were almost 58 percent higher than in Chicago. Fifteen years later, the gap had shrunk to barely 16 percent. For industries involved in world trade, the consequences were staggering. The new competition exerted relentless pressure on prices and profits.

How Globalization Spoils Drug Dealers' Margins

Today, the forces of globalization are also felt in places one would hardly suspect. Take, for instance, the market for heroin and cocaine, in which prices have fallen through the floor over the past 15 years. Since the early nineties, hard drugs have become 50 to 80 percent cheaper in Western industrialized countries. According to a U.N. drug report, in 1990 a single gram of cocaine costed $175—today it is worth less than $100. On the European black market, heroin can be had for $75 a gram—15 years ago, it was more than $250. A similar price slump has been observed in the United States.

The law of supply and demand alone does not account for the price decline, argue Claudia Costa Storti of the Portuguese central bank and Paul De Grauwe from the Catholic University

Leuven in Belgium. Production costs of drugs play only a minor role for prices in the black market; in the case of cocaine they account for just about 1 percent of its street value. Demand for hard drugs in the United States and Europe has risen, if anything. Taken by itself this would argue for higher instead of lower prices—especially since the global supply of cocaine and heroin has more or less held steady.

Falling prices may be due to globalization, economists surmise. Just like any other market, it has made the drug trade more competitive and efficient. "Lower transport costs and the use of the new IT have allowed to dramatically improve the efficiency of the distribution of drugs," write Storti and De Grauwe. Furthermore, communication between the supply and demand sides have become simpler and safer, the authors explain: They allow dealers to manage their inventories more efficiently. Finally, the risk premium for dealers has come down since the opening up of China, India and Russia has increased the supply of poor, low-qualified workers. Some may have been attracted by the extremely high margins of the drug business.

"The spectacular decline in the retail prices of cocaine and heroin can only be explained by what happened with the intermediation margins in these markets," the researchers write. In the early nineties, dealers in Europe made $120 on a gram of heroin, today it's no more than $40. The spreads between producer prices and wholesale prices have narrowed even more.

Globalization According to Crustaceans

Powerful economic forces are at work to drive the international division of labor. A British private investor who made a quick fortune as a stock broker was the first to recognize an important aspect of globalization: David Ricardo in 1817 published the slender tome "On the Principles of Political Economy and Taxation."

In his booklet, Ricardo was the first to describe a phenomenon that was to become a cornerstone of economics: the "comparative cost advantage." Put in simple terms, it means that international trade pays off for all countries participating.

Comparative advantages arise where nations are differently situated in terms of capital and labor. In Sweden, for example, growing grapes would hardly be rewarding, and the raising of reindeer in France just as futile. Both countries can enhance their wealth when concentrating on the production and export of goods they can manufacture at lower cost compared to other nations, while importing what other countries can supply more economically.

In theory, the benefits of free trade are incontestable. Yet to this day economists are hard put to provide empirical evidence of these effects and calculate them to the last dollar. Isolating the impact of customs duty on the supply of goods and prices is a methodically ambitious task. Peter Debaere, economist at the Darden School of Business, University of Virginia, was one of the first to succeed. Taking as example the global market for shrimp, he demonstrated that, by introducing protective customs and imposing other trade restrictions, nations only harm themselves. Consumers in these countries pay higher prices for fewer goods.

The global shrimp market is ideally suited to demonstrate this logic of globalization. The shrimp business is very international: Almost 80 percent of the worldwide product volume is produced in developing countries like Thailand, China and Vietnam—60 percent of the product is consumed in the United States, Europe and Japan.

In 1997, the E.U. introduced import duties on shrimp from Thailand. In subsequent years, it further imposed strict import controls to protect consumers from antibiotics residue in the product. The United States, by contrast, levied no customs on crustaceans until the end of 2002 and their regulations regarding antibiotics were less restrictive.

This caused massive distortions on the global market for crustaceans, Debaere showed. The Thai shrimp farmers increasingly exported their product to America; as a consequence of the significant rise in shrimp supply, U.S. prices fell through the floor.

If we discount potential health risks for consumers due to antibiotics residue and focus on purely economic consequences, one thing is very clear: Pricewise, American consumers benefited greatly from the European policy of implementing protective tariffs. One year before the change in E.U. policies, the prices of shrimp (exchange-rate adjusted) were 20 percent higher in the United States than in Europe. They have since continued to fall until shrimp became cheaper in America than in Europe. These developments, however, put enough of a burden on U.S. producers of crustaceans for protective measures against shrimp imports to be revived—duties on Asian shrimp were reinstated by the United States.

Trade without Comparative Cost Advantages

To fully understand the process of globalization in today's world, however, we must go beyond Ricardo. After all, nearly 70 percent of total exports worldwide are transacted between developed nations—29 countries comprising a mere 15 percent of the world's population account for over two-thirds of exports worldwide. At the same time, the difference in factor endowment among industrialized nations is hardly worth mentioning nowadays, and hasn't been for quite some time. "Since the major trading nations become similar in technology and resources, there is often no clear comparative advantage within an industry," write economists Paul Krugman and Maurice Obstfeld.

The key to explaining the ongoing trading boom is economies of scale. Simply put, the concept means that the greater the quantities manufactured by a company, the lower the average cost of each individual item. This is true in particular for knowledge-intensive industries. For example, the development costs for computer programs or pharmaceuticals may run into the billions; once the product is ready for the market, however, it can usually be mass-produced at minimal cost. Or, to use economist lingo, fixed costs are high and marginal costs are very low. Under such conditions, free trade becomes highly attractive to companies, enabling them to serve larger markets and reach a greater number of customers.

This rise in free trade, driven by increasing economies of scale, offers consumers a much broader product selection in conjunction with lower prices. In theory, Krugman has noted this as early as 1979. And in reality these "gains from variety" prove to be immense indeed, as researchers Christian Broda (Graduate School of Business, University of Chicago) and David Weinstein (Columbia University) demonstrate, using the United States as an example. Using detailed analysis of import and export data, they were the first to analyze foreign trade at the level of individual products.

The results were quite impressive. Since 1972, U.S. imports have risen from 5 percent to 12 percent of economic output; at the same time, product variety has increased at an astounding rate. In the early seventies, the United States used to import 70,000 types of product; meanwhile, this same figure has risen to 260,000. One of the reasons is that Americans now buy from a much greater number of nations.

This policy has made U.S. customers better off. According to Broda and Weinstein's estimate they add up to the equivalent of at least $250 billion, or roughly 2.6 percent of America's gross domestic product. Prices of goods imported to the United States have risen at a slower rate since 1972 than indicated in official statistics, where the greater product variety has not been properly accounted for. According to the researchers' calculations, the price increase of imports was actually 1.2 percent lower per year than was reported officially.

No Reason to Fear "Made in China"

Pleasant as globalization may be for the consumer in industrialized nations—what does it mean for the manufacturing sector and the people earning a living there? Pessimists fear that manufacturing industries in high-wage countries are doomed, and along with them, millions of jobs.

Peter Schott, an economics professor at Yale, sounds an "all clear," albeit with reservations. While our industries must be prepared for severe disruptors, they should be able to face the new competition head-on, says Schott. He bases his conclusion on the development of world trade over the last three decades: During that period, competition from China has grown by leaps and bounds, yet businesses in high-income nations have persevered—not least because they managed to develop superior, innovative products that outperform China's offerings.

Similar to the studies of Broda and Weinstein, Schott has evaluated detailed data from U.S. foreign trade statistics. This enabled him to analyze U.S. imports at the level of individual merchandise groups and products. At first glance, the naked figures appear disturbing. Across all imported industrial products, the share of Chinese goods has increased drastically, from near 0 percent in 1972 to almost 20 percent at present. In consumer products like clothing and toys, China's market share has reached as much as 36 percent.

Another result of Schott's appears troubling: The Chinese range of products seems to have grown increasingly similar to that of Western nations, at least at first glance. Today, Chinese enterprises compete against those from high-income countries in almost all product categories. In 1972, by contrast, Chinese products were found in only 9 percent of all manufacturing product categories on the U.S. market. Today, the number has risen to 68 percent. "No other country's growth in product penetration comes close to this increase," the economist writes.

Upon closer inspection, the findings appear in a somewhat different light. In addition to the different product groups, Schott also compared individual segments of each group in detail. Here he detected something quite striking: Within a given product group, differences between goods from China and those of Western countries have not diminished but actually increased. The scientist refers to this phenomenon as "vertical product differentiation," illustrating it by using the following example: "Japan and China might both produce and export high definition televisions, but the Japanese televisions might employ more sophisticated technology, be of much higher quality, or contain a richer set of attributes than the ones exported by China."

Differences of this kind do not appear in trade statistics, as they could not be compiled and measured within acceptable budgetary limits. The Yale professor therefore attempts to capture them by taking an indirect route: "These vertical differences should manifest in prices," he notes, "with Japanese televisions fetching a much higher price in the U.S. market than Chinese televisions, due to consumers' willingness to pay for them."

And this is exactly what Schott manages to prove for most of the major U.S. imports. Within the given merchandise groups, he writes, products from China are invariably much cheaper than those from developed economies. In the chemicals group, for instance, the "Made in China" discount is 23 percent, in machinery even 60 percent. Over the years, these price differences have not decreased—on the contrary: "These discounts have widened over the past five to ten years."

In Schott's view, this goes to prove that qualitative differences existing between Chinese products and those of other industrial nations have markedly increased. "The gap between Chinese and OECD export prices suggests that competition between China and the world's most developed economies might be less direct than their overlap in product markets implies."

Central to his argument is the premise that price differences do not result from lower Chinese production costs, but are due to consumers' willingness to spend more money for the higher-quality Japanese TV sets.

Aside from all economic theory, history is a witness. Economic historians established that for homogeneous goods with minor quality differences, such as wheat, prices already converged during the world trade boom of the nineteenth century—notwithstanding persisting differences in the cost of production. Accordingly, the fact that industrial nations are able to sell goods of the same merchandise group at higher prices than China can probably be viewed as evidence of their ability to respond to the new competition with better and more sophisticated products. Schott's overall conclusion sounds encouraging: "If that is the case, there is hope that manufacturing in high-wage developing countries will continue to survive competition from low-wage countries like China."

Global Competition Can Be Crippling

For companies or industries no longer at the leading edge of technology, new foreign competition can become a matter of survival. This point is made by a research team led by Harvard economist Philippe Aghion.

Using the United Kingdom as an example, the scientist managed to show that new entrants from abroad do not always stimulate innovations in domestic industries—sometimes it is quite the opposite. In some British industries, the team found growing foreign competition to have a crippling effect on innovation and productivity. Setting out to find an explanation for this phenomenon, they came up with the following hypothesis: How domestic companies respond to new vendors mainly depends on how far the established firms are technologically trailing behind the best in class.

Aghion refers to this phenomenon as the "Technological Frontier": It is defined by the very best and most advanced production processes the world has to offer. The further behind domestic companies find themselves, the more remote their prospects of outmaneuvering the new competitor with better products and more refined technology. "Incumbents that are further behind the frontier have no hope to win against a potential entrant." In those cases, says Aghion, increasing competition depresses returns on investments in research and development.

In the United Kingdom, the impact was substantial. According to the study, productivity in technologically leading sectors—such as capital goods for the electronics industry or the media—grew twice as much as in industries with average technology when faced with increased competition. In backward industries like brewing or automotive components, productivity growth actually declined as competitive pressures grew. The study's conclusion for economic policy: "Policies aiming at decreasing or removing entry barriers alone may not be sufficient to foster productivity growth of incumbent firms in all industries, even when such policies can be shown to be growth-enhancing on average."

The question is, why does free trade make businesses more productive in the first place? Economists' standard reply is: Competitive pressures rise when previously protected markets are opened. In order to prevail against new competitors from abroad, established companies cannot help but improve their products and production processes. A case in point is what happened to the German automotive industry in the 1980s: When Japanese manufacturers started quickly penetrating international markets with better and cheaper cars, Mercedes,

BMW, et al. were forced to further enhance their vehicles, which they did with appreciable success. Conversely, the leading American carmakers counted on their dominance of the domestic markets and fell back in the competitive race.

Greater competitive intensity, though, is neither the only nor the most important way in which free trade makes companies more competitive: This is a finding from a study by Mary Amiti (Federal Reserve Bank of New York) and Jozef Konings (Catholic University Louvain in Belgium) in which Indonesia served as an example.

The Southeast Asian country joined the World Trade Organization (WTO) in 1995 and, over the following ten years, lowered all customs duties by 40 percent or more. Owing to uniquely detailed statistics on industrial enterprises in Indonesia, comprising more than 300 industries, the scientists were able to explore at the level of individual companies how employment, sales and productivity changed. They also had information on the share of imports of intermediate goods the companies had sourced in. To isolate the effects of customs, the researchers took advantage of the fact that trade barriers had been dismantled to different degrees in different industries.

As Amiti and Konings point out, economists have been overlooking one important reason why free trade makes companies more productive: It is the import of intermediate inputs from abroad. When, for example, import duties on compressors for refrigerators were lowered, the productivity of Indonesian companies benefiting from it—such as refrigerator manufacturers—would rise disproportionately. When duties on imported inputs fell by 10 percent, Indonesian companies would register a 12 percent gain in productivity. By contrast, the effect was much less for duties on consumer goods, such as fully assembled refrigerators: Depending on the industry, productivity gains were between 1 and 6 percent (for the same 10 percent decrease of duties).

Again, the main reason why the import of input goods and services makes businesses more productive is probably variety gains: On the world markets, businesses have a much wider selection of components and are free to pick the best and cheapest.

The World—A Village?

No question, globalization has changed the world we live in at breakneck speed. Yet how profound a change has it been? *New York Times* columnist Thomas L. Friedman has an answer: "The world is flat," he asserts in his 2005 bestseller.

According to Friedman's central thesis, the computer and the web have shrunk the world. Long distances are no longer an issue for businesses. "Professionals everywhere, from China to Costa Rica, can work from home as if they were in offices next door to each other [...] which requires us to run faster in order to stay in the same place."

As obvious as this may sound, in economic terms the world is far from being a village. At least this is the contention of two Dutch foreign trade economists, Steven Brakman and Charles van Marrewijk. They put Friedman's thesis to the test and found: "The world is not flat, nor is distance dead. We show that indeed geographical trade and investment patterns illustrate the importance of distance."

Using a simple example, the scientists demonstrate how crucial a product's location is to its value: Production costs for a Barbie doll are less than a dollar in China—in the United States, the same doll sells for ten dollars and more. The manufacturer's profit margin alone does not account for the difference, the researchers show; transportation and marketing continue to play a significant role.

Analyzing trade flows between countries, the researchers show that the geographic distance between two nations, along with their economic prowess, is still a core determinant for trade volume. "[A] 10 percent increase in distance reduces trade by about 9 percent," the study finds. The reason why distance is still an issue, the authors argue, is that the sheer costs of transportation are not all that matters in international trade. In addition, there are costs resulting from direct or indirect trade impediments, language barriers and differing legal systems.

There is plenty of scope left for further globalization—that much is clear from the research. Should we ever get close to the point where distance is meaningless for international trade, our economies will look quite different. Until then, companies will have no choice but to keep adapting to evolving international trade linkages.

Africa's Sad Secret

One continent has largely been missing out on globalization—Africa. South of the Sahara, an economic tragedy has been happening since 1970: The number of people who have to live on less than $1.50 a day has risen by more than 200 million, according to an estimate by Xavier Sala-i-Martin, professor of economics at New York's Columbia University.

Some explanation can be found in the continent's sad history. Without a functional political system guaranteeing a minimum of infrastructure, legal protection and stability, it is impossible for a nation to prevail in international trade and generate major development leaps. In many regions of Africa, these indispensable requirements are lacking. According to Harvard economist Nathan Nunn, this is not happenstance but a fateful, long-term consequence of the slave trade. Slavery, he argues, has profoundly damaged the social and societal fabric of Africa.

For almost 500 years—from the fifteenth until deep into the nineteenth century—the slave trade had dramatic proportions: Almost 18 million Africans were sold as slaves during this period. Two-thirds of them went to North America, the remainder toward the Red Sea, the Indian Ocean and within Africa. Without these abductions, Africa would have had twice the population in the nineteenth century.

From many sources, Nunn has collected all available data on the slave trade. Important records are the logs of slave vessels transporting the hapless out of Africa. Nunn knows the ports of embarkation of almost 35,000 sea transports that took place between 1514 and 1866, and the number of slaves aboard. From registers, notations made on markets and court documents, he gathered information as to the slaves' probable ethnic backgrounds.

On this basis, the economist managed to extrapolate the number of people abducted from each region. Hardest hit was Angola with 3.6 million victims, followed by Nigeria (2 million), Ghana (1.6 million) and Ethiopia (1.4 million). Other countries had practically no slavery—among them, Namibia, South Africa and Botswana. Nunn managed to prove that the more a country was affected by the slave trade, the worse off it is today, economically speaking.

Per se, this does not say much about cause and effect: It might well be that slave trading boomed in economically weak regions that have remained that way to this day. In that case, slavery would have been the effect, rather than the cause of economic weakness.

Nunn succeeds in debunking this theory, providing abundant evidence of slavery having caused the region's problems. His calculations show that the manhunt was prevalent not in especially impoverished but in rather wealthy areas of Africa. "Because the more prosperous areas were also the most densely populated, large numbers of slaves could be efficiently obtained," the economist writes.

But how is it that events that took place several hundred years ago still show aftereffects today? According to some evidence, slavery has deeply and permanently poisoned the social and societal structures in the regions affected. The slave hunters had strong incentives to stir up conflicts and civil wars, since that would ease their work. Existing nations, such as the kingdom of Congo, became destabilized to the point of collapse.

What's more, the breakdown of state institutions is likely to have been coresponsible for the extreme ethnic fragmentation of the continent. As tribes were the only organizational units affording some protection against slave hunters, they continued to increase in stature during those times. "An important consequence of the slave trades was that they tended to weaken ties between villages, thus discouraging the formation of larger communities and broader ethnic identities," Nunn writes.

In today's world, these kaleidoscopic societal structures prove to be a great disadvantage. After all, the secret to success of modern, market-economy-based societies is in the division of labor, along with anonymous market transactions. Both will function only while strangers trust and cooperate with one another.

What Happened to All the Money?

One testimonial to Africa's misery is the interstate road A109 in Kenya. It runs from the coastal metropolis Mombasa at the Indian Ocean to the capital, Nairobi, over 300 miles (500 kilometers) away. The road is famous—for never having been completed. Even though a vital artery for the country, it is only partially paved. For long stretches, it consists of almost nothing but potholes. Wilfred Kigen, the Kenyan marathon superstar, could easily outpace the trucks laboring down those road sections. Now if the primary seaport of a country is not accessible via a reasonably surfaced road, how can that country fully exploit the opportunities of world trade?

For many years, Kenya was one of the major recipients of economic aid—during the nineties, such aid accounted for roughly 10 percent of the gross domestic product. Evidently, this was not enough to improve the country's most vital overland connection, to at least approach the level of an American country road. "Where has all the money gone?" is a question explored by three U.S.-based economists, Santanu Chatterjee (University of Georgia), Paola Giuliano (Harvard) and Ilker Kaya (University of Georgia).

They are not only referring to Kenya but to foreign aid in general. Numerous studies have shown that the amount of development aid has no influence on the economic growth of recipient countries. On principle, development aid is supposed to promote growth. To make sure it works that way, donor nations usually attach the condition that the money flows into growth-sustaining investments—like the road from Mombasa to Nairobi.

The researchers evaluated data on 67 developing countries covering the period from 1972 through 2000. Their thesis of development aid's failure to kick-start growth was confirmed. Skeptics might argue that this is because slow-growing countries receive particularly generous amounts—an argument the authors disprove citing numerous facts. Apparently, the main reason that development aid does not contribute to growth is that, in many cases, it displaces the recipient countries' own efforts. An extra million dollars of development aid allocated for roads, bridges or schools raises government outlays for such infrastructure investments by only $100,000. In other words: For each additional million, the governments of recipient countries reduce their self-determined infrastructure expenses by $900,000. The money "saved" thanks to the aid flows into consumptive government expenditures instead.

References

Aghion, Philippe, Richard Blundell, Rachel Griffith, Peter Howitt and Susanne Prantl (forthcoming): "The Effects of Entry on Incumbent

Innovation and Productivity," in: *Review of Economics and Statistics.*

Amiti, Mary and Jozef Konings (2007): "Trade Liberalization, Intermediate Inputs, and Productivity: Evidence from Indonesia," in: *American Economic Review*, Vol 97, pp. 1611–1638.

Brakman, Steven and Charles van Marrewijk (forthcoming): " 'It's a Big World After All': On the Economic Impact of Location and Distance," in: *Cambridge Journal of Regions, Economy, and Society.*

Broda, Christian and David Weinstein (2006): "Globalization and the Gains From Variety," in: *Quarterly Journal of Economics*, Vol. 121, pp. 541–585.

Chatterjee, Santanu, Paola Giuliano and Ilker Kaya (2007): "Where Has All the Money Gone? Foreign Aid and the Quest for Growth," Institute for the Study of Labor (IZA) discussion paper no. 2858.

Debaere, Peter (2005): "Small Fish—Big Issues. The Effect of Trade Policy on the Global Shrimp Market," Centre for Economic Policy Research discussion paper no. 5254.

Krugman, Paul (1979): "Increasing Returns, Monopolistic Competition and International Trade," in: *Journal of International Economics*, Vol. 9, pp. 469–479.

Krugman, Paul and Maurice Obstfeld (2006): "International Economics: Theory and Policy," Amsterdam: Addison-Wesley Longman.

Nunn, Nathan (2008): "The Long-Term Effects of Africa's Slave Trades," in: *Quarterly Journal of Economics*, Vol. 123, pp. 139–176.

O'Rourke, Kevin H. and Jeffrey G. Williamson (2002): "When Did Globalization Begin?" in: *European Review of Economic History*, Vol. 6, pp. 23–50.

O'Rourke, Kevin H. and Jeffrey G. Williamson (2005): "Did Vasco Da Gama Matter For European Markets? Testing Frederick Lane's Hypotheses Fifty Years Later," National Bureau of Economic Research working paper no. 11884.

Schott, Peter K. (2008): "The Relative Sophistication of Chinese Exports," in: *Economic Policy*, Vol. 53, pp. 7–49.

Storti, Cláudia Costa and Paul De Grauwe (forthcoming): "Globalization and the Price Decline of Illicit Drugs," in: *International Journal of Drug Policy.*

8

Financial Markets—Totally Efficient or Totally Crazy?

Financial markets are efficient, students are taught in Economics 101. Any information publicly available—or so the textbooks tell us—has already been incorporated in the stock prices. Thousands upon thousands of investors, in their chase for returns, will have made sure that no opportunities for extraordinary profits have been left on the table. This hypothesis has made Chicago economist Eugene Fama both famous and a perpetual Nobel Prize candidate. If you believe in efficient financial markets, anyone presuming to call an equity underpriced or overpriced will seem nothing but a fool to you.

Yet some economists have noticed that what happens in financial markets is not always in line with the efficient market hypothesis. This comes as no surprise, really: Just like *Homo oeconomicus,* the completely rational, coolly calculating investor is an artifact. Financial markets are made up of humans—with all their faults and weaknesses, their greed and their fear of risks, their urges to follow the crowd, and their limited intellectual capacities.

There's No Fool Like a Stock Market Fool

If financial markets were truly efficient, investors would be reasonably safe from making serious mistakes—even those thinking they can outfox the market by buying "cheap" equities and selling "overpriced" ones. Market efficiency should assure that each paper—regardless of the pick—is priced more or less correctly.

Far from it, says Lawrence Harris, professor of finance at the University of Southern California. "Market efficiency will not protect you. If you don't know the ropes, your only protection is not trading," he warns. Harris should know what he is talking about: He used to be chief economist at the Securities and Exchange Commission (SEC). According to Harris, market efficiency goes no further than establishing a price level. En route from one level to another there are countless traps, often set by professional traders trying to manipulate the market, for instance, with bluffing strategies.

It works as follows: A trader quietly accumulates shares in an issue. When some news transpires about the stock, he again steps in to increase his position, pushing up the price. Irrespective of how pertinent the news may be, the trader draws attention to the stock (or, in traders' lingo, "puts it into play"). Others see the momentum as being the result of good news, and pile in. Chart technicians are especially vulnerable to this type of trick, as they mainly track stock price movements and compare them to historical patterns. Once the ruse takes on a life of its own, more investors will jump aboard, dragging others with them. This is the moment for the bluffer to sell his shares in small tranches and reap a handsome profit.

Those with a more unlawful bent may expand this strategy by entering commentaries about the company on internet forums under a false name. And while this kind of bluffing is illegal in most countries, even without the forged commentaries, supervisory authorities find it exceedingly difficult to prove rule violations.

These goings-on are not unusual, but a daily occurrence at the exchanges, Harris points out: When traders say they wish to "test the mood of the market" by their trading presence, or "gauge the sentiment of the market," it is no more than a polite way of saying they will look for ways to manipulate it. Successful funds managers with a great deal of public exposure have other options in their arsenal. If they wish to exit a position, for instance, they can seek opportunities to give interviews hyping the specific investment.

What this means for retail investors, or institutional investors not conversant with these shenanigans, is: Market efficiency will only protect you from making wrong investment decisions if you do not pretend to be quicker and smarter than the market. In other words, equity purchases and sales should not be hitched to the latest price move or analyst recommendation, or the company's most recent press release or the information cluttering chat-rooms and message boards. Anything you could find out there is either contained in the price, or irrelevant, or even deceiving.

What the Eye Does Not See, the Heart Cannot Grieve Over

The Italian economists Luigi Guiso and Tullio Jappelli support this advice with a scientific investigation. Using the customer data of a large Italian bank, they tested whether well-informed investors achieve higher returns at the stock market. They had information on how much time the bank's clients would spend on gathering information, and on the revenues in customers' portfolios. As a measure of investment returns they used the "Sharpe ratio," which indicates the units of revenue received for a given risk. In simple terms, this means that a security paper with wide price swings must achieve a higher return to reach the same Sharpe ratio than a less risky alternative, such as treasuries with short maturities (T-bills).

According to classic financial market theory, a rational investor would seek information to help him avoid shares of weak companies, thus enhancing his chances to pick future winners. But since the collection of information involves costs and effort, he would stop as soon as he would realize that the cost of an additional piece of information exceeds its value. An investor would not waste time and money on information that is worthless.

If investors acted according to these principles, there would be a close correlation between portfolio gains and the costs of information expensed by the investor. The opposite is the case: According to Guiso and Jappelli, investors who spend two to four hours per week plowing through financial information have a 25 percent lower Sharpe ratio than those who do not spend even a minute. Intensive research would be rational only if the investors considered the collection of information—such as the purchase and perusal of investor literature—to be a pastime, not a cost factor. The authors were unable to find any signs for the hypothesis that doing research is a pleasure for investors, though. There is plenty of evidence that the difference in the Sharpe ratio is due to investors' resultant excessive self-confidence. Lab tests repeatedly confirmed that men have a greater tendency than women to overestimate their abilities. Guiso and Jappelli's findings fit into the picture: Additional consumption of information is reflected in poorer returns for men than for women.

The researchers also found that the more information investors acquire, the more trading they will do. If investors were entirely rational, this, again, would lead to higher returns—or, more precisely, to a better Sharpe ratio. The very opposite was true for the Italian bank's clients. And there is yet another mistake investors are prone to when accumulating information: They will not diversify sufficiently. This means that they assume risks for which there is no commensurate reward.

The First Shall Be the Last

The phenomenon can be explained by investors basing their decisions on unreliable information. Could it be that only investors getting their information from reliable sources will achieve gains? One of these reliable sources should be those who, as corporate analysts, specialize in tracking the strategy and business development of certain corporations and making enlightened forecasts about the futures of those companies. Whoever is successful at this should be able to turn a profit—for himself, his employer and the readers of his analyses. An obvious strategy, then, would be to listen only to analysts with a proven track record of successful predictions.

But, the conclusion of a study by Giles Hilary of Hong Kong University and Lior Menzly of Vega Asset Management, New York, suggests the opposite. Together they investigated what an analyst's past performance says about his future success. By evaluating almost 50,000 quarterly forecasts, they found that analysts who have predicted revenues and earnings with particular accuracy in the past may not be able to duplicate their performance in the future. To the contrary: Having had an above-average run of forecasts come true, they will tend to go out on a limb with future predictions—and fail. The fall-off happens to experienced analysts as much as to neophytes, independent of whether they work for a large or small bank.

Over time, an analyst who makes great calls for a certain period is apt to see himself as somewhat of a genius. It may cause him to dismiss publicly available information in favor of excessively relying on his own intuitive feelings. His predictions will increasingly diverge from the consensus and become vulnerable to errors in judgment.

What this means for investors is, they should view the rankings by financial market analysts with caution. When choosing between two analysts of equal ability and experience, it is best to follow the advice of the one who delivered forecasts of average quality in the past. Predictions of analysts who have been riding a hot streak should be treated carefully.

Lemmings to the Sea—Many Analysts Just Follow the Crowd

While some analysts overestimate their abilities, others are afraid to voice independent opinions. They base their own forecasts on what a majority of their peers is predicting. One indicator of this is if recommendations, when revised, tend to migrate toward the consensus—as revealed in a study by Ivo Welch, professor of finance at Brown University.

From the vantage point of an analyst, it seems sensible to plagiarize his peers. Those too far out of step with the majority risk ridicule and scorn. Albert Edwards, chief strategist of Société Générale, experienced such a reaction firsthand in the summer of 2001, when he (correctly) predicted the end of the boom in the United States. He was working for the investment bank Dresdner Kleinwort at the time. On the bank's online forum, he suffered more than his share of scorn. One investor even demanded that the bank "send this old, sclerotic, dangerous man into retirement."

As long as an analyst sticks with the consensus, the danger of getting negative attention is much smaller. If you are wrong, you have plenty of company. And the risk of getting caught plagiarizing is low. You can always defend yourself by saying it's not your fault if others read information the same way.

But the excuse does not work across the entire analyst caste, as two economists from the Unites States and South Korea showed in a recent study. After investigating analysts' herd instinct with a rather creative approach, Narasimhan Jegadeesh and Woojin Kim's conclusion is "that recommendation revisions are partly driven by analysts' desire to herd with the crowd."

The study was based on a capital market model following Fama's efficient market hypothesis: Rationally acting individuals in such (financial) markets will evaluate new information at the moment it transpires, and price it into their quotes. The market's response to these latest recommendations will then permit conclusions as to the extent of "herding," the researchers state. If information is processed efficiently and analysts follow their herd instincts, some stock recommendations will be more valuable to investors than others—to wit: those that diverge from the consensus. These analysts are likely to have specific information valuable enough to outweigh their desire to follow the majority.

This hypothesis was proved in theory with the researchers' model: In the absence of a herd instinct among analysts, and in efficient markets, it would not matter for a stock's performance whether a new buy or sell recommendation will lean toward the consensus or away from it. By contrast, when investors assume that financial market analysts behave like lemmings, new buy or sell recommendations diverging from consensus will impact a stock's price more severely than those in consonance with the majority.

With those theoretical insights in the bag, the scientists then investigated how analyst forecasts move prices in practice. Their database was comprised of almost 50,000 buy and sell recommendations for U.S. shares from the years 1993 through 2005. The analysis revealed the same pattern for real-life situations as was found in the herd instinct model: Analysts diverging from the majority opinion with a new recommendation would indeed cause greater moves in share prices than those staying close to the consensus. Jegadeesh and Kim considered this to be proof that many analysts actually crib from their peers. Financial markets seem to take implicit account of that by giving less weight to forecasts in line with the general consensus.

The instinct to follow the majority is stronger when it comes to downgrading a stock: "We find stronger herding effects for downgrades than for upgrades, which suggests that analysts are more reluctant to stand out from the crowd when they convey negative information," Jagedeesh and Kim write.

The surprising part is that analysts from large and renowned financial institutions are more prone to the herd instinct—evidently, smaller banks are more willing to take the chance to voice unconventional opinions.

Why Analysts Speak in Two Tongues

In summary, investors are better off not putting their blind faith in analysts, especially stock analysts. After all, there are rarely surveys of analyst forecasts that don't see the markets higher on average than could be reasonably expected over the long haul. You will hardly ever find a majority forecasting a drop in share prices, even though price losses are anything but unusual.

For regulatory agencies and financial market researchers, the question as to how objective analysts really are has been of particular concern since the Internet bubble of the nineties. And the reply from science is sobering: Rose-colored glasses seem to be an indispensable tool of the profession. Analyst opinions are invariably skewed to the bright side, a number of studies show.

What could be the reason for that? Do analysts subconsciously overestimate the prospects of a company? Or do they deliberately issue optimistic reports due to conflicts of interest? After all, the employers of these market mavens make a lot of money on the listed companies—through IPOs, capital increases and bond issues.

Ulrike Malmendier (Berkeley) and Devin Shanthikumar (Harvard) submit scientific evidence to support the fact that many analysts are methodically and purposefully embellishing their recommendations to ingratiate themselves with the businesses they follow. In their analysis, the scientists take advantage of the fact that the analysts' touting of shares has its natural limits. When dealing with institutional investors like insurance companies or funds, market mavens have an incentive to give unbiased opinions: For one, professional investors are important clients for the analysts' employers—investment banks and major broker-dealers—as they handle much larger investment volumes than retail clients. In addition, institutional investors have greater insight into the market and will not easily be led by the nose. Once an investment bank is rumored to be overly enthusiastic in its opinions, large clients will take their business to the competition.

Malmendier and Shanthikumar found that analysts use two different channels to communicate with investors: Straightforward stock recommendations like "buy," "hold" and "sell" are mostly intended for the retail trade and are widely followed by this type of investor. Institutional investors mostly disregard these pronouncements, focusing on more complex forecasts that are detailed in the extensive reports addressed to them, such as the future earnings per share.

In their study, the scientists examine at the level of individual analysts whether messages destined for the retail investor differed from those targeted at institutions. Compiled from several sources, their database covers individual analysts' "buy," "hold" and "sell" recommendations for individual stock, together with the respective earnings estimates and market responses. In addition, they checked if and when the analyst's employer had obtained investment banking business from the respective corporation. The optimism of an analyst was measured by how far he strayed from the consensus estimate in the financial markets.

Their conclusion: "Security analysts speak in two tongues." Apparently, analysts exaggerate less when talking to professional investors than toward the retail crowd—the two scientists found their messages for market pros to be noticeably more accurate. And if there is an investment banking relationship between the analyst's employer and the respective business, he will take a much more bullish stance toward retail customers than his peers do.

What is particularly noteworthy is that analysts with potential conflicts of interest will raise their forecasts only when the majority of their colleagues are optimistic—then, however, they will remain bullish much longer. By the same token, they wait much longer before lowering their outlook following bearish news on the company. Their earnings forecast of the same company, however, is generally no different from other observers' outlooks. The researchers found a tantalizing detail here as well: Shortly before a company publishes its latest figures, analysts with potential conflicts of interest will tend to downplay its earnings prospects, so the company appears to exceed market expectations—another indicator of banks trying to curry favor with their clients.

An altogether different picture emerges for analysts whose employers have no active investment banking relations with businesses evaluated. Where conflicts of interest are not an issue, there are no systematic gaps between recommendations for retail customers and institutional investors—nor any other conspicuous details. All of this points to the same thing: The firewalls between investment banking and research, which regulators require to safeguard against improper trading, do not seem particularly thick or high.

The Dirt on Coming Clean

Ever since the scandals surrounding Enron, WorldCom and others, investors are alerted to potential conflicts of interest. Every analyst report today is accompanied by page-long disclaimers.

However, such warnings can do more harm than good. Three American economists and psychologists, Daylian Cain, George Loewenstein and Don Moore, showed test subjects a glass jar filled with coins from a distance, and asked them to estimate its value. The closer a subject came with his guess, the higher the reward would be. Each of them had an adviser assigned to them who was allowed to inspect the contents from close up. As the advisers' reward would go up in proportion with the subjects' estimate, they had a similar conflict of interest as stock analysts do at a bank: The bank will earn commissions from the stock purchases of its clients; so when an adviser discourages clients with bearish forecasts, he is doing his employer a disfavor, since positive outlooks will boost business. The researchers informed half of the clients about their advisers' conflict of interest (in the advisors' presence); the other half was not explicitly informed.

As could be expected, most advisers exaggerated the amount of money in the jar. But could the better-informed group of estimators defend their interests more effectively? They could not. Advisers with a known conflict of interest exaggerated the jar's contents even more than their peers, on the premise that their clients would subtract something anyway. The estimators, on the other hand, who knew of their advisers' conflict of interests, trusted them almost as much as those unaware. In the end, the informed group came out worse than the uninformed one. The advantage went to the advisers who, on top of everything, did not even need to have any feelings of guilt since their clients had been in the know.

So Let Us Predict the Past

As we have seen, reading analyst reports isn't only a tedious chore—its benefits are doubtful, too. Even when there's no reason to suspect a hidden agenda, analysts' forecasts often do not seem to be worth the paper they are printed on. Markus Spiwoks (Wolfsburg University of Applied Science) and Oliver Hein (Goethe University of Frankfurt) examined analyst predictions for the debt market and found: Of 33 financial institutions attempting to forecast the yield from ten-year U.S. treasury bonds (T-bonds) for twelve months down the road, none did better than the so-called naive forecast that simply extrapolated the current yields. Spiwoks, who used to work as a bond analyst himself, was not very surprised after what he had seen in practice. By rights, everyone should have a 50:50 chance of coming out better than the naive forecast. The probability of nobody succeeding would then be a fraction of a percent.

In fact, analyst forecasts follow current quotes pretty closely, and forecast curves tend to mirror the most recent developments. When share prices go up, analysts will raise their twelve-month forecast accordingly, and they will lower their forecasts when prices fall. So what they predict is in fact the price charts of the post, Spiwoks and Hein point out. Analysts, in other words, are smart enough to stay close to the naive forecast.

This does not explain, however, why the share of those leaning in the right direction, at least coincidentally, is not larger. The reason probably lies in the interaction of prevailing analyst opinions and market positioning. If, for example, most analysts predict rising interest rates, in agreement with the majority of the big market players, then most of them can be expected to hold positions reflecting this conviction. Funds managers will have fewer debt securities or shorter maturities in their portfolio than would be customary. Should interest rates decline contrary to expectations, a process will take effect that aggravates the forecast error. Funds managers on the wrong side of the market will step in with buy orders to avoid getting into deeper trouble. The consequence of all this is that interest rates—initially the subject of forecasts—will depend on these very forecasts, and they will do so to the disadvantage of the forecasters. Whenever they make mistakes, their market position will exacerbate them.

The famous Austrian economist Ludwig von Mises picked up on the problem of making forecasts almost 50 years ago: Even if we could predict economic developments of the future, it would not work out, he pointed out, for people would align their actions with these predictions and thus change the future. There is also a proven trading strategy to take advantage of market positioning, which is called contrarian investing. In the long run, you will make better profits if you position yourself adversely to current market sentiment. When most analysts predict an upward momentum in prices, you will be better off leaving those securities alone; when they are out of favor with analysts, you might consider buying.

Rational Bubbles Burst Rationally

To some extent, prices in the financial markets are simply subject to coincidence. Innocuous bits of information can trigger events totally out of proportion to their significance—even with a perfectly rational public. This is the result of an analysis by Franklin Allen (University of Pennsylvania), Stephen Morris and Hyun Song Shin (both at Princeton). The researchers take up an idea going back to John Maynard Keynes: As early as in 1936, the grand old man of macroeconomics compared the stock market with a beauty contest, at which jurors may gain some reward when their favorite gets the most votes. As a result, they do not vote for who they view to be the most beautiful of contestants, but for the one they believe is fancied most by the other members of the jury. In reference to financial markets, Keynes wrote: "We have reached the third degree where we devote our intelligences to anticipating what average opinion expects the average opinion to be."

On this basis, Allen, Morris and Shin constructed a financial market model in which the current price quote is determined by the average estimate on tomorrow's estimate regarding the future development of prices. Here, we encounter the problem of lacking time consistency; that is: The estimation of what will be tomorrow's estimate on long-term price development is not necessarily consistent with today's estimation of long-term price directions.

An example may clarify how this time inconsistency can lead to price bubbles: Let's say I believe that most investors think of the market as being overvalued. I also know, however, that most investors have not yet sold out. My conclusion from that is that they expect a price increase, at least for the short term, and are therefore unlikely to sell tomorrow. I will step up and buy.

The same will occur tomorrow, with the effect that my daily predictions for the next day's average market assessment will not be in line with my long-term forecast of the average market assessment. The discrepancy grows wider with each day, as observant investors have an incentive to "ride the bubble."

Obviously, the trend evolving this way will be prone to an abrupt reversal. Bits of innocuous public information can bring about a change in direction, for rational investors—rightfully—attach greater significance to publicly available information than to their own, private information. Only public information is meaningful for the formation of investors' average market assessment.

Yet both types of information are unreliable. For instance, an upward blip in the U.S. core inflation may be no more than a slight aberration. If financial markets function akin to Keynes's beauty contests, however, this bit of commonly available information can have very significant consequences. All investors will notice the upward move in inflation rates—and all will know that everyone else sees it, too. As a result, many investors might expect others to sell—and begin to exit their own positions as well. What caused exaggeration on the way up is now likely to cause exaggeration on the way down.

Of Black Swans and Black Days in the Market

We don't like to think about the days when the markets go haywire, yet they are absolutely decisive for an investor's success or failure. Javier Estrada, professor of finance at the IESE Business School in Barcelona, showed this much in a study analyzing long-term price trends on exchanges in 15 countries.

His calculations show: Someone having invested a fixed daily amount in the Dow Jones index since 1900, but having missed the ten most profitable trading days, would have lost 65 percent of all returns. By contrast, someone having managed to avoid the ten worst trading days would have increased his gains by 206 percent. "These magnitudes are enormous, given that ten days account for only 0.03 percent of the days considered," Estrada writes. Results are similar when viewed in the context of shorter time spans. "A negligible proportion of days determines an enormous creation or destruction of wealth and, therefore, the odds against successful market timing are simply staggering," is Estrada's conclusion. Investors might as well abandon their efforts at making money through market timing.

Rather alarmingly, extreme upward or downward spikes are much more frequent than assumed in fund managers and analysts' models. Alas, the same is true for the models of banks' risk managers, which are designed to protect financial institutions from market swings. These models assume that violent market movements follow the famous Gaussian bell curve, or normal distribution. If this were so, the Dow Jones index would almost never deviate more than about 3 percent up or down in a single session. On 99.73 percent of all trading days, the index would decline by no more than 3.17 percent or climb by no more than 3.22 percent. Wider fluctuations could only have occurred 79 times during the 29,190 trading days between 1900 and 2006. In point of fact, they occurred 461 times, six times more frequently than the Gaussian normal distribution would have it.

Perhaps even more impressive is this: If the Dow Jones index would follow the Gaussian normal distribution, a gain of more than 9.2 percent within one trading day would occur only once every 1,003,561,397,831,590 years. In reality, price increases of 9.2 percent and more occurred ten times over a total of 107 years.

These numbers should set off alarm bells in the minds of investors, financial institutions and regulators—the usual mathematical models all presume a normal distribution for returns on securities. Whoever relies on that will seriously underestimate the actual risks, and is in serious danger of running into nasty surprises at some point.

Returns on Stocks Are Lower Than You'd Think

As investors, despite all this contrary evidence, will not let go of trying to time the market, they make much less money at the stock exchange than they hypothetically could. This is the sobering conclusion of a study by Ilia Dichev, economics professor at the University of Michigan. Over the past decades, U.S. investors have on average earned only half of valuation gains that the increases in the major stock market indices would imply.

There is a simple explanation for this finding: A stock's performance is not all that determines how much its owner will earn. Another crucial factor is the time at which shares are bought or sold and in what quantities.

The phenomenon is best illustrated by a numerical example: Imagine you buy 100 shares of a stock at $10 in early 2005. One year later the price has climbed to $20. Because things are going well, you add another 100 shares. One year later, the stock falls back to $10 a share.

The hypothetical return on your stock between 2005 and 2007 is zero. Your portfolio, though, shows a debit position of $1,000—you bought $3,000 worth of stock that now has a value of only $2,000. The reason is that you were twice as heavily invested during the stock's decline than you were during its rise.

The performance of a stock is not synonymous with its actual profitability for the investor, as Dichev emphasizes. "While conventional buy-and-hold returns reflect the return experience of stocks, the return experience of investors is also affected by their capital flow timing."

When taking into account its fluctuating market capitalization, investors at the NASDAQ obtained returns of only 4.3 percent in the period from 1973 through 2002—although the unweighted price appreciation of listed shares was more than twice as large, with 9.2 percent per year. At the NYSE, the spread was not quite that wide: Between 1926 and 2002, investors earned 8.6 percent a year; the unweighted average return was 9.9 percent.

Evidently, in the economist's quintessential judgment, a typical investor will systematically enter or exit the market at the wrong time. He will buy in the wake of rising prices—and stay away after the end of a bear market. Retail investors, he points out, do much better with passive investment strategies: Not only do they save on commissions, they also avert the risk of jumping in at the wrong time.

References

Allen, Franklin, Stephen Morris and Hyun Song Shin (2006): "Beauty Contests and Iterated Expectations in Asset Markets," in: *Review of Financial Studies,* Vol. 19, pp. 719–752.

Cain, Daylian, George Loewenstein and Don Moore (2005): "The Dirt On Coming Clean: Perverse Effects of Disclosing Conflicts of Interest," in: *Journal of Legal Studies,* Vol. 34, pp. 1–25.

Dichev, Ilia D. (2007): "What Are Stock Investors' Actual Historical Returns? Evidence from Dollar-Weighted Returns," in: *American Economic Review*, Vol. 97, pp. 386–401.

Estrada, Javier (2007): "Black Swans, Market Timing, and the Dow," IESI Business School working paper.

Fama, Eugene F. (1970): "Efficient Capital Markets: A Review of Theory and Implication for Stock Market Efficiency," in: *Journal of Finance*, Vol. 48, pp. 65–91.

Guiso, Luigi and Tullio Jappelli (2006): "Information Acquisition and Portfolio Performance," Center for Economic Policy Research discussion paper No. 5901.

Harris, Lawrence (2005): "Market Efficiency—The Microstructure Perspective," lecture held at the symposium "Market Efficiency Today" of the Center for Financial Studies (CFS) on October 6, 2005, at Frankfurt am Main.

Hilary, Gilles and Lior Menzly (2006): "Does Past Success Lead Analysts to Become Overconfident?" in: *Management Science*, Vol. 52, pp. 489–500.

Jegadeesh, Narasimhan and Woojin Kim (2007): "Do Analysts Herd? An Analysis of Recommendations and Market Reactions," National Bureau of Economic Research working paper No. 12866.

Malmendier, Ulrike and Devin Shanthikumar (2007): "Do Security Analysts Speak in Two Tongues?" National Bureau of Economic Research working paper No. 13124.

Spiwoks, Markus and Oliver Hein (2005): "Forecasting the Past: The Case of US-American Interest Rate Forecasts," Wolfsburg working paper.

Subprime Surprises—Or: The Anatomy of the Financial Crisis

For almost four years, from 2000 to 2004, Horst Köhler was managing director of the International Monetary Fund in Washington, D.C.—not a job for someone who distrusted international financial markets. During that time, Köhler had often cautioned against excessive regulation—to him, modern financial products were superb risk-spreading tools.

All the more noteworthy is how, four years later, Köhler speaks of the same subject in his function as German federal president. "The international financial markets have turned into a monster we must hold at bay," he said in an interview in early summer 2008. Indeed, the world financial markets were turned upside down as of early 2007.

The name of the crisis stems from a special segment of the U.S. mortgage market—the market for subprime loans. Before the turn of the millennium it had been a market niche of limited importance; less than 10 percent of mortgage loans were granted to Americans with poor credit standing. Then the market exploded. Between 2000 and 2006, the annual volume of loans granted tripled to more than $600 billion. The share of high-risk borrowers rose from 9 to 20 percent of all new mortgage loans—even though the volume of "better" ("prime") loans also increased during that period. At the same time, real estate prices in the United States climbed to record heights. Since the end of the nineties, they had more than doubled.

The housing market collapsed and took the economy down with it. The Federal Reserve had to lower the base rate to 2 percent within a matter of months. As a complementary measure, the American government hurried to set up a fiscal stimulation package. Still, the crisis deepened. All major investment banks either failed, were taken over or changed their status. Major financial institutions, including Fannie Mae, Freddie Mac and insurer AIG had to be bailed out by the government. Eventually, the government was forced to set up a huge $ 700 billion dollar bail-out fund. In Europe, similar upheavals took place.

Why did this happen and who was to blame?

What Kind of a Monster?

Princeton economist Markus Brunnermeier leaves no doubt as to where he sees the root cause of the disaster. In his survey article in the *Journal of Economic Perspectives* he writes: "The transformation from a classical banking model to an 'originate and distribute' model led to a deterioration of lending standards, contributed to the recent boom in house prices, and fueled the credit expansion behind the recent bonanza in leveraged buyout markets."

Securitization is the key word here. In his 1999 bestseller *The Lexus and the Olive Tree,* Thomas L. Friedman gave one of the best nontechnical descriptions of the process. Referring to the beginnings of the securitization in the 1970s, Friedman writes: "Investment banks started approaching banks and home mortgage companies, buying up their whole portfolio of mortgages, then chopping them up into $1,000 bonds that you and I and Aunt Bev could buy."

Securitizers pool illiquid assets, such as mortgage loans, and transform them into securities that can be sold to capital market investors. By 2006 the value of securities related to mortgage loans alone had increased to more than $3 trillion, according to some estimates.

Theoretically, securitization is a good thing. It allows issuers to cater to the specific risk appetites of different investors. If things go wrong, numerous individual investors, each holding a small slice of the risk, would be affected just a little, instead of one lender being severely affected. This was supposed to make the financial system more stable.

In the last decade, investment bankers developed a number of fancy new financial instruments, further facilitating securitization. Some of these products were so complicated that even financial institutions investing in them did not fully understand them. The new investment vehicles allowed banks to shift more risks to off-balance-sheet entities, which were not subject to banking regulation. Hence, banks could do more business and take on more risks with less capital. In essence, a huge shadow financial system was created.

The background of the subprime boom is not a fundamentally justified development but an explosive mix of greed, cheap money and new financial products—this is the conclusion of a whole series of studies. "Lending standards were relaxed to generate high yielding loans to meet securitization demand," write John Kiff and Paul Mills, economists at the International Monetary Fund (IMF), in one of them. "Safeguards ensuring prudent lending were weakened by the combination of fee-driven remuneration at each stage of the securitization process and the dispersion of credit risk, which weakened monitoring incentives."

Americans with low educational levels, low incomes and a poor credit standing were lured with shifty special offers from mortgage banks and effective interest loads were disguised—all for one purpose only: generating loan volume to satisfy the near-insatiable investor demand. Initial interest rates were kept artificially low. When these teaser offers expired, however, the rates would leap to market level and the load could easily double. As long as real estate prices went up, such "adjustable-rate mortgages" were not a problem. People running into a pinch could simply take out another loan—or sell their houses at a higher price. When real estate prices fall, however, the house of cards collapses.

Two research teams, independently of each other, investigated the goings-on in the U.S. subprime market in greater detail. Their studies take us on a fascinating trip to the crisis' ground zero—and paint a merciless picture of how the financial sector's excesses caused the market's demise.

Atif Mian and Amir Sufi of the University of Chicago's Graduate School of Business analyzed the regional development of subprime markets, using detailed data for individual postal code regions. What they found was that the subprime boom was highest in regions where loan requests had previously been denied with above-average frequency. What's particularly astonishing: Income levels and unemployment rates took a more unfavorable turn in these regions than they did in the rest of the country, which means that the average creditworthiness deteriorated in relative terms. But that didn't matter much to the mortgage institutions—it was the very loans from those regions that they passed on to financial investors, rather than keeping them in their books.

In addition, the granting of subprime loans followed a perverse mechanism, according to IMF economists Giovanni Dell'Ariccia, Deniz Igan and Luc Laeven: The more applications submitted in a region, the lower the loan denial rate. The exact opposite was the case for "prime" loans to customers of good credit standing: In this group, the denial rate increased as banks took care to pick the best debtors. In regions with a particularly large number of subprime lenders, more of these loans would be granted—as was the case in regions where real estate and housing prices increased at above-average rates.

These findings suggest that banks granted loans regardless of the consequences. "Nowadays, a bank faces only a 'pipeline risk.' That is, only risks that are not yet passed on and are still in the bank's pipeline are the bank's concern," Brunnermeier writes. As a consequence, the risk of a loan going sour lost most of its dread for the banks—after all, they did not have to put their heads on the block.

A team of four researchers managed to furnish evidence of just that causality. Using the data on over one million real estate loans granted in the United States between 2001 and 2006, Benjamin Keys (University of Michigan), Tammoy Mukherjee (Sorin Capital Management), Amit Seru (University Chicago) and Vikrant Vig (London Business School) were able to prove that when a bank knew that a loan would remain on its books, it would apply much more scrutiny in examining the applicant's creditworthiness than it would when the loan could be securitized.

The researchers took advantage of the fact that there is a threshold rating score for households above which it becomes significantly easier to securitize a loan. Loans to borrowers with scores slightly above the threshold were twice as likely to be securitized as loans to borrowers with scores very slightly below. Typically, a loan to a household with a better credit score should be slightly safer. Default rates, however, show the opposite. The default rate of loans to more solvent borrowers—those that could be securitized—was 20 percent higher two years after origination. Mortgage originators apparently put less effort into screening the slightly better borrowers, since these were much more likely to remain on their own balance sheets.

Unfortunately for financial institutions, the other theoretical advantage of structured finance turned out to be an illusion, too. According to the textbook story, securitization would allow the risks to be distributed to investors outside the banking system. In reality, most of these risks never really left the banking system. "Banks, including sophisticated investment banks, were among the most active buyers of structured products," notes Markus Brunnermeier.

Not everybody in the business was completely unaware of the dangers. Even people in the top echelon knew there would be a problem but felt that their hands were tied by the very short-term nature of modern finance: Chuck Prince put it nicely at the beginning of the crisis, shortly before he was ousted from his job as CEO of Citigroup due to the large losses of his bank. "When the music stops in terms of liquidity, things will be complicated. But as long as the music is playing, you've got to get up and dance. We are still dancing," he told the *Financial Times* in July 2007. He did not fall hard when the music stopped. His severance package of about $140 million softened the blow.

How Rating Agencies Fed the Monster

The financial products based on subprime mortgages were rather complex. The reason they held so much appeal to investors was that they had received the rating agencies' seal of approval. According to them, a large part of these securities was almost as safe as U.S. treasury bonds: Both were rated AAA.

Since the rating agencies used the same letter code for mortgage-backed securities as they used for regular company or government bonds, they became a logical option for the asset managers. "AAA" is "AAA," the rating agencies insisted, no matter what type of security it refers to. Adam Ashcraft and Til Schuermann, two economists at the Federal Reserve Bank of New York, point out that this is wrong: Structured products like asset-backed securities have a very different risk profile. In particular, their default risk is much more dependent on the business cycle and the housing market. The market knew that, which is why "AAA"-rated mortgage-backed securities offered a much higher yield than "AAA"-rated bonds.

Asset managers knew it too, but it did not matter to them. If a pension fund tells its asset managers to buy highly rated securities only, they will buy those highly rated securities with the highest yield. This way they can make sure they will beat the performance benchmark and keep their jobs. The same is true for a bank and its security traders.

The rating agencies made a killing—and had strong incentives to be nice to their clients. They were hired and paid by the institutions interested in selling structured securities. Rating agencies charged twice as much for the assessment of these papers than they would for traditional securities, according to Ashcraft and Schuermann. At the peak of the subprime frenzy, Moody's achieved 44 percent of its sales this way—with a handsome 50 percent profit margin at that.

The rating agencies would closely collaborate with the investment banks. In the end, they could hardly pass for independent evaluators—rather, they acted like consultants helping to tailor products so they would get an AAA rating. "The rating agency is an active part of the structuring of the deal. In practice, arrangers will engage in a process that is iterative and interactive, informing the issuer of the requirements to attain desired ratings in different tranches and largely defining the requirements of the structures to achieve target ratings," write Joseph Mason, professor of finance at Drexel University and finance professional Joshua Rosner. The exaggerated ratings had repercussions all the way from the end product to the loan seller at the start of the securitization process. In each stage of the process, they would quash all incentives for scrutiny.

Scrutiny, a.k.a. due diligence, is important, because in the securitization process, asymmetry of information is abundant. In non-economic terminology one might also call them "opportunities to cheat." One example is the so-called predatory borrowing: A home buyer may know something about him- or herself that would make lenders deny the loan if they were aware of it. Predatory lending is also possible. Lenders understand much more about mortgages than their costumers do. Their sales people may talk customers into taking a mortgage they cannot afford, or that will aggravate their financial situation. Mortgage lenders know more about the quality of the loan portfolio they are selling than the buyers do. Those who buy the loan portfolios and turn them into mortgage-backed securities still know more about the loan quality than the buyers of these securities. At every step of the process some information about the quality of the original loans gets lost.

The asset managers had no incentive to question the ratings. Since the arrangers of the securities faced strong demand from asset managers and investors, they saw no need to perform due diligence on the sellers of the loans portfolios. And the mortgage institutions, knowing they could sell any loan portfolio quickly, had no reason to show any restraint with regard to whom they would give a loan. They became complicit in predatory borrowing and started to engage in predatory lending. Volume was everything.

Securitization had created a large class of non-bank, single-purpose mortgage lenders. They are thinly capitalized and do not even have much of a reputation to protect. These companies could follow their incentives for creating as much mortgage volume as possible with near indemnity. The business was very profitable while it lasted. According to a news agency report, the CEO of Countrywide, one of the largest mortgage institutions, took home $50 million in compensation in 2006.

Whenever things went wrong, operations would simply be closed down. According to IMF economists, between mid-2006 and mid-2007 many of the poorly capitalized non-depository firms went out of business. These companies were responsible for about 40 percent of 2006 subprime originations. Most customers who might want to sue for predatory lending will be out of luck.

Did the Fed Egg the Monster On?

The search for culprits did not stop short of a person who had achieved the status of a finance god, and then left office just in time not to see the crisis break out: Alan Greenspan. He is now being criticized for having kept rates too low for too long, thereby encouraging the housing bubble and lending excesses.

One of the critics is John Taylor, the doyen of monetary policy at Stanford. Using a simulation model, the creator of the famous Taylor rule of monetary policy determined that a tighter monetary policy could have prevented much of the real estate boom—as well as the excessive granting of subprime mortgages. "From 2002 to 2005, the short-term interest rate path deviated significantly from what the experience of the preceding two decades would suggest is appropriate," Taylor writes. His simple model of the housing market tells him that exceedingly low rates "may have been a cause of the boom and bust in housing starts and poor credit assessments on subprime mortgages may also have been caused by this deviation."

Not even the Federal Reserve would deny this. Greenspan is on record as saying that the Fed was very concerned about the possibility that the economy might slide into deflation after the dotcom bubble had burst, and took the calculated risk of inflating the housing market in order to avoid this dreadful scenario. There was no deflation, so in retrospect this might seem like a mistake. However, so far nobody has been able to show that the Fed's concern, which was widely shared at the time, was unfounded.

A number of economists and some central bankers have gone as far as suggesting that central banks should actively try to prevent asset price bubbles by raising rates if they see one. According to this view, the failure to "lean against the wind" during the dotcom frenzy of the turn of the millennium, and during the recent housing price boom, would make the Fed guilty by omission.

Perhaps unsurprisingly, Professor Frederic Mishkin, in a paper he wrote while he was a member of the Federal Reserve Board in 2007, comes down squarely on the side of Alan Greenspan. Greenspan made the point that raising interest rates to prevent an asset price bubble would do more harm than good. In order to use rate policy to fend off asset price bubbles, a central bank has to know how to adjust rates in order to achieve the desired result. "By definition, bubbles are departures from the behaviour normally incorporated within models; it is heroic to expect the tools of monetary policy to work normally in abnormal conditions," writes Mishkin. Greenspan had said something similar, arguing that small increases in interest rates might even make investors more confident, believing that everything is fine and under control, while large increases would excessively harm the economy.

Katrin Assenmacher-Wesche of the Swiss National Bank and the Frankfurt-based Swedish economist Stefan Gerlach have supported Greenspan and Mishkin's arguments with empirical data. The two researchers analyzed the data of 17 industrialized countries to find out how quickly and by how much inflation, economic growth, share prices and real estate prices will typically respond to changes in the federal funds rate. What they found was that economies often have to pay dearly for their attempts to prevent real estate prices from skyrocketing: A central bank raising base rates, aiming to suppress real estate prices by 15 percentage points compared to what they would be without the intervention, must reckon with economic growth being slowed down by 5 percentage points. Similar correlations were found for equity prices. Price fluctuations by 15 percent and more are far from unusual in real estate and stock markets.

Another finding is even more alarming: The effects of interest policies on stock prices and on real estate prices differ greatly in terms of timing: Stock prices respond immediately, then the effect slowly fades. Real estate prices respond with considerable delay. Here, the price effect builds over approximately four years—by that time, the effect on share prices has long been gone. "As a consequence of this difference in timing, it is not possible to use monetary policy to stabilize both residential property and equity prices," according to Assenmacher-Wesche and Gerlach.

Regulation Matters

While the Fed has enough arguments at hand to fend off any criticism blaming their monetary policy for the subprime crisis, Greenspan and his colleagues may be quite guilty on another account: As with most central banks, the Fed has a significant role in supervising financial institutions.

The Fed did not see any need for regulatory action to curb the excesses on the market for subprime loans, and for credit derivatives in general. Nor did they advocate scrutiny by the other supervisors and lawmakers. The general consensus was that market forces would ensure the necessary discipline in the financial markets, and help prevent predatory lending, predatory borrowing and excessive risk taking—so regulators did nothing to stop the financial services industry, writes Christopher Whalen of Institutional Risk Analytics. Policymakers confined themselves to issuing cautionary but inconsequential guidance.

IMF economists Kiff and Mills, even after writing their detailed account of the numerous market failings leading to the financial turmoil, still argue against more regulation in response to the subprime crisis. Their reasoning could perhaps be another explanation for the hands-off approach of regulators and legislators all along. "Caution is warranted to avoid unintended consequences for both future mortgage availability and the attractiveness of U.S. capital markets for foreign investors," they argue. And since a large share of mortgage-backed securities had been bought by investors abroad, "a proportion of the losses is no doubt accruing to foreign investors." According to a study by the Institute of International Finance, a Washington-based banking group, of the $387 billion of credit losses banks had owned up to spring 2008, a stunning $200 billion was suffered by European banks and only $166 billion by U.S. banks.

In contrast to the IMF's staffers, former IMF chief economist Kenneth Rogoff, now teaching at Harvard, and his coauthor Carmen Reinhart attribute a large proportion of the blame for the subprime crisis to amateurish and misguided regulators. Perhaps the freedom of speech increases once people leave the Washington bureaucracy. Governor Mishkin, who joined the Fed only after most of the excesses had already happened, agrees that by using their regulatory powers central banks can and should lean against financial excesses. "If elevated house prices are leading to excessive risk-taking on the part of financial institutions, the central bank can encourage financial institutions to have appropriate risk-management practices in place," writes Mishkin in his 2007 article. In May 2008 he reiterates: "It falls on the regulatory policies and supervisory practices to help strengthen the financial system and reduce its vulnerability to both booms and busts in asset prices." It seems the Fed did not perform particularly well on this account. Mr. Greenspan had never made a secret of his opinion that markets are best left alone, and that is what the Fed did.

When banks verge on financial collapse, regulatory authorities and economic politicians face a dilemma: By coming to their aid they might avert a severe wave of panic, which otherwise might do serious harm to the economy—but that, in turn, could lead overprotected banks to accept too much risk, some economists warn. The institutions would then act like rental car customers, driving rather carelessly in the safe knowledge that they have comprehensive insurance coverage. In political economist jargon this is called a moral hazard.

In the cases of Northern Rock and Bear Stearns, authorities mainly opted for quick damage containment—perhaps rightly so, writes Princeton economist Markus Brunnermeier.

Charles W. Calomiris, an economics professor at Columbia University, New York, disagrees: For long-term stability of the banking sector, he argues, it is important that banks be exposed to the risk of failure. "Research on the banking collapses of the last two decades of the twentieth century have produced new empirical findings indicating that the greater the protection offered by a country's bank safety net, the greater the risk of a banking collapse," Calomiris writes in a survey article for the *Oxford Handbook of Banking*.

Calomiris's argument contradicts the famous hypothesis by Milton Friedman: Together with Anna Schwartz, the Nobel laureate had stated in 1963 that the bank collapses in the United States during the 1930s had mainly been due to their clients' irrational behavior. Financially sound institutions, according to Friedman and Schwartz, had had their necks broken by "bank runs." Calomiris's view is that the panic factor as a cause of banking crises is greatly overrated: When banks collapse, he argues, it is usually due to fundamental discrepancies in their balances. "Empirical research on banking distress clearly shows that panics are neither random events nor inherent to the function of banks or the structure of bank balance sheets," Calomiris writes, pointing out that this was equally true for the Great Depression.

There is one question, however, that Calomiris does not address: Are governments able at all to cope with the "moral hazard" problem? Once a bank is in financial misery, threatening to pull the economy down with it, past promises are quickly forgotten.

If authorities come to the conclusion that a bail-out cannot be refused, the necessary consequence is regulation: Regulators will then need to look over banks' shoulders and make sure they won't take excessive risks. If, however, regulators choose to pursue a hands-off approach and banks can nonetheless count on a bail-out, it is a recipe for boom and bust.

How Bad Will It Get?

How much and how long will the world economy suffer from the fallout of the real estate crisis? Expert opinions are divided. Fed governor Mishkin has done the math in the early phases of the subprime crisis, finding several indicators of noticeable but, all in all, relatively moderate damage to the economy. Using the Federal Reserve's macroeconomic model, Mishkin simulated the effects of U.S. real estate prices plummeting by 20 percent within two years.

According to his findings, the GDP would be 0.5 percentage points lower after three years than it would have been without the crisis. Even if Americans responded twice as strongly to this price drop than the Fed usually assumes, the losses in growth would amount to a moderate 1.5 percentage points, and unemployment would increase by 0.6 percentage points. If, however, the Federal Reserve responded timely with noticeable base rate decreases, as it did, it could further limit the damage to the real economy, says Mishkin.

Former Fed chairman Alan Greenspan is much less optimistic. "The current financial crisis in the U.S. is likely to be judged in retrospect as the most wrenching since the end of the second world war," he writes in a *Financial Times* guest column in March 2008.

Another study, published in the *American Economic Review* in the same month, supports Mr. Greenspan's pessimism: Valerie Cerra of the International Monetary Fund and Sweta Chaman Saxena of the Bank for International Settlements find that banking sector turbulences do considerable damage to economic wealth, particularly in industrialized countries—and over a very long period of time. Their study evaluates occurrences of the past 40 years. If results are transferred to the current situation, there is every indication that the next few years may get pretty unpleasant economically.

For a total of 190 cases, Cerra and Saxena analyzed the impact of banking, financial and national crises on economies' growth and wealth over the period of 1960 to 2001. Besides immediate losses in economic growth, the two researchers also looked at how long it took for countries to recover. What they found is that, if countries are able to cope at all with the consequences of a currency or banking crisis, it will take them several years. And if banks are in trouble, the country will lose 7.5 percent of its economic output on average.

Carmen Reinhart and Ken Rogoff, in comparing the subprime crisis to 18 earlier banking crises in industrialized countries, reach a similarly alarming conclusion: "If the U.S. crisis will prove similar to the most severe industrialized-country crises, growth may fall significantly below trend for an extended period." Historically, the countries affected had to take a growth loss of 2 percentage points in real per-capita income, the scientists write, pointing out that it takes an average of two years for economies to weather the consequences of a crisis.

Reinhart and Rogoff also note that the run-up in equity and housing prices, which ultimately led to the subprime crisis, closely tracked the average of earlier crises. And, they do not share Governor Mishkin's optimism regarding the Fed's ability to significantly alleviate the problems for the economy. According to experiences from past crises of this sort, they write, the central factor is how large the shock to the financial system will be, with the efficacy of political countermeasures ranking only second in importance.

Further adding to the complications, the speculation bubble in the real estate market had reached a historical high, according to Yale professor Robert Shiller. "It may be hard to understand from past experience what to expect next, since the magnitude of the boom is unprecedented," Shiller points out. "The implications of this boom and its possible reversal in coming years stand as a serious issue for economic policy makers." The significance of the real estate and construction sector for the U.S. economy as a whole can hardly be overrated, says Edward Leamer, a UCLA economist. Eight of the ten post-war recessions in the United States were preceded by massive problems in the real estate industry.

A much more cheerful conclusion comes from three economists who work for, or advise, Deutsche Bank in America: Michael Dooley, David Folkerts-Landau and Peter Garber. Beginning in 2003 they wrote several academic papers, laying out the Bretton-Woods-II hypothesis, which has been widely discussed in policy circles: It says that the world is presently governed by a currency arrangement resembling the Bretton Woods fixed-rate system. Big emerging markets, notably China, pursue an export-oriented development strategy that rests on stable and competitive exchange rates vis-à-vis the dollar. They run large current account surpluses, resulting in ballooning dollar reserves that need to be invested.

Five years after they promoted Bretton Woods II, the team is still standing by its initial prognosis that the system will last until 2013 at minimum, since there is still an enormous pool of very cheap labor in China and India waiting to be integrated into the world economy. This implies that a persistent influx of capital into the United States will keep interest rates down, helping to limit the damage resulting from the liquidity crisis. The authors draw attention to the fact that interest rates on the capital market have fallen, not risen, in response to the credit crises, along with interest rates on conventional mortgages, leading to a wave of refinancing to lock in low fixed rates.

What this shows is that foreign investors, having lost a lot of money through a depreciating dollar and subprime losses, keep pouring in money instead of withdrawing it. Since the riskier or even fraudulent borrowers are now rationed, ordinary safe borrowers can reap more of the benefit.

References

Ashcraft, Adam B. and Til Schuermann (2008): "Understanding the Securitization of Subprime Mortgage Credit," Federal Reserve Bank of New York, staff report 318.

Assenmacher-Wesche, Katrin and Stefan Gerlach (2008) "Ensuring Financial Stability: Financial Structure and the Impact of Monetary Policy on Asset Prices," working paper.

Brunnermeier, Markus K. (forthcoming): "Deciphering the 2007–08 Liquidity and Credit Crunch," in: *Journal of Economic Perspectives.*

Calomiris, Charles W. (forthcoming): "Bank Failures in Theory and History: The Great Depression and other 'Contagious' Events," in: *Oxford Handbook of Banking,* edited by Allen Berger et al.

Cerra, Valerie and Sweta Chaman Saxena (2008): "Growth Dynamics: The Myth of Economic Recovery," in: *American Economic Review,* Vol. 98, pp. 439–457.

Dell'Ariccia, Giovanni, Deniz Igan and Luc Laeven (2008): "Credit Booms and Lending Standards: Evidence from the Subprime Mortgage Market," International Monetary Fund working paper 08/108.

Dooley, Michael P., David Folkerts-Landau and Peter M. Garber (2008): "Will the Subprime Crisis Be a Twin Crisis for the United States?" National Bureau of Economic Research working paper no. 13978.

Friedman, Thomas L. (1999): *The Lexus and the Olive Tree,* New York: Anchor Books.

Keys, Bejamin, Tammoy Mukherjee, Amit Seru and Vikrant Vig (2008): "Did Securitization Lead to Lax Screening? Evidence from Subprime Loans," working paper.

Kiff, John and Paul Mills (2007): "Money for Nothing and Checks for Free: Recent Developments in U.S. Subprime Mortgage Markets," International Monetary Fund working paper.

Leamer, Edward (2007): "Hosing IS the Business Cycle," National Bureau of Economic Research working paper no. 13428.

Mason, Joseph R. and Joshua Rosner (2007): "Where Did the Risk Go? How Misapplied Bond Ratings Cause Mortgage Backed Securities and Collateralized Debt Obligation Market Disruptions," paper presented at the Hudson Institute, May 2007.

Mian, Atif, and Amir Sufi (2008): "The Consequences of Mortgage Credit Expansion: Evidence From the 2007 Mortgage Default Crisis," National Bureau of Economic Research working paper no. 13936.

Mishkin, Frederic, S. (2007): "Housing and the Monetary Transmission Mechanism," National Bureau of Economic Research working paper no. 13518.

Reinhart, Carmen and Kenneth Rogoff (2008): "Is the 2007 U.S. Subprime Crisis so Different? An International Historical Comparison," National Bureau of Economic Research working paper no. 13761.

Shiller, Robert (2007): "Understanding Recent Trends in House Prices and Home Ownership," National Bureau of Economic Research working paper no. 13554.

Taylor, John B. (2007): "Housing and Monetary Policy," National Bureau of Economic Research working paper no. 13682.

10
Managers Are People, Too

Some celebrity CEOs may have trouble believing this, but even senior executives are creatures of flesh and blood. Accordingly, the human factor has increasingly come to the fore of management science. Scientists have determined that our preoccupation with status, coupled with an inbred aversion to loss, a propensity toward overconfidence and other human weaknesses all contribute to businesses' suboptimal performance.

Take, for instance, information processing. Here we frequently encounter a phenomenon that was described by none other than Jesus: "Nowhere is the prophet held in less esteem than in his native land, among relations and his family," reads Mark 6:4.

Today, management researchers speak of a "preference for external knowledge." Ideas are taken most seriously when coming from experts outside the organization or from competitors. Ideas developed by in-house staff, by contrast, have a hard time getting a fair hearing. The phenomenon is fairly common in contemporary business, as shown by Tanya Menon of the University of Chicago and Jeffrey Pfeffer of Stanford University. For instance, the management of the American fast food chain Fresh Choice was especially impressed with the strategies of its competitor Zoopa—but only until they took it over in 1997. After that, the Fresh Choice upper echelon exhibited much less appreciation for their Zoopa colleagues. The reverse occurred in the mid-nineties at Xerox: Management for years dismissed an Internet strategy devised by its own research department—until competitors began to bring similar concepts to market.

From a management economics perspective, this preoccupation with outside know-how is highly detrimental. "People in groups and organizations have the incentive to reinvent the wheel over and over again, rather than learn from one another. Such outcomes are a tremendous waste of resources," write Menon and Pfeffer.

Conducting experiments, they found the phenomenon to have psychological roots: If good ideas come from a peer, many people perceive them to be a threat. After all, by learning from colleagues or, worse yet, from subordinates, one would be forced to admit that their ideas were better than one's own.

"The threats that a rival poses to a person's self-views affect their willingness to capitalize on that rival's knowledge," the researchers write. Many employees fear a coworker with creative ideas will climb the totem pole faster than they will. Another fear is being seen as a dumb copycat when adopting a coworker's concepts. To avert that kind of loss in status, we react defensively to bright ideas from our fellow workers and associates—we either gainsay their flashes of genius or ignore them altogether.

An experiment with over 130 MBA students, 30 years old on average and with six years of professional experience, showed this: "The more threatened a person feels when coping with an external rival, the more likely he or she is to pursue the knowledge of the rival." The exact opposite is the case for in-house rivals. This remarkable phenomenon occurs irrespective of whether the rival is an individual or another department.

But there is a remedy: Reluctance toward a co-worker's ideas will vanish if the person in question has experienced self-confirmation shortly before. People feeling sure of themselves are much less afraid to lose their status due to an in-house rival's brainwave.

The study furnishes an important explanation as to why it is so difficult to transform a company into the much-talked-about "learning organization." Knowledge management is far more than a question of technology—it involves a great deal of psychology as well.

To overcome these barriers, managers must work on how threats to the ego are perceived in the company, the authors recommend. Only then will the vision of an organization in which everyone shares their knowledge have a fighting chance.

Why Employees Run Away after Mergers

The ego and self-esteem of employees plays a particularly large part in the wake of a merger or takeover. Quite frequently a power struggle ensues between the staffs of the merged organizations, as an investigation by economists Valerie Smeets, Kathryn Ierulli and Michael Gibbs reveals.

Following a merger, the deck is reshuffled for workers—from the formal chain of command to the personal employee networks. Frequently, people tend to give preference to colleagues from their old firm.

The staff of the smaller firm will be more likely to fall on hard times because they have fewer allies in the new organization. In extreme cases, people from the smaller firm wind up in situations akin to that of discriminated minorities in society. Using business data collected in Denmark, the authors demonstrate that after a merger, it is mostly people from the smaller company who leave.

The study was based on a set of unique data from the Danish statistics office. Since 1980 the agency has been maintaining a detailed business data bank that is updated annually. It contains information on each business's ownership structure and staff composition. In addition to staffing levels, the statisticians also keep information on individual employees, such as age and gender, education, profession and salary. The kicker of it all is that the individual career path of each employee can be tracked over the course of years.

For 640 mergers and takeovers that took place in Denmark between 1982 and 1998, the researchers analyzed the staff turnover in the affected businesses before and after. "We find that the more one firm dominates the other in terms of number of employees, the more successful are its employees post-merger," the study concludes. "The majority does tend to drive out the minority after the merger." And: "The relative power of the two firms matters to how the merger plays out."

One year after a given merger, 22 percent of the smaller firm's staff had left the new organization—but only 17 percent of those having worked at the larger organization had left. Three years after the merger, 51 percent of the smaller partner were gone, versus 41 percent of the acquirer.

The effect is even greater when merging businesses operate in different industries. In that case, many more employees of the weaker partner bail out—over three years, their departures are twice as numerous than those of the stronger partner's employees.

Surprisingly, people in the lower echelons of the hierarchy are more likely to leave the new company. The authors assume that senior employees are less vulnerable in the case of a merger—even if they belonged to the weaker partner before.

How to Keep Cocky Managers in Check

A chief executive without an outsized ego—it's almost a contradiction in terms. Someone reaching the very top without being convinced that he is better suited and has greater skills than anyone around him? Hard to imagine—and that is the way it should be. Psychologists have found that optimists and people with self-confidence are movers and shakers, whereas realists tend towards inactivity and self-doubt. On the other hand, numerous companies have dug themselves a deep hole because confident CEOs, convinced of their own genius, wasted money on unprofitable projects, buyouts and mergers.

Two economists, Ulrike Malmendier (Berkeley) and Geoffrey Tate (University of Pennsylvania) have developed a sophisticated approach to test whether there are objectively determinable traits in executives that cause them to make wrong decisions.

The scientists focused on the question of how companies should finance investments. It is an area in which managers frequently make mistakes: They will overinvest when ample cash-flow reserves enable the company to finance machinery, equipment or buildings on its own. Conversely, managers are likely to underinvest when they have to tap credit lines or go to the capital market.

The researchers found that with excessively self-confident senior managers, a company's investment activities are particularly geared to its current cash position. The reason is that these kinds of chief executives tend to believe that they and their company are underappreciated—and its share price is undervalued. Whenever they would have to seek outside financing for investments, they would curtail investments because the borrowings seem too expensive. At the same time, they would overestimate the profitability of pet projects and invest too much when abundant cash flow makes them easy to finance.

As an indicator of managers' self-confidence, the two economists used information on the timing of their option exercises. The reasoning is this: A realistic and risk-conscious manager will exercise his options at the earliest time possible since his assets and income are already disproportionately tied to the fortunes of a single company. An over-confident manager will often believe the company's shares to be undervalued. He will tend to hang on to his options and even buy additional stock in the company.

Under this scheme, the researchers divided 477 chief executives from the largest American companies into a "neutral" and an "overoptimistic" camp—and detected a clear pattern with regard to investment attitudes: Executives of the latter group geared their investments much more to current liquidity than did the former.

To pinpoint possible problem cases, company boards do not have to rely on the (sometimes rather complex) analysis of top management's capital market deals: The two economists identified other indicators that are easier to track. One danger signal is a chief executive's interest in amassing various titles—for instance, when he insists on wearing the hat of "president" or "chairman of the board" in addition to CEO. Education also plays its part: Engineering professionals have an above-average tendency to let their investment decisions be guided by liquidity considerations, while those with a business management background are less prone to commit this type of fallacy.

Why Good Managers Are Reluctant to Correct Their Own Mistakes

Even the best of managers with a realistic self-image can turn into a headache for the company. The reason is that in certain cases, especially talented managers have a strong incentive to ignore the consequences of their own mistakes, instead of proactively taking countermeasures early on. Particularly managers of above-average ability tend to stick with faulty decisions even if they hurt the company. In extreme cases, the company owners may be forced to have a manager fired—not despite, but because of his being very capable, as the German personnel economist Dirk Sliwka has discovered.

A striking example is the behavior of the former chief executive of BMW, Bernd Pischetsrieder. The takeover of the British carmaker Rover, which he had engineered in the nineties, turned out to be a flop that cost the company billions. And although the problems were evident at an early stage, Pischetsrieder chose to sit tight and do nothing, and it took his successor to bring the Rover adventure to an end.

Pischetsrieder acted quite rationally, Sliwka argues, reasoning as follows: Due to inequitably distributed information, company owners can never fully control whether their CEOs really pursue their companies' best interests or their own. Managers, however, are not only concerned about their organizations' best interest but also about their own reputation—which, in turn, does not merely depend on how much the business thrives but also on his or her self-marketing to the public. Thus, the true virtues of a CEO can only be judged circumstantially by outsiders.

Now if a manager, based on proprietary information, becomes aware of a probably false decision on his part, he is faced with a dilemma: If he takes countermeasures, the damage to the company may be contained. On the flipside, he will admit his mistake and thus damage his reputation in executive recruiting circles.

An individual acting selfishly will correct his mistakes only if his own gain, resulting from the expected upward development of the company, is likely to outweigh the inevitable loss of reputation. One thing is important to note here: At the moment when this manager decides whether or not to rectify his mistake, he cannot know for sure if he has really made a mistake. All he knows is: It looks like one.

In a given situation, the probability of a management mistake is not independent of the manager's qualities. A CEO who has proved his outstanding leadership capabilities rightfully enjoys a confidence premium, even though it may appear that he made a mistake. For this reason, good managers have more to lose by changing course than bad ones, in particular since the odds they have made the right decision are higher. A good manager will therefore have more cause to believe that the signs of a possible failure in a project will turn out to be a false alarm. With less competent managers the probability is higher that they have chosen the wrong direction from the very beginning, which is why they are quicker to respond to any information portending the failure of a project. The result of this asymmetry is that in cases where a change of course would be absolutely right from the company's perspective, a particularly skilled manager is more likely to miss the crucial moment of taking remedial action. His worries about a possible loss of reputation among executive ranks are only partially counterbalanced by the hope that correcting his original decision will set the company on a better course.

The lessons for real life are: A company's owners or board of directors should not blindly rely on a good manager to always make the best decisions for the company. In a crisis scenario, it may even be in the owners' best interest to fire a proven and capable manager—thus making way for a successor to clean up the sins of the past, without having to worry about his reputation.

Company Leaders Are Not Born That Way

Much more frequently than having to fire managers, company owners are faced with the problem of finding capable ones. If they set their criteria too narrowly they run the risk of harming the business. For instance, family-run businesses will often make the mistake of locking themselves so that the eldest son can become the senior manager: This is one of the findings of a study conducted by Nicholas Bloom (Stanford) and John van Reenen (London School of Economics).

On average, enterprises organized under recognized management principles are more productive than others, the researchers demonstrated. Their sales grow faster than those of competitors managed by gut feel—and they go bankrupt less frequently.

The researchers interviewed senior executives of 732 industrial businesses in the United States, the United Kingdom, France and Germany. They asked in detail about how the companies' production and other processes were organized. As a guideline for evaluating management practices, they used the canon of practices recommended by a large international management-consulting firm.

American managers came out on top—"good" management practices are most deeply entrenched in U.S.-based business. German managers are not much worse on average, whereas their French and British counterparts clearly bring up the rear.

According to the study, German managers are especially good at systematically working out process improvements, continually monitoring performance, and dealing with low-performing individuals or teams. Weaknesses concern the introduction of advanced production methods and the rewarding of truly outstanding employees.

The United Kingdom and France have a surprisingly large number of businesses that garnered the worst grades in almost all disciplines. Their managers will oftentimes order semi-finished products in bulk and keep them in stock for half a year; production problems are investigated only when a crisis has already set in; and they do not pay too much attention to either their excellent or their lower-performing employees.

A high proportion of utter misfits is the chief reason for the great differences between the countries in terms of managerial quality. In the middle and upper-quality levels the differences are less substantial.

How do badly managed businesses like these survive in the market? Bloom and van Reenen's reply is twofold: These enterprises either operate in markets with low competition—of which there are more in Europe than in the United States—or they are family-owned. The latter account for 30 to 40 percent of companies in the three European countries, which is about three or four times as much as in the United States.

Family ownership by itself is not the problem, though. In Germany, most owner families hire professional managers from the outside. Not so in France or Britain: There, businesses are frequently run by family members, with the eldest son of the owner at the helm. According to the economists' findings, the fact that the choice of candidates for company leader comes down to one single family member is particularly problematic. While there are certainly top performers and a lot of average performers among the family businesses run by the eldest sons, the share of outright failures in this group is alarming.

What Businesses Can Learn from Heart Surgeons

To be sure, what management consultants recommend is not necessarily the ultimate wisdom in all instances. Businesses following the standard recommendation by management consultancies like McKinsey to outsource tasks wherever possible may be making a mistake. The lure of outsourcing is flexibility and low cost. But the process carries inherent risk—especially when contractors must cooperate with salaried employees. In such cases, outsourcing can lead to considerable frictions resulting in quality issues.

Robert Huckman and Gary Pisano of Harvard Business School illustrate the problem by using cardiac surgeons as an example. U.S. hospitals have been following the outsourcing trend for years: An increasing number no longer have heart surgeons on their salaried staff, preferring to work with free-lance doctors instead. The two economists' study reveals that freelancing surgeons do not perform equally well in each hospital studied. Their success rate in a given hospital corresponds to the number of operations they perform in that particular hospital. The number of operations they carry out in another hospital is almost irrelevant to their performance.

The study is based on detailed data about heart operations in Pennsylvania during 1994 and 1995, collected by a government agency for the purpose of increasing cost control in the health-care system. For more than 38,000 coronary bypass surgeries, the economists have the records of which doctor in what hospital did the procedure and whether the patient survived.

Individual surgeons' performance was measured based on how many of their patients died following the operation. To ensure the figures were comparable, they were adjusted by patients' individual characteristics, like age and previous illnesses. This prevents a systematic distortion of surgery data, such as when topflight surgeons focus on difficult cases that, irrespective of a doctor's skills, have a higher risk of mortality.

Initially, the analysis confirmed a predictable pattern: The more experience a surgeon has with certain types of operations, the fewer mistakes he or she will make. On the average, 1.77 percent of all patients in Pennsylvania did not survive coronary bypass operations, the study shows. The risk declines with doctors' increasing experience: When a doctor performs one additional surgery every three months, the probability of mortality goes down 0.015 percentage points.

This effect, however, is essentially limited to a surgeon's experience gathered in one and the same hospital. With each additional operation the surgeon performs in a clinic, the mortality factor of his or her patients there drops by 0.018 percentage points. When that doctor performs an operation in another clinic during the same three-month period, patients' death rates decline by only 0.001. "We find a substantial degree of firm specificity in surgeon performance," the authors write, observing that "surgeon performance is not fully portable across organizations."

The success of a bypass operation does not only depend on the individual surgeon's skills, the researchers conclude. Another highly important factor is how well the heart specialist interacts with the support staff in the respective clinic.

Put in economic terms, the surgeon's human capital and that of the operating team are complementary production factors. The more frequently a surgeon works with the same team, the fewer misunderstandings and mistakes will occur—the "team-specific human capital" increases. Heart surgeons who, as free-lancers, work with frequently changing teams of nurses and anesthesiologists are unable to fully exploit this learning curve effect—as a consequence, there will be more mishaps in their surgeries, which some patients pay for with their lives.

The phenomenon of company-specific performance also remains relevant when the question of outsourcing is left aside. What this means is that even if you hire away the competitor's top employee, you are not guaranteed to be successful. "Particularly when a highly skilled worker must interact with a complex array of other assets—human and physical—within a given firm, the performance of that worker may not be easily transferred across organizations."

What Bosses Can Learn from Monkeys

When bosses wish to motivate their underlings, trouble is brewing. The business of giving rewards and motivating is a tricky one, and plenty of errors occur. How many is revealed by two interdisciplinary studies, one focusing on capuchin monkeys, the other on people.

Behavioral economists have long been aware that the subject of incentives has many hidden traps. For instance, there is a considerable risk of material rewards crowding out employees' intrinsic performance motivation. Where they used to have an inner urge to do well, the introduction of a reward system may blunt these ambitions unless extra remuneration is forthcoming. There is also a risk of setting incentives so high as to damage team spirit or even encourage sabotage.

A social creature appreciates rewards not only because of their (monetary) values, but also as a manifestation of the high regard in which he or she is held. Much depends on how we are situated relative to others.

This even holds true for monkeys, as biologists and psychologists have found out in joint experiments. By using pieces of cucumber as rewards, the researchers managed to teach capuchin monkeys quite reliably to fulfill the task of handing testers a rock. Once a monkey noticed, however, that another monkey in an adjoining cage received a tastier grape instead of a drab cucumber for the same task, he would go on strike—just as he would if a cohort had to do less for the same cucumber morsel.

Similar experiments were conducted on humans by brain researchers and economists of the University of Bonn. In this instance, they glimpsed into the test person's brain to find out what was going on.

In pairs, the test subjects were asked to resolve guessing games while their brain activity was measured with MRI. Based on the blood flow, the researchers measured the degree of activity of the brain's "reward center." High activity is associated with an enjoyable exercise, which we are motivated to repeat.

The testers simultaneously showed images with varying numbers of dots to two subjects at a time. The subjects had to answer questions like: "Are there more or less than 24 dots in this picture?" It turned out that the very start of the experiment, combined with the imminent opportunity to win a reward, triggered increased blood flow in the brain's reward center. Those guessing poorly were "penalized" by their reward center with a drop in brain activity. Those guessing well were rewarded by their brain with an extra dose of euphoria.

The effect became really noticeable only when the other test person had failed. In that case, the successful participant's brain activity held steady, independent of how high the actual reward. The reward centers of those winning $30 were just as agitated during the exercise as those getting $60. By contrast, when both were equally successful and received identical rewards, the motivational effect was small, even with the $60 reward. When one candidate received $30 for a good guess while his opponent failed, his reward center was clearly more active than in cases where he pocketed $60, but the other person got the same amount.

Those who received $60 for a correct guess but learned that their partner had made $120 suffered a drop in activity of the reward center; those who got the $60 knowing that the other person received only $30 felt much better than if the payout had been equal.

What this shows is that indiscriminately dispensing praise and rewards does not get you much return. When everybody gets patted on the back, nobody feels special. On the other hand, if you reward or praise somebody, you need to take into account that others may feel pushed to the sidelines and become demotivated. The same applies in a team effort where some members contribute more than others, but all members are compensated equally.

To add to the complications, for people to get motivated it does not matter what is objectively fair, but rather what they perceive to be fair. This is a difficult issue to solve. Only managers well versed in psychology can expect to reap more benefits than damage from their rewarding systems.

Bosses, You Need to Talk More with Your People

Imagine you work at a telecom company and handle orders for broadband Internet connections. It's important for your employer that you do a good job. That means you should really give it your all, for when the business runs into trouble, your job could be in peril, too.

However: You are not the only one responsible for whether a customer gets his broadband Internet access quickly and without a hitch—your coworkers need to help manage the process as well. If just one of them goofs off, it won't matter how hard you are trying—the order will not go out in time.

If you reckon that others are taking it easy, you will also slack off over the long haul—especially if the chances of getting caught and called on the carpet are remote. This is what economists call "failure of coordination": Actors do not cooperate even though it would be to everyone's benefit.

A Spanish American research team has investigated how such dilemma can be overcome, mainly focusing on two questions: What are the consequences for performance levels when management offers more money? And what is gained when superiors and employees maintain better lines of communication?

The two scientists, Jordi Brandts of the Institut d'Anàlisi Econòmica in Barcelona and David Cooper of Florida State University, created a test environment closely resembling our telecom example. They simulated enterprises with groups of five test persons—four were employees, the fifth was the boss. With regard to sales and profit, they created a rule by which the employee making the least effort determined the company's output and thus its profits.

Each individual could determine for himself how much effort to expend. As in real life, greater commitment was unpleasant to a certain degree, and could bring with it "employee grief."

161

The boss, although aware of the state of employee morale, did not know who was the biggest loafer among his people.

First, Brandts and Cooper analyzed what happened when the company paid a fixed salary and the manager was not able to communicate with his people: With clock-work regularity, companies would fall into a crisis. After only a few rounds, employee morale began to nosedive—as did the sales and earnings of the firm.

To find out how best to pull a business out of crisis in such instances, the researchers gradually handed the managers several tools.

For one, they introduced bonus payments and also encouraged multilevel communication between the management offices and shop floor. The surprising result: Money alone was hardly a motivating factor for better performance. Instead, it would only speed up the collapse in earnings because personnel costs would rise while sales would not.

What proved to be much more effective was talking to people. When managers were able to send electronic messages to their employees, the team's performance level rose noticeably. The laziest employee would try twice as hard as before, when communication wasn't possible. Better still if communication was more than a one-way street and employees were able to send back text messages to their superiors. In that case, the minimum effort was four to five times higher than during times of noncommunication.

The scientists then went to great lengths to analyze the message contents and found three things to be particularly effective. First, managers should openly plead with all employees to show maximum commitment. Second, they should stress the benefits of strong commitment for both sides. Third, they should emphasize that outstanding performance will be appropriately rewarded by the company. With this kind of communication strategy, managers were able to raise their companies' earnings by an average of 30 percent—even though personnel costs rose simultaneously.

The researchers caution against interpreting these results too superficially. Drawing the conclusion that monetary incentives are unimportant would be wrong, they point out. To the contrary: Money is at the heart of the matter—but only when coupled with good communication. "Directly raising incentives is a poor managerial strategy," Brandts and Cooper note, "but pointing out to employees that everyone can make more money if all work harder is quite effective."

The Best CEOs Manage the Largest Firms

CEO pay is one of *the* most emotional topics. In the last decades management compensation has skyrocketed. One common thesis is that managers' unchecked greed and the failure of corporate governance are to blame. While there is ample anecdotal evidence that these factors do play a role, two American professors of finance, Xavier Gabaix (Princeton) and Augustin Landier (New York University) offer a framework that provides an alternative, economic justification for the large increases in CEO pay.

Contrary to the usual reasons given for high managerial pay, the authors do not argue that option programs and other lavish perks are required as incentives for executives to do their very best. Instead, they argue along the lines of the so-called "matching theory."

The basic idea is this: There are differing levels of managerial talent and effectiveness enhancing a company's market value. In large companies where sales, profits and market capitalization are high, executives of outstanding ability can make a great deal of difference, simply because asset growth in absolute terms is larger than in medium-sized businesses. It makes perfect economic sense, then, for the best executives to join the largest companies, since, in absolute terms, these companies will profit the

163

most from good managerial decisions and thus be able to offer them the highest pay.

The researchers fed data from all over the world into their model. What they found was that in general, companies' market capitalization corresponds fairly closely to the CEO's salary. In other words, a business twice the size will pay its CEO twice as much. And the fact that CEO compensation at the 500 largest U.S. enterprises has increased six-fold in real terms between 1970 and 2003 can be explained with the concomitant appreciation of these companies' market capitalization in the same period. According to the scientists' calculations in the context of their abstract matching model, this very correlation appears to be optimal.

By contrast, they found little evidence for the alternate thesis in which a lack of corporate governance is blamed for the differences in compensation. Corporations ranking among the lowest 15 percent on a corporate governance index pay their CEOs 5 percent more on average than do medium-ranking enterprises.

The only paradox in CEO salaries that the two scientists detected is that corporations seem to consider the differences in managerial talent to be marginal—or else they would compensate the best much more generously.

According to a calculation by the two scientists, if the best executive in a large U.S. corporation was replaced by the one in two hundred-and-fiftieth place on the quality scale, the firm's asset value would decline by no more than one-and-a-half-hundredth of a percent. Although this appears to be a negligible difference, the fact that the largest U.S. corporation has such a high asset value still justifies a CEO compensation that is six times higher than the one offered by the two hundred-and-fiftieth biggest corporation.

Gabaix and Landier conclude: "CEOs are no supermen or women, just slightly more talented people who manage huge stakes a bit better than the rest and, in the logic of the competitive equilibrium, are still paid hugely more. Substantial firm size leads to the economics of superstars, translating small differences in ability into very large differences in pay."

Lots of Money, Lots of Anxiety

CEOs of the strongest-selling corporations today earn 367 times more than the average American, according to a recent analysis by Paul Krugman of Princeton University. Thirty years ago, it was only forty times more. While salaries in that range may boggle the imagination of John Doe, some investment bankers in London and New York make much more in a decent year, thanks to year-end bonuses. With these astronomical yet incentive-based incomes, companies want to retain the cream of the crop and motivate them to deliver top-level performance. After all, one of the basic laws of economics says that higher incentives lead to greater commitment and better performance.

A team of U.S. scientists voice strong doubts about the premise, though. Led by the management professor Dan Ariely (MIT) and the organizational psychologist George Loewenstein (Carnegie Mellon), the team managed to demonstrate in a series of experiments that exorbitant incentives can have perverse effects on performance—and deteriorate it instead of improving it.

For part of their experiments, the researchers traveled to India. In a remote town, they paid test persons to resolve problems that required skills, concentration and creativity. Pay was geared to how well they did. Unknown to the test subjects, the researchers had divided them into three groups with different maximum amounts for these rewards.

For some of the test subjects, the researchers set a ceiling of 2,400 rupees—around $56—for excellent performance. By Indian standards this is a lot of money, corresponding to what people in the region on average have at their disposal for consumption in a six-month period. The other two groups had a ceiling of only 24 and 240 rupees for the same activity.

The results were surprising: Test persons standing to earn 2,400 rupees performed significantly worse. Only 20 percent of them managed to earn the maximum. In the other groups, more than 35 percent did—although the task and performance requirements were identical.

Now, it is fair to ask to what extent poor Indian farm workers, having to solve games of skill and concentration for the first time in their lives, can be representative of highly trained and experienced specialists with much more complex tasks to fulfill.

To cross-check the test results from India and get to the bottom of the surprising phenomenon, researchers in Chicago and Boston subjected students to similar, more refined experiments. The test persons had to solve arithmetical problems, and press on a computer keyboard the "n" and "v" key as often as possible within four minutes. While the math part called for cognitive ability, the typing was purely a matter of manual skill.

The researchers intentionally chose activities familiar to the students, who were also given the opportunity to practice prior to the experiments. One group could earn $30 at maximum, the other up to $300. To raise the incentive stakes, the scientists scheduled the experiments close to the semester break—they counted on the students being especially strapped for cash at that point in time.

As before, the math question outcomes showed a clear difference in performance. In the $30 group, 60 percent of participants showed excellent results—but when $300 was beckoning, only 40 percent came through. It was different, though, with the inane typing test: Here the share of top performers in the high incentive group doubled from 40 to 80 percent.

According to the scientists' assumptions, the reason is that in jobs where concentration or creativity is called for, high incentives will distract the individual, but not so during repetitive, annoying routines that can be done without much thinking.

Aside from all the debates around income differences and envy, the study could prompt boards and shareholders of large corporations to put on their thinking caps—if the performance of top managers and businesses can be improved by limiting incentives for senior executives, excessively high bonuses for specialists and CEOs would be less than desirable.

References

Ariely, Dan, Uri Gneezy, George Loewenstein and Nina Mazar (2005): "Large Stakes and Big Mistakes," Federal Reserve Bank of Boston, working paper no. 05–11.

Bloom, Nicholas and John Van Reenen (2007): "Measuring and Explaining Management Practices Across Firms and Countries," in: *Quarterly Journal of Economics,* Vol. 122, pp. 1351–1408.

Brandts, Jordi and David Cooper (2007): "It's What You Say, Not What You Pay: An Experimental Study of Manager-Employee Relationships in Overcoming Coordination Failure," in: *Journal of the European Economic Association,* Vol. 5, pp. 1223–1268.

Fließbach, Klaus et al. (2007): "Social Comparison Affects Reward-Related Brain Activity in the Human Ventral Striatum," in: *Science,* Vol. 318, pp. 1305–1308.

Gabaix, Xavier and Augustin Landier (2008): "Why Has CEO Pay Increased So Much?," in: *Quarterly Journal of Economics,* Vol. 123, pp. 49–100.

Huckman, Robert and Gary Pisano (2006): "The Firm Specificity of Individual Performance: Evidence from Cardiac Surgery," in: *Management Science,* Vol. 52, pp. 473–488.

Malmendier, Ulrike and Geoffrey Tate (2005): "CEO Overconfidence and Corporate Investment," in: *Journal of Finance,* Vol. 60, pp. 2661–2700.

Menon, Tanya and Jeffrey Pfeffer (2003): "Valuing Internal vs. External Knowledge," in: *Management Science,* Vol. 49, pp. 497–513.

Menon, Tanya, Leigh Thompson and Hoon-Seok Choi (2006): "Tainted Knowledge vs. Tempting Knowledge," in: *Management Science,* Vol. 52, pp. 1129–1144.

Sliwka, Dirk (2007): "Managerial Turnover and Strategic Change." in: *Management Science*, Vol. 53, pp. 1675–1687.

Smeets, Valerie, Kathryn Ierulli and Michael Gibbs (2006): "Mergers of Equals and Unequals," Institute for the Study of Labor (IZA) discussion paper no. 2426.

Wolkenten, Megan von et al. (2007): "Inequity Responses of Monkeys Modified by Effort," Proceedings of the National Association of Sciences (PNAS), November 2007.

11

The High Art of Buying and Selling

In most textbooks on economics, it takes only one sentence to describe the science's fundamental assumption concerning behavior. "People choose the best bundle [of goods] they can afford," are the succinct words used in the classic *Intermediate Microeconomics* by Hal R. Varian. To date, (market) economists take for granted that human beings will invariably choose what is best for them; consumer autonomy is one of the pillars of the discipline.

Now a paradigm shift seems imminent, since there is mounting evidence that people do not always make the best choices for themselves. Apparently, we have a tendency to voluntarily overpay, and our buying and consuming decisions are often influenced by irrelevant factors. All of this makes us susceptible to the machinations of marketing experts.

The Winner's Curse

Online auctions are among the most impressive Internet success stories. A case in point is eBay, which has evolved from a small startup into a global retail giant in less than ten years. Goods worldwide change hands to the tune of $2,000 a second on the platform.

One of the reasons Internet auctions are so popular is that bidders feel they can get the most for their money online. But auction experts warn that this perception may be a fallacy. Studies reveal that in the heat of bidding, the winners often go over the top, overbid and end up overpaying.

The experts even have a technical term for this. They call it the "winner's curse." It is based on the insight that whoever made the highest bid for an object is likely to be the person who most overestimated its value. The curse affects up to three-quarters of all auction winners, according to a study conducted by a research team from Stanford University and Berkeley.

"Winning at an auction means that all other bidders felt the object to be of less value," Cologne economist Axel Ockenfels states. He demonstrates the dilemma to his students by using an empty candy jar filled with pennies, which he auctions off during one of his classes. "In the mean, the bids approached the jars's legitimate value fairly closely," the professor recounts. "The highest, winning bid, as a rule, is conspicuously over the top, though."

How much the curse of winning weighs on real eBay auctions is a matter of debate among economists. After countless studies, Ockenfels's conclusion is: "In general—but not always—you can get good deals at eBay auctions." The probability of getting your money's worth is especially high when an object, such as a collector's piece, holds greater value to you than to other bidders, or when you can be sure that there are only a few competing bidders equally qualified to assess the true value of an object.

Yet the fact remains that it is easy to be caught in the overbidding trap. How easy indeed was demonstrated by researchers Hanh Lee (Stanford) and Ulrike Malmendier (Berkeley). As their study object they used an item the value of which should pose no problems to eBay users: the popular board game Cashflow 101. The game, normally sold for $195 by its manufacturer, was offered for $129 by two reputable dealers on eBay during the period of analysis.

For six months, the economists observed almost 700 eBay transactions around Cashflow 101. What they found was that, if shipping costs are left out of the picture, in 42 percent of all auctions the final transaction price was above the readily available buy-it-now price. If shipment is included, 73 percent of bidders paid too much. Every other auction winner overpaid by $10 including shipment, every fourth by $30.

The exaggerated bids come from a small minority of eBay users—only 12 percent of bidders make such mistakes. However, since the highest bid wins it takes only a small group to skew the entire pricing picture. "Auctions select precisely those consumers as winners who overbid and thus amplify the effect of biases in the market," according to Lee and Malmendier. In their opinion, the results of the study can be generalized, and their conclusion is that "In order to maximize their revenues, sellers should pick the auction that maximizes their chances of attracting overbidders to participate in the auctions."

Snipers Buy Cheaper

While sellers at eBay have fun with naive overbidders, the latter are an annoyance for anyone wanting to find a good buy at online auctions. To come to grips with the problem, it is advisable to keep in mind what a study by Axel Ockenfels and his Harvard colleague Alvin Roth recommends.

Until recently eBay advised bidders to enter the maximum amount they are willing to pay for a certain article at their first (and only) bid. In any case, what the successful buyer will ultimately pay is only the price that the last co-bidder had offered before dropping out. After a bidder has entered her maximum bid, an electronic bid assistant continually stores up bids that are just a tad above the competition's current offer—until that maximum limit is reached. In theory, so-called snipers—that's the jargon for bidders who become active immediately before an auction's end—only risk being too late. Supposedly, there's nothing to gain by joining an auction at the last minute.

Wrong, say the two economists, pointing out several good reasons why over 10 percent of all bids are made within the last five minutes, and why it is mainly experienced eBay users who put in their bids last-minute.

To begin with, every auction has bidders who don't really master the game. They believe their highest bid to be payable and go about it as if they were at a horse auction. Every time they are outbid, they enter another, higher bid. This kind of sequential bidding can also be a trick of fraudulent sellers wishing to push the price up. By bidding very late, snipers avoid being outbid by such sequential bidders. In addition, last-second bidding helps to sidestep a battle with other snipers.

Second, there is a specific reason to be late at actions, valid in particular for bidders with a nose for the true value of an article; for instance, in the case of antiques. They have reason to be concerned that others will become aware of their greater experience—for example, by checking out their rating profiles—and will ride their coattails. Experts putting in their bids very late make it harder for such copycats to push up prices.

To empirically test the practical implications of these theoretically derived reasons, Ockenfels and Roth compared bid histories at eBay and Amazon auctions. It helped that Amazon uses a different modus for the closure of an auction. While eBay sets an irrevocable date, Amazon's deadline extends for ten minutes beyond the preliminary closing date until no further bid is incoming. Bidders gain another ten minutes to react to sniper bids.

The two researchers compared auctions of computers and antiquities at both auction platforms. A computer's value is easily determinable, while in cases of antiques, the bidder's know-how is essential. What they found is that late bids are much more frequent at eBay than at Amazon. In addition, late bids at eBay are mostly placed by experienced users, while at Amazon it's the other way a round. And finally, bids for antiques are submitted much later at eBay than for computers. In summary, these findings support the theory that experienced, knowledgeable bidders guard themselves against copycats by bidding late. In other words, snipers know what they are doing.

This does not resolve the question, though, of whether eBay or Amazon has the better rules in place. On the one hand, Amazon users probably reckon with a higher price since it is harder for experienced bidders to protect themselves from getting outbid; on the other hand, this effect may well be counterbalanced by the fact that experienced and active bidders probably prefer eBay for this very reason. It is fitting, then, that antiques auctions at Amazon have pretty much dried up.

The Illusion of a Strong Will

It is not only at online auctions that people tend to overpay. Most of us also have problems in situations where there is a time lag between the costs of a decision and its benefits.

One example is the relatively innocuous question of what type of contract to choose at a fitness center. The large majority of clients in American health clubs opt for contracts under which they pay way too much, according to the findings of Stefano Della Vigna and Ulrike Malmendier of Berkeley. They conclude that "These and additional empirical findings are hard to reconcile with standard preferences and beliefs."

Their analysis was based on detailed data of 8,000 clients from several health clubs. Each of these clubs offered three payment options: Clients could buy a pass good for ten visits, paying $10 per visit, or sign a monthly contract at $80 per month that automatically renewed if not canceled. The third option was an annual contract at $800 that automatically expired after 12 months. Now if clients acted rationally they would sign a monthly or annual contract only if they were reasonably certain that they would use the gym often and regularly. Anyone going less than seven or eight times a month would do better with a ten-visit pass.

In fact, almost 90 percent of clients choose a monthly contract, even though they visit the gym no more than four or five times a month—which translates into a price per visit of $17. A ten-visit pass would cost them only $10 per visit. Even at the beginning of a membership, when the motivation for regular exercise is highest, the contractual commitment is not worth it: On average, new members work out five and a half times a month, thus paying almost $16 per visit. After a few months, when the initial euphoria has faded, the number of monthly work-outs drops to a little more than four, which means that the price per visit rises to almost $19. All in all, the average client with a monthly contract gives away $700 over the life of his or her membership.

Another paradox is that clients with monthly contracts pay a somewhat higher fee for the right of cancellation, although they are usually the most loyal clients: The probability that they will stay with the health club for more than a year is 18 percent higher than with members who have annual subscriptions. What's more, they allow two months to pass between their last work-out and their cancellation of the contract. During that time, the fitness center makes another $185 off of them.

The scientists' conclusion is that people habitually overestimate their own self-discipline when they sign on. After all, visiting a health club means instant physical exertion, which at some future point will be rewarded with better health or a trimmer physique. At the moment of the actual decision to sign a contract, people have that desired future effect in mind. Later, however, when in the midst of one's daily routines the question arises as to whether to visit the health club, the immediate effort is rated higher and the future reward appears lower. Put in abstract terms, people's eagerness to visit the gym depends on the time lag between the present and the intended work-out. Or, to use economist jargon, preferences are time-inconsistent.

Businesses can take advantage of this human weakness by structuring contracts accordingly, explain Della Vigna and Malmendier. Whenever time-inconsistent preferences play a major role, as is the case with fitness training, it will make sense to offer a flat-rate contract and strongly emphasize its benefits to clients. For customers, in turn, this means that they should be very cautious when offered flat-rate contracts, and calculate precisely whether these are worth the money.

Tallying Is a Matter of Luck

Suppose your bank offered you a credit opportunity. What would have a greater impact on your decision—the snapshot of a pretty woman adorning the letter, or a knockout interest rate? Should your reply now be that it would clearly be the interest rate, you are a specimen of the coolly calculating *Homo oeconomicus*, the same one that economists have been basing their models on. Yet fortunately for the banks, you are either completely atypical or wrong in your self-assessment.

In fact, banks hardly compete on interest rates. Above all, they rely on advertising and other soft factors. How well this strategy pays off—and how far man is from being a *Homo oeconomicus*—is a question that a group of economists and psychologists of leading U.S. universities investigated by means of a unique field test.

The researchers engaged a leading provider of loans for low-income South Africans for their experiment. Fifty thousand letters were sent out to customers who had previously taken out credit, offering them a new loan—at monthly interest rates that ranged anywhere between 3.25 and 11.75 percent. In most cases, the offer was better than other alternatives available to the customers. In addition, the scientists randomly used various marketing tools in their letter to test a number of psychological hypotheses.

The study, entitled "What's Psychology Worth?," produced astonishing findings: When the offer's addressee was a male, the snapshot of a woman had as much impact as a reduction in credit interest of 4.5 percentage points a month—equivalent to around 1.5 percent of the addressee's monthly income.

A rather effective—though expensive—approach is to ask customers beforehand if they would be interested in a credit offer. Of those approached this way, a much higher share will bite. Another ruse is to suggest ways to use the credit. Acceptance of the offer also rises considerably if the bank's letter states—although unsubstantiated—how much more the customer would have to pay at competing institutions. Expressing the same difference in terms of money saved is less effective.

By contrast, it is highly ineffective to offer several contract options with different maturities and credit amounts, instead of one sample offer only. This finding is in great contrast to economists' assumptions of rational behavior—after all, the bank saves customers the time and effort required to figure out alternate products by themselves, and more information should always be in the customer's best interest. Psychologists and marketing experts have long known that, when people have to choose between similarly attractive options, they lean toward delaying their ultimate decision. It takes a substantially reduced interest rate to neutralize this information overload.

All the offers' variations are no more than so-called framing effects—essentially irrelevant information that, from the recipient's point of view, places the offer into different psychological contexts. Now it would be fair to argue that what may be typical for South African low-income people may not be applicable to well-off sophisticated citizens of industrial countries. The authors' counterarguments are: First, these psychological elements are based on peculiarities that were also corroborated by lab experiments in industrial countries; second, the study revealed no connection between educational levels or income and the significance of these psychological factors.

Equally telling is the slack price competition in the banking sector, which has repeatedly been documented, in conjunction with its high advertising budgets. To summarize, economists researching and consulting in relevant fields, such as industrial and competitive policies, would be well advised not to blindly base their analyses on the exalted model of an autonomous, rational consumer with unshakable preferences.

The Customer as King—Ungrateful and Unforgiving

All of this does not mean, though, that customers are at the suppliers' mercy and unable to judge the quality of products. The opposite is the case, as a study by two American economists reveals. For several years, Debanjan Mitra (University of Florida) and Peter Golder (Stern School of Business) kept tabs on 214 products in 46 merchandise categories, and the reactions of American customers to objective quality changes in a product.

Their conclusion: Quality wins—but it takes time. Before changes in quality actually register in consumers' heads, a lot of water will pass under the bridge. How slowly and how strongly they will react varies from one product category to another. With refrigerators, it takes seven years until quality changes have filtered down to the customer's awareness level; for automobile tires, it takes as long as ten years. With personal computers and diapers, though, the full effect can be felt after roughly three years.

In painstakingly detailed work, the researchers tapped several sources of information for their study. As a measuring rod for the objective quality of a product, they chose the test results printed in *Consumer Reports* magazine, taking into account only products that had been tested at least four times between 1989 and 2000. The quality ratings for each of these products were compared to consumer surveys, in which 30,000 Americans were polled on their opinions about the products of individual manufacturers. Based on the results of these surveys, the researchers analyzed how strongly and how quickly quality changes in a certain product will resonate in the public's perception of that product's quality.

A key result of the investigation was that customers' response to quality changes is not symmetrical. Deteriorating quality will enter the public's conscience faster than will quality improvements. "Because firms will generally promote increases in quality but not decreases, these results underscore the importance of word-of-mouth and media reports," the researchers write. After all, one would assume that companies, with all the professional marketing tools at their disposal, have the means to disseminate information about quality improvements faster.

In products that need to be replaced frequently—diapers or paper towels, for instance—improvements and deteriorations reflect faster on the image. The same applies to merchandise groups in which quality inconsistencies across products are particularly pronounced.

Preconceived notions customers have of a manufacturer play an important part in how quickly and clearly they will notice a higher or lower product quality. Customers are quicker to notice quality improvements in well-reputed branded goods than in no-name products. Conversely, quality deterioration in low-priced products is noticed much earlier, impinging even more on the name's less-than-stellar image.

Apparently, well-reputed companies benefit from the fact that people will accept and believe information much more readily if it confirms their preconceived notions. The good news for premium brands is that consumers do not penalize them excessively for quality slippage. The scientists had expected image losses to be more pronounced for high-standard enterprises in cases of product deterioration.

The marketing researchers draw several conclusions relevant for managers: For one thing, businesses facing quality problems should react quickly to stem the tide. As consumers are slow to become aware of qualitative inconsistencies, the manufacturers have a window of time in which to contain the damage to their reputation. Furthermore, it is advisable to deliberately develop a top-notch brand reputation, as it builds a lot of goodwill among customers.

Brand Image Pays Off Twice

In the long run, only happy customers are good customers. But things can quickly get complicated when you try to explore the connection between customer satisfaction and how much people are willing to pay. Are satisfied customers prepared to pay more? Are they more willing to go along with a price increase?

A research team around the Mannheim, Germany–based marketing professor Christian Homburg investigated these questions in two experiments. In the first, they gave subjects a detailed account of a restaurant visit and asked them to rate their impressions on a satisfaction scale. For instance, the researchers would describe the inside temperature as a bit too cool, the ambient noise level as somewhat high, the service as good, the menu as elaborate and the ingredients as very fresh. Each subject then rated a variety of these imaginary restaurant visits and indicated how much he or she would be willing to spend on a certain menu at that place.

In the second experiment, the economists offered students learning software that they could test out. Different individuals were given versions of varying quality and ease of use. Following the test, the researchers questioned the students about their satisfaction level and the maximum amount they would be willing to spend on such software. Using an elaborate procedure, they made sure their test subjects were truthful in stating these maximum amounts.

Although both experiments were structured quite differently, results were identical: The connection between customers' satisfaction and their willingness to spend money is very strong, but not linear. When customers have been very unhappy with a product, their spending inclination will steeply increase with a rising satisfaction curve. The same is true for customers who are already quite happy with the product and notice a quality improvement. In the medium satisfaction range, spending readiness changes very little with a comparable change in satisfaction. What this means in practice is that businesses with satisfied customers will find it much easier to raise their prices. Their customers will be much more inclined to believe they have valid reasons for a price hike, such as cost pressures or quality improvement. This is essential, as customers attach great importance to business relations being fair, and it does not sit well with them if the pursuit of profits is the only reason for higher prices. Dissatisfied customers are particularly sensitive to price increases, and quick to infer disingenuous motives.

"Our research supports the managerial belief that satisfied customers—those receiving higher quality service or who feel better about the product—are, in fact, willing to pay more for it," the authors write. Pricing policies should therefore never be implemented regardless of customer satisfaction. At weak satisfaction levels, it may be wise to shelve price increases until steps to improve customer satisfaction have borne fruit.

Moreover, in many cases it may be worthwhile to focus on improving satisfaction levels of customer segments whose willingness to pay is particularly sensitive to changes—that is, the highly satisfied and the highly dissatisfied.

Join Christina Aguilera in the Winner's Circle

Businesses do not always resort to legitimate means in their marketing tactics. The lightning career of singer Christina Aguilera is a case in point. A specialty agency hired by the singer's record label had plastered the fan websites of pop star Britney Spears with recommendations drawing attention to the emerging artist. The agency's staff mimicked the target group's jargon adroitly enough that most of the time no one realized this was covert advertising. And sure enough, Aguilera's debut album made it to the top of the U.S. pop charts.

The phenomenon intrigued economist and Yale professor Dina Mayzlin, causing her to scientifically research the issue: What happens when companies issue manipulative product recommendations, indistinguishable from genuine user recommendations, on the web?

Mayzlin built a complex theoretical model to analyze this question, and came to a very differentiated conclusion. On the one hand, companies with inferior products do more hidden online advertising than their competitors with superior products; on the other hand, general incentive and cost structures are such that superior products will still garner more positive than negative comments—even if Internet users can remain anonymous. In other words, if you follow online recommendations you have a better than 50:50 chance of choosing the right product.

Three factors are responsible for the result. First, businesses cannot produce hidden online advertising at no cost. To be somewhat credible, the messages must be posted manually on message boards or chat forums, which makes this form of marketing quite expensive. Second, truly superior products get more genuine recommendations from customers. And third, returns per additional positive recommendation diminish as the number of recommendations increases.

By and large, however, hidden online marketing operates under different economic laws than traditional advertising. For instance, the textbook wisdom that companies with better products advertise more actively does not apply. With traditional advertising, businesses with inferior products cannot count on recouping high advertising expenses with booming sales figures, while firms offering good products can. An extravagant ad campaign, thus, signals to the customer that the company believes in the quality and sales prospects of its product. With anonymous online advertising, by contrast, customers are unable to determine the originator or budget volume; therefore, the positive signal effects of high advertising expenses are lost to companies with superior products.

With hidden online advertising, it makes more sense for companies with inferior products—and less cost-free praise from genuine customers—to ramp up their marketing. After all, the revenues of a business depend on the likelihood of a potential customer coming across a positive recommendation.

Yet marketing expert Mayzlin shows that although hidden online advertising dilutes the informational content of product recommendations on the Internet, they do not become worthless for the user. The reason is that the marginal cost of producing an additional hidden message rises; consequently, the number of messages for the inferior product will usually not approach the level of the better product, which enjoys the additional support of actual users.

With regard to the question of whether hidden online advertising should be prohibited for certain products, the study offers some pointers. Loss of welfare by anonymous advertising is greatest when quality differences between products are large and the market is small. One example is treatment methods for rare diseases. Since there will only be a limited number of genuine patient reports, the vendor of a useless therapy will profit the most from posting manipulative reports on the web, and do most harm to the deceived consumers.

Information Is Power

Naiveté and blessed ignorance can be just as costly on the web as in traditional commerce. On balance, however, the Internet shifts power from the vendor to the customer. Consumers can choose from a greater number of vendors and make easier price comparisons.

Using the U.S. new-car market as an example, a research team from Yale and Berkeley has managed to show that customers who thoroughly plan their purchase over the web pay significantly less than those getting their information from offline sources only. On average, Internet users save 1.5 percent. This is equivalent to about 22 percent of the dealer's gross profit margin, as Florian Zettelmeyer, Fiona Scott Morton and Jorge Silva-Risso show in their study.

The empirical investigation was based on dealer records of over 5,200 new-car sales in California. To obtain information on buyers' web usage and other characteristics, the scientists additionally quizzed them exhaustively about their buying habits.

Three out of four new-car buyers used the Internet in planning their purchase—mostly to visit the manufacturer's website and independent information services. Only every third Internet user went to the sites of individual dealers.

Online information proved especially beneficial for customers with an aversion to haggling. The web boosts their "offline" negotiating position in two ways: First, it is fairly easy for U.S. consumers to find dealer prices on the Internet, which means that they also know the dealer's acceptance limit. Those knowing the dealer price paid 0.61 percent less on average than customers who were in the dark.

Price search engines are a second major driver of price slippage. These so-called online buying services have regional exclusive agreements with selected dealers, who will respond to customers' online inquiries by submitting a price offer. Car buyers using these services saved an additional 0.72 percent.

The dealers go along because, via these buying services, they can reach a much larger sales territory than they do when using traditional channels. Thus, a car sale facilitated by a price search engine is very likely to represent an additional deal. And there is another reason why dealers are willing to make concessions: If their online business is slow, the search engines will cancel their exclusivity agreements and give them to competitors.

Ultimately, according to the economists, price search engines don't haggle just for current buyers but also for future ones. How about that for a revolution?

References

Bertrand, Marianne, Dean Karlan, Sendhil Mullainathan, Eldar Shafir and Jonathan Zinman (2005): "What's Psychology Worth? A Field Experiment in the Consumer Credit Market," National Bureau of Economic Research working paper no. 11892.

Della Vigna, Stefano and Ulrike Malmendier (2004): "Contract Design and Self-Control," in: *Quarterly Journal of Economics,* Vol. 119, pp. 353–402.

Della Vigna, Stefano and Ulrike Malmendier (2006): "Paying Not to Go to the Gym," in: *American Economic Review,* Vol. 95, pp. 694–719.

Homburg, Christian, Nicole Koschate and Wayne Hoyer (2005): "Do Satisfied Customers Really Pay More?" in: *Journal of Marketing,* Vol. 69, pp. 84–96.

Lambrecht, Anja and Bernd Skiera (2006): "Paying Too Much and Being Happy about It: Existence, Causes and Consequences of Tariff-Choice Biases," in: *Journal of Marketing Research,* Vol. 43, pp. 212–223.

Lee, Hanh and Ulrike Malmendier (2007): "The Bidder's Curse," National Bureau of Economic Research working paper no. 13699.

Mayzlin, Dina (2006): "Promotional Chat on the Internet," in: *Marketing Science,* Vol. 25, pp. 155–163.

Mitra, Debanjan and Peter N. Golder (2006): "How Does Objective Quality Affect Perceived Quality? Short-Term Effects, Long-Term Effects, and Asymmetries," in: *Marketing Science,* Vol. 25, pp. 230–247.

Ockenfels, Axel and Alvin Roth (2002): "Last Minute Bidding and the Rules for Ending Second-Price Auctions: Evidence from eBay and Amazon on the Internet," in: *American Economic Review,* Vol. 92, pp. 1093–1103.

Zettelmeyer, Florian, Fiona Scott Morton and Jorge Silva-Risso (2006): "How the Internet Lowers Prices: Evidence from Matched Survey and Transaction Data," in: *Journal of Marketing Research,* Vol. 43, pp. 168–1841.

12

The Athlete as a Guinea Pig—Or: Why Economists Love Sports

What determines who will win at Wimbledon? Do football teams on fourth down make the right decisions? How much does a team's success depend on its superstar? Do soccer referees favor the home team? And how important is the coach for a professional sports team's performance?

Questions of this kind are not just vexing to the average sports fan. Increasingly, they have been catching the attention of economists, too. Be it tennis or baseball, football or soccer—for years, economists have systematically dissected all types of sports. It is more than mere amusement to them—more than anything else, professional sports lends itself to the analysis of certain economic phenomena.

To quote Dutch economists Franc Klaassen of the Tinbergen Institute and Jan Magnus of Tilburg University, "sports statistics (and sports economics) has developed from an anecdotal field where one collects statistics (so many double faults, so many aces) to an almost-respectable discipline. An important reason for this development is that sport statistics can help answer behavioral questions."

Compared to everyday life, studying sport has several advantages: Rules of the game are less complex, there is one clear-cut goal—winning—and results are definite. When incentives change, causes and effects can easily be pigeonholed—rules are the same for all players and matches take place in a controlled environment. In his book *The Baseball Economist,* J. C. Bradbury, a professor at Kennesaw State University, writes: "Baseball is a game full of well-defined benefits and costs, which makes it a fantastic laboratory for economists." To top it off, hundreds of games are played each year in the pro leagues of team sports, and for many years, each player's stats have been minutely recorded. It affords economists easy access to a comprehensive collection of data.

The productivity of a top-line player, for instance, can be measured much more easily than that of an office worker. Labor market researchers can take advantage of this in analyzing which factors determine an employee's compensation in real life. In particular the highly charged question of whether whites are paid more than blacks or Hispanics for equal performance is investigated using the U.S. pro leagues as a basis. However, results are not as unequivocal as one would think. Older studies from the eighties and nineties, using the National Basketball Association (NBA) as an example, came to the conclusion that white athletes earned significantly more than black players with comparable skills. For the National Football League, however, these findings could not be confirmed by other researchers, nor does ethnic background seem to be a factor in the recognition of players in baseball. A team of three researchers showed that the probability of a player being elected to the National Baseball Hall of Fame by sports journalists is entirely predicated on his past performances on the baseball diamond—irrespective of whether he is black, white, or Hispanic.

Football Teams Don't Play It Right

Sometimes the great, fundamental questions of their discipline cause economists to search for answers in the stadiums. For example, do businesses really maximize their profits? This is a central assumption in practically all theoretical models the discipline has at its disposal. Verification in the real world is anything but easy—first, because the decisions that the management of a chemicals or automobile company has to make are highly complex, second, because scientists rarely catch a glimpse of a company's internal data.

It is easier with professional football teams. David Romer, a professor at the University of California at Berkeley, has evaluated strategic decisions of NFL teams as to whether they were maximizing their odds of winning. Romer focused on a key moment regularly facing football players on the field: the behavior of the offense when facing a fourth down. At this stage, there are three options open to the team: First, they can continue to play out their set of downs and try to gain the balance of the necessary ten yards for continued ball possession. If they fail to get a first down, or a touchdown, the ball goes over to the other team. Second, if the offense is within distance, they can try for a field goal through the uprights, which, if successful, scores three points. The third option is to punt, which will not get them any points but, when properly executed, forces the opposing team into an unfavorable field position, closer to its own goal line.

In his study, which was published in the well-regarded *Journal of Political Economy* in 2006, Romer presented a sophisticated computer program. Based on data from 700 NFL games, the software permitted him to estimate the value of each field position—what is the worth of a first down, or of a punt? In a second step, he compared these theoretical values with the actual decisions made. The teams graded out rather poorly: Players and coaches were quick to punt and pass up many promising opportunities. "On the 1,068 fourth downs for which the analysis implies that teams are on average better off going for it, they kicked 959 times," the economist writes. Even on fourth down with a yard to go, a team will often play it safe and punt instead. In other words, the teams act much more defensively than a sober-minded profit maximizer would. "The behavior of National Football League teams on fourth downs departs from the behavior that would maximize their chances of winning in a way that is highly systematic, clear-cut, and statistically significant," the researcher concludes.

Cricket Players Learn Very Slowly

In cricket, there is also a type of decision that the teams do not seem to handle well. V. Bhaskar, a game theorist at University College London, has examined the choice cricket captains make when they have the option to decide who is batting first. The option to make this choice is awarded by a coin toss, making it nice and random, something empirical economists love. Cricket teams attach quite a lot of importance to the decision on who will bat first, since the conditions for batting or fielding can vary over time, with variation in the weather and conditions of the natural surface on which the game is played.

At cricket, one team bats first and sets a score; then it is the other team's turn to bat and try to exceed the first team's batting score. Bhaskar calculated the percentage at which nine international teams chose to bat first. It turns out that in one-day games that are played entirely in daylight, most teams chose to bat first roughly half of the time. But according to Bhaskar's study, the conventional wisdom about the importance of batting first is wrong. Three teams chose to bat first a lot less, the West Indies team in particular only about a quarter of the time. And the West Indies were the undisputed champions in most of the years analyzed.

Bhaskar found that captains winning the coin toss often did not make the right decision. On average, they chose to bat first too often. For teams who "won" the coin toss and chose to bat first, the likelihood of winning actually was below 50 percent. That is, the captain chose to put his team at a disadvantage.

There is more evidence suggesting that teams must be making mistakes. It turned out that whenever a team playing against the West Indies, or against the two other teams who liked to bat second, won the coin toss, they would choose to field first more rarely than they should. Remember that the West Indies team liked to field first and were highly successful, so their opponents had no reason to assume the West Indies were making a mistake with their choice. Consequently, the right thing to do would have been to field first and take that option away from the West Indies team. As it turned out, the other teams chose to bat first almost half of the time and let the West Indies have their preferred choice. The same mismatch occurred with the other two teams who liked to field first.

Bhaskar has a favorite theory to explain why cricket captains make wrong choices so often. In cricket, unlike baseball, the ball is bounced off the ground by the bowler. For the chances of the batter to hit the ball, the state of the pitch, the central strip of the cricket field between bowler and batter, is important. Until 1970, international test match cricket was played in a different format, in which the pitch deteriorated a lot during the game, which lasted several days. This conferred a clear advantage on the team batting first. Therefore, prior to 1975, captains chose to bat first 87 percent of the time, which gave them a 55 percent chance of winning—a fairly large advantage. During a one-day game on today's better-quality pitches, the pitch does not deteriorate nearly as much as during the five-day matches decades ago.

The captains might not adjust their decision appropriately, because their decision is evaluated by cricket commentators and selectors of the team, both of which are usually former cricketers. The evaluators may have outdated information, with a consequent bias against batting first. Bhaskar cites former England captain Mike Brearley, who writes: "[I]t is irrationally felt to be more of a gamble to put the other side in [to bat]...decisions to bat first, even when they have predictably catastrophic consequences, are rarely held against one." If this is true, captains who choose to bat first when there is a small advantage to fielding first may well survive longer than those who choose optimally.

Game Theorists Playing at Wimbeldon

Are tennis players smarter than football or cricket players? It almost seems so. Mark Walker and John Wooders managed to show that professional tennis players at the Wimbledon tournament did master a similar conundrum fairly well.

Test participants (or weaker players) regularly fail in what game theoreticians call "mixed strategies." Therefore, before Walker and Wooders had published their analysis of Wimbledon tennis in 2001 in *American Economic Review,* there had been some consensus that flesh-and-blood people would be overstrained if they tried to apply optimally mixed strategies as configured by game theoreticians. Such mixed strategies contain a probability component: For instance, the best strategy may be to pick variant A with a 75 percent probability and variant B with a 25 percent probability.

Apparently, however, the world's best tennis players are up to the task: At serve they act pretty much the way game theory prescribes.

Walker and Wooders investigated the serving players' decision making on whether to hit into the opponent's forehand or backhand. To play optimally, the player at serve must calculate the power of the opponent's forehand relative to his backhand. With a weaker backhand, more balls should come in its direction but not so many for the second player to confidently adjust his stance accordingly. An unexpected ball here and there to the forehand enhances the chance to capture the point. Walker and Wooders found most players capable of varying their serves to the forehand and backhand randomly enough for both variants to have an almost equal chance to garner the point.

But even tennis stars are not absolutely perfect game theoreticians. It would be optimal if the decision to serve into the forehand or backhand were left completely to coincidence—totally independent of how previous serves went. This makes the serves harder for the opponent to return. To play in such a vein is hard since nobody carries a coincidence generator in his brain. Walker and Wooders found that when compared with its hypothetical ideal, serves alternate too often between fore- and backhand. It is a mistake committed regularly by people trying to imitate randomness.

Of Incentives and Their Side Effects

Sports grounds are particularly good places to study the impact of incentives. Using soccer teams as an example, a research team around Zurich, Switzerland, economist Bruno Frey showed: Large discrepancies in income within a team are counterproductive. "The larger the income differences are, the lower is the performance," Frey's study sums up. This effect is particularly pronounced in top teams. Exorbitant salaries paid to some superstars do not spur on the other players but instead have a demotivating effect—thus the economists' interpretation.

This observation confirms Frey's hypothesis that, rather than the absolute amount of their income, it is their relative position compared to others that matters to people. The result is equally relevant away from the soccer field, wherever pay is directly coupled with performance—for instance, with insurance agents or financial advisers. Any attempts to spur on the members of marketing teams by concocting internal performance rankings could backfire, the economists warn.

Even though inequality of salary may inhibit the performances of soccer teams, money plays an overriding part in a team's success. The bigger a club's payroll, the higher the likelihood of the team doing well, the Munich economists Markus Kern and Bernd Süßmuth show, citing the German premier league. How much a club will invest in its coach is secondary—teams with outlandishly paid star coaches hardly fare better on average than others.

New Brooms Don't Sweep Any Better

Clubs and their fans seem to overestimate the importance of the coach. A chronically unsuccessful team will invariably fire the coach—but only in the rarest of cases will this change the team's fortunes for the better, according to a study by Bas ter Weel. The economist from the University of Maastricht analyzed whether clubs in crisis will play more successfully after a change in coaches. His conclusion: New brooms don't sweep any better.

The hopes that a new coach will work wonders by motivating players to deliver a better performance is almost always misplaced: As ter Weel points out, there is only a very short-run shock effect picked up by the popular media, but this effect does not last very long. In most cases, the team's performance will pick up measurably only in the first game under the new coach—only to drop back to its previous level afterward.

For his study, ter Weel analyzed data from the Dutch pro soccer league Eredivisie for the years 1986 to 2004. During this period, 81 coaches were fired and another 103 did not have their contracts renewed. Ter Weel observed "a relatively steep hazard rate for trainers, since during the average season, over 50 percent of the teams are replacing them; 44 percent of all separations have been forced."

Following an extended series of defeats, the likelihood of a coaching change rises steeply. When a team plays worse than its seasonal average for four straight games, the coach will have to worry about his job—even more so if he had signed many new players prior to the team's drop in performance, or if his contract expires soon anyway. When a series of defeats push down the team's position in the standings, compared to historical averages, the coach will equally find himself on the hot seat.

But why is it that a new coach can rarely bring about a change in direction? Is it because the team simply plays lousy, or because the coach's personality has little impact on the team's performance? To come up with an answer, the economist used a trick—he put together a control group of clubs that also experienced a breakdown in form but held on to their coaches. As a measure for the teams' success on the field, the economist used the number of points per match that a club accumulates over the last four games.

Ter Weel's surprising finding was that teams standing by their coach in crisis regain their bearings sooner than those making a change. And he came across more interesting phenomena. For instance, coaches who have been in the business for many years and those who have been players before are less able to turn around a club than those with less professional experience.

"The estimates suggest that manager quality measured by the manager's previous achievements as a player, years of managerial experience and number of spells does not significantly matter for predicting turnover and does not explain much of the performance increase after resignation," ter Weel concludes. The scientist is convinced his results can be transferred to regular businesses. He uses them as a powerful rejoinder against the conclusions of several management research studies that found that a change in management will frequently lead to a certain recovery of business performance. "Manager quality might not be as important as put forward by other studies," ter Weel warns.

Even experienced soccer coaches are not beyond strategically wrong decisions, an investigation of economists Christian Grund and Oliver Gürtler reveals. A popular mistake is this: When their own team is trailing, coaches will often strengthen the offensive by bringing in additional forwards. Along with improving the odds of catching up, however, this strategy also increases the risk that the opposing team will score more goals. According to Grund and Gürtler, the second effect will usually prevail: In their analysis of 1,700 substitutions during the German Bundesliga season of 2003–2004 they found that, when a coach switches to a more offensive tactic after his team has fallen behind, the opposing team will increase its lead in 40 percent of all cases. Only in 21 percent of games did the trailing teams manage to equalize. By contrast, teams that were left unchanged caught up in 35 percent of cases, and in only 30 percent were scored on again.

Slowing Down Others Will Get You There, Too

One of the important insights of recent economics research is that higher incentives often cause undesirable side effects. There is plenty of evidence for that in sports arenas as well. One case in point is the change of rules that the World Soccer Association (FIFA) introduced a few years ago. In an attempt to heighten the suspense (and the number of goals) in soccer matches, the incentives for victorious teams were increased: They are now awarded three points instead of the previous two. A tie will bring each team one point, as before.

The two economists Luis Garicano and Ignacio Palacios-Huerta analyzed how the change affected game behavior and results, based on data from the Spanish Primera pro soccer league. As a control group, they used the same teams' games in the Spanish Cup competition, where the three-point rule is not in force.

What they found is: The number of games ending in a tie did come down noticeably following the rule change and the shots on goal and corner kicks rose—but the expectation of more goals scored did not pan out. "Teams are less likely to tie, but they are also less likely to win by a "useless" (but possibly quite entertaining) large number of goals," the scientists write.

To wit, the new incentives only work during the initial phases of the game; later on, they reverse. The team ahead—rather than being anxious to score more goals—will then focus its efforts on stopping the opponent from scoring. For good reasons: If the opposing team ties the score, two points will be lost now instead of a single one, as used to be the case. In other words, the introduction of the three-point rule caused teams to become much more defensive—through fair and unfair means.

After having gone ahead in scoring, a team will substitute forwards for defenders more often than it used to, and its unsportsmanlike behavior will increase. The number of fouls, in conjunction with the number of yellow and red cards, clearly rose after the rule change.

By comparing the development with that in cup tournaments, the economists show that this phenomenon cannot be explained away with a generally rougher style of play. The increase in fouls committed and warnings issued is evident only in league games, where the new rules apply. Contrary to FIFA's intentions, the higher reward for the victor seems to have led to an increase in sabotage and disruption on the pitch.

When Referees Are Taking Sides

Not only are players taken to the test by economists—so are referees. The relationship between them and the sports association paying their salaries is an instructive example of a so-called principal-agent relationship. Under this heading, economists discuss problems that arise from the fact that you cannot do everything in life by yourself. Some chores get done only when they are delegated to another individual.

In the eyes of economists, referees are "agents" acting on behalf of a "principal"—the soccer association. This is where the rub lies: Due to an uneven distribution of information, the principal will often find it difficult or well nay impossible to check how conscientiously the agent is going about his work. A referee is supposed to be impartial and enforce the rules of the game. A selfish agent, however, will also have incentives to surreptitiously pursue his own instead of his principal's interests.

One example is the scandal around the German referee Robert Hoyzer, which shook the country in 2005. The German Soccer Association had commissioned him with enforcing the rules of soccer during ongoing matches—instead, he followed his own interests. Hoyzer rigged matches so his buddies could rake in profits by betting on these games.

While this kind of criminal energy is surely an exception, countless studies by economists have shown that referees systematically favor the home teams. This, too, is a violation of their sworn duty: Instead of ensuring a fair game, their whistles blow for whatever makes the crowd happy. When the hosts trail by a single score after 90 minutes the injury time played is significantly longer than it otherwise would be—in Spain more than two minutes, in Germany a bit over half a minute. This is the finding of an analysis by Matthias Sutter of the University of Innsbruck and Martin Kocher of the University of Munich. Based on the data from 306 games played in the first and second Bundesliga division, as well as the regional league, in the 2000–2001 season, the two researchers showed: Referees also favor the home team when awarding penalty kicks. Using the judgment of soccer experts at the *Kicker* sports magazine as a yardstick, Sutter and Kocher's evaluation shows: On the question of "penalty or no penalty," German referees make the right decision in 81 percent of instances if it favors the home teams. They decide correctly in favor of the visiting teams in only 51 percent of cases.

Within a fitting institutional framework, soccer associations should be able to come to grips with the principal-agent issue, according to economists Neil Rickman and Robert Witt of the British University of Surrey. In an empirical study they show the quality level in referees' decisions to have measurably improved in the English premier league since the introduction of professional referees.

In England, the compensation of premier league referees has been raised substantially since the 2001–2002 season: Instead of a few hundred pounds plus expenses, they now receive an annual salary of £33,000 plus £900 per match. In return, they must attend biweekly meetings at which their decisions are analyzed—for those who commit too many errors, sanctions are in store up to the point of suspension.

It definitely helped: One year later, the systematic favoring of home teams had ceased. Prior to the introduction of professional referees, home teams in England had also benefited from unabashedly preferential treatment; injury times would be dragged out when the host trailed by one goal after 90 minutes of play. When a score in the final second could avert a home defeat, the referees, just like in Germany, on average allowed 30 seconds more added time than they did with matches unequivocally settled at the end of normal time.

Following the reforms, the two economists could no longer detect any significant connection between the scoring at the end of 90 minutes and the length of extra time played. It seems that the introduction of professional referees generated strong enough financial incentives to influence referees' behavior. Better pay and strict censure make errors in judgment by referees an expensive proposition—those blowing their whistles at the wrong moment face a painful loss of income.

References

Bradbury, J. C. (2007): *The Baseball Economist—The Real Game Exposed,* New York: Dutton Adult.

Bhaskar, V. (forthcoming): "Rational Adversaries? Evidence from Randomized Trials in One Day Cricket," in: *Economic Journal*.

Dohmen, Thomas (2005): "The Influence of Social Forces: Evidence From the Behavior of Football Referees," Institute for the Study of Labor (IZA) discussion paper no. 1595.

Frey, Bruno S., Benno Torgler and Sascha L. Schmidt (2006): "Relative Income Position and Performance: An Empirical Panel Analysis," Institute for Empirical Research in Economics (IEW), University of Zurich working paper no. 282.

Garicano, Luis and Ignacio Palacios-Huerta (2005): "Sabotage in Tournaments: Making the Beautiful Game a Bit Less Beautiful," Center for Economic Policy Research discussion paper no. 5231.

Jewell, Todd R., Robert W. Brown and Scott E. Miles (2002): "Measuring Discrimination in Major League Baseball: Evidence from the Baseball Hall of Fame," in: *Applied Economics*, Vol. 34, pp. 167–177.

Kern, Markus and Bernd Süßmuth (2005): "Managerial Efficiency in German Top League Soccer: An Econometric Analysis of Club Performances On and Off the Pitch," in: *German Economic Review*, Vol. 6, pp. 485–506.

Klaassen, Franc and Jan Magnus (2006): "Are Economic Agents Successful Optimizers?: An Analysis Through Strategy in Tennis," (May 2006). Tilburg University Center discussion paper no. 2006-52.

Rickman, Neil and Robert Witt (forthcoming): "Favouritism and Financial Incentives: A Natural Experiment," in: *Economica*.

Romer, David (2006): "Do Firms Maximize? Evidence from Professional Football," in: *Journal of Political Economy*, Vol. 114, pp. 340–365.

Sutter, Matthias and Martin G. Kocher (2004): "Favoritism of Agents—The Case of Referees' Home Bias," in: *Journal of Economic Psychology* Vol. 25, pp. 461–469.

Walker, Mark and John Wooders (2001): "Minimax Play at Wimbeldon," in: *American Economic Review*, Vol. 91, pp. 1521–1538.

Weel, Bas ter (2006): "Does Manager Turnover Improve Firm Performance? New Evidence Using Information from Dutch Soccer, 1986–2004," Institute for the Study of Labor (IZA) discussion paper no. 2483.

13

In the Dark Recesses of the Market Economy

"It is not from the benevolence of [the] butcher, the brewer, or the baker that we expect our dinner, but from their regard to their own interest." This line from the pen of Adam Smith is one of the most famous quotes in the field of economics. It illustrates a fundamental hypothesis of market-based thinking: Each individual actor on the economic stage is free to act egoistically—the "invisible hand of the market" will steer matters so that results will be in everyone's best interest.

Some preconditions must be present, however, for everything to go so smoothly. Competition must flourish and businesses must not have market power. And everybody must play by the rules—the referees as much as the players—in order for the pursuit of one's own interests to serve the common weal. For a long time, economists showed little interest in what will happen if these conditions are not met. But changes are afoot. With increasing frequency, studies are published using the tools of economics to explore what goes on in the dark recesses of economics, to determine who has what power and how it is wielded. There are entrepreneurs profiting from their connections with politicians, rating agencies and banks abusing their power, and international financial organizations that have more than development and crisis management on their political agendas.

Betting on Hitler

Businesses and lobbying groups spend millions of dollars each year tending the political landscape. Political scientists have been arguing for the longest time over the impact of party sponsorship and campaign contributions on the democratic decision-making process. What about the economic consequences?

From the viewpoint of contributors the money should be well invested—not so from the perspective of the overall economy. This is the conclusion of a number of recent economic studies that shine a spotlight on the value of political ties for businesses.

For companies, having good political connections is usually of great benefit, according to the researchers' unanimous conclusion. When they are in cahoots with politicians their business will clearly prosper. They pay lower taxes, are eligible for better credit terms, and, when in a pinch, will more readily receive government assistance. As a result of all this, they are more profitable and their stock will enjoy higher quotes at the exchanges.

The studies also reveal that in the national economy as a whole, political patronage will lead to noticeable distortions—not the least because less profitable enterprises are saved from failure at the taxpayer's expense. In general, political patronage apparently encourages businesses to become slothful. One indication is that their annual reports contain much less information.

Even in modern democracies there is a close connection between political contributions by a business and its commercial success: This is the result of a study by U.S. scientists Michael Cooper, Huseyin Gulen and Alexei Ovtchinnikov, based on U.S. data from the years 1979 through 2004. The more financial contributions a business showers on candidates during congressional election cycles, the rosier its prospects for the future. "Contributions to political parties lead to abnormal returns," the authors point out.

The insight seems equally valid for a great variety of social systems. A both fascinating and chilling example for how political ties can be rewarding for companies is provided in a study with the catchy title "Betting on Hitler," published in the *Quarterly Journal of Economics*. The economic historians Thomas Ferguson (University of Massachusetts, Boston) and Hans-Joachim Voth (University of Pompeu Fabra, Barcelona) showed that businesses that maintained close ties to the Nazi Party (NSDAP) before 1933 clearly had the inside track after Hitler's rise to power.

To begin with, the two researchers noted that there was a remarkably tight relationship between the German business world and the Nazis before 1933. This contradicts a fairly recent hypothesis by the U.S. scientist Henry Turner, according to which it is untrue that large parts of the German industry promoted Hitler from early on and helped him come to power. Ferguson and Voth dissent: One out of seven companies listed on the Berlin exchange was intimately involved with national socialism prior to the takeover—members of executive committees or supervisory boards contributed money to the NSDAP, advised Hitler on questions of economic policy, or acted on his behalf behind the scenes. Hitler's support was especially strong in large-sized corporations: "When weighting the companies according to their market capitalization, there were senior executives with Nazi ties in more than half of all corporations listed on the Berlin exchange."

Next, the researchers checked how the Nazi-connected companies' share prices fared compared to others: "Firms that had 'bet on Hitler' benefited substantially." In the two months following his rise to power, their share prices rose between 5 and 8 percent more than those of companies without Nazi connections. These findings cannot be explained away with fundamental factors like size, profitability, or a boom in the industry.

On moral terms, contributions to democratic parties cannot be equated with support for criminal dictatorships—nonetheless, for donors such transactions prove beneficial, irrespective of the type of regime. This is the conclusion of a study by Mara Faccio of Vanderbilt University, published in the *American Economic Review*. Ties are particularly tight in countries suffering from endemic corruption that is likely to keep foreign investors at arm's length, the researcher says. In today's Russia, more than 85 percent of listed companies are cheek-to-jowl with the country's political class; in Germany it is only 1.2 percent. How much a business will benefit, however, also depends on the type of relationship: Only if board members decide to assume political roles will their company increase in market value, the U.S. scientist found.

Economists also have an answer to the question of precisely how and through what channels corporations will profit from political nurturing: If firms find themselves in difficulties, government will come to their aid much quicker if they have political ties. Based on the data of 450 well-connected firms from 35 countries, Mara Faccio (along with two coauthors) shows in the *Journal of Finance* that between 1997 and 2002, 11.3 percent of these corporations received public funds from their governments—in a comparative group of ailing companies without political contacts, only 4.4 percent did.

More often than not, politically well-connected firms that have been rescued by the government will run their business affairs poorly afterward. "Bailouts of connected firms are even more wasteful than bailouts in general," is the authors' verdict.

Next to tax breaks, politicians will also make favorable credits available. Using Indonesia as an example, Christian Leuz (University of Chicago) and Felix Oberholzer-Gee (Harvard) show that companies maintaining good relations with the Suharto regime sought equity or credit on foreign capital markets less often. Apparently these well-connected firms had enough access to cheap financing in their home markets and did not need to tap the international capital market.

Political patronage can also be a hazard. With a sudden change in regime, what used to be a godsend can turn into a curse overnight. Leuz and Oberholzer-Gee conclude this much: Companies that maintained close ties with Suharto found themselves in deep trouble following his toppling, and were forced to seek more capital on foreign markets.

Investors, Check the Obituaries

Mara Faccio and David Parsley of Vanderbilt University used a particularly original approach to demonstrate the economic value of political patronage—and the concomitant risks when the benefactor vanishes: They investigated how the unexpected death of a politician affects companies located in his home district.

The two researchers cast a wide net. Not only did they check cases in which close political ties were in the records, they treated each business headquartered in the departed politician's district as a potential recipient of preferential treatment on his part—be it tax breaks or public rescue efforts in case of financial problems, well-disposed treatment from government agencies, or custom-tailored laws. In total, the researchers evaluated 123 deaths and the share prices of over 7,000 companies. Only cases of unexpected, sudden deaths were considered; other cases do not give a reliable picture of their impact on stock price. For each politician, roughly 60 firms with the prospect of potential privileges were lined up.

Despite their broad study layout, the authors noticed a strong, statistically significant correlation: A politician's unexpected passing depresses the share price of a company with headquarters in his district. The stock of the affected firms would lag behind the overall market's direction by almost 2 percent. And this is likely to be a rather conservative estimate of a political connection's total value, for not every politician favors all businesses in his home district. Furthermore, any political links unrelated to geography are exempted.

On a general note, it is advisable for investors to react promptly when news of a politician's death becomes public. The stock market's response will build up slowly over the ten days following the event.

There are individual differences, though. For instance, companies with dominant family ownership benefit more from political connections—their shares will soften more with a politician's unexpected demise. This seems plausible, since the nurturing of political relations over a long time is easier for a family-owned business than one with a broad ownership base and frequently changing management.

In countries where corruption is a fact of life, the death of a protagonist will push down a stock's value even more, as can be expected. The study's result, however, is not entirely driven by developments in developing and emerging markets. Industrial countries dominate the cases investigated because data are more available there. Of the 123 deaths, three-fifths occurred in industrialized countries.

Finally, share prices of smaller businesses suffer proportionately more from a loss of sponsorship. The authors' explanation is that large enterprises have the resources to construct entire contact networks with politicians. In the United States, it is not unusual for a company to financially support the election campaigns of two competing candidates or parties. It makes large enterprises less dependent on an individual's patronage.

To test the robustness of their results, the authors did a similar study focusing on companies with documented familial ties to unexpectedly deceased politicians. The result: The loss in share price is only slightly higher than for organizations with purely geographic links. This points to the fact that geographic connections are of comparable importance to familial connections.

The Power of Rating Agencies

Rating agencies play a vital part in keeping financial markets supplied with up-to-date information. They tell investors all there is to know about a company's or a country's creditworthiness. This enables smaller investors, in particular, to assess risk more accurately—and the credit markets to operate more smoothly.

So much for theory. In practice, there are several problems with regard to credit agencies, as documented by Mark Carlson of the Federal Reserve and Galina Hale of Yale University. The few recognized rating agencies pack quite a punch, owing to a peculiarity of their business model: They grade a company's creditworthiness—not its ability to pay back borrowed money. The latter would not change in response to an agency's judgment. Creditworthiness, however, is made up of the ability to pay off outstanding loans and to take on new debt—for companies frequently take out new loans to roll over prior debt. Credit institutions, however, only go along with such practice when the enterprise has an appropriate rating. And this is where the cat bites its tail: When a rating agency decides a business's credit standing to be impaired, this will turn out to be the truth (within certain limits)—simply because many potential credit institutions will follow the agency's assessment and withhold further credit. In that case the company may become illiquid, whereas it would have had no problems when rated positively. In other words, a positive rating could have been just as correct.

In economist lingo this means that there is not one equilibrium of supply and demand but two—one for high creditworthiness and the other for low. The rating agency has a hand in deciding where the balance will lie. This gives it a great deal of power, which it can either use to the benefit of the organization and the recipients of its rating, or abuse for its own advantage. If, for instance, rating and consulting services are not sufficiently segregated, it is not beyond the realm of possibility that the agency will issue benign ratings in return for lucrative consulting assignments. Or they award ratings to companies commission-free, possibly hoping that business will come through with a paid rating order. The paid rating might turn out to be more positive, after all. As long as the assessment seems plausible, it won't cost the rating agency anything—not even its reputation: Due to the self-fulfilling prophecy, the creditworthiness of a well-rated business will be accordingly high.

Why Banks Don't Like to Google

Not only with credits will financial institutions flex their muscles, but also when companies go public. Investment banks, for instance, will occasionally use raw power to get their hands on lucrative consulting assignments—this is the outcome of a study by three economists from Switzerland, France, and the United States.

The problem was highlighted during the IPO of Google in 2004: Much to the surprise of most investors, the Internet company chose an auction to float their shares. At the time, market traders knew only the so-called book-building method, which is handled by investment banks, although auctions are actually an excellent pricing tool in free markets. In theory, they should also be much more appealing to the company going public: Underwriting fees are lower and, more important, prices at issuance are usually much higher, meaning that the companies or their owners get more money for the shares they issue.

Why, then, are almost all IPOs done via book building? According to François Degeorge, François Derrien and Kent Womack, it's simply a matter of investment bank interests.

The process begins with the banks functioning as lead underwriters, setting a trading range for the shares. During the subsequent book-building phase, investors put in their bids of how much stock at what price (within the predetermined band) they would order. The price is generally set low enough for demand to clearly exceed supply. As a result, whoever has shares allotted to him from the underwriters can count on safe and sometimes spectacular gains during the first trading day.

Banks are essentially free to allocate the goodies as they see fit—a nice privilege. American courts have found some U.S. institutes to take unfair advantage: In return for share allocation, they had buyers retain their investment banking services, or they collected excessive commissions and fees.

No wonder, then, that banks are partial to the book-building process. Still, one question remains unanswered: Why are there not more Googles? Degeorge, Derrien and Womack have an explanation: because the banks reciprocate the advantages derived from book building with voluminous and positive analyst reporting and media coverage. As evidence of this, the researchers present an econometric evaluation of French IPOs in the nineties. Only in France and only during that time were book building and auctioning used in equal measure for initial public offerings.

As the analysis revealed, underwriting banks issued clearly more favorable analyst reports and recommendations on stocks they brought public via book building than on those auctioned off. The same pattern emerged with banks not part of the underwriting consortium—especially when the lead underwriter regularly brought businesses public and had favors to disburse. Also, stock brought public by book building received many more "booster shots"—which is traders' jargon for buy recommendations issued by analysts when a stock is tanking following its IPO.

The media, too, reported much more exhaustively about the former group of companies than those that took the auction route. The difference only became evident, though, after the modus of going public had been decided. Before, both types of company were of equal interest to the media. This may be one reason why the Google IPO was greeted with deprecating comments from the analyst community, yet the shares quintupled from their issue price. What a strange miscalculation by the market experts.

How Investment Funds Buy Good Press

Other economists do not give the press very good grades, either. In some parts of the media, there no longer is a clear separation between editorial content and advertising. American investor magazines seem to write what important advertisers want to read. Such is the conclusion of Jonathan Reuter from the University of Oregon and Eric Zitzewitz of Stanford University.

The researchers analyzed the reporting on equity funds of five important U.S. media, focusing on one fundamental question: Will the issuer of funds receive favorable treatment in return for placing numerous ads? The authors concentrated on the financial industry because it is better suited than others for proving journalistic bias: Contrary to many other products, the quality of an equity fund can be objectively judged both ahead of time and in retrospect. Subjects of analysis were the newspapers the *New York Times* and the *Wall Street Journal,* together with investor magazines *Money, Kiplinger's Personal Finance* and *Smart Money.* Almost half of the advertising expenses of investment funds went to these five publications.

For the years 1997 through 2002 the economists obtained data on the ad volume allotted to each of the five publications. They also evaluated how positive or negative each paper's reports were about each fund. The results were astounding. At the newspapers, the separation of editorial and advertising content seemed to be maintained—the economists could not detect any kind of journalistic favouritism at either the *New York Times* or the *Wall Street Journal*. Not so at the investor magazines: In *Money, Kiplinger's Personal Finance* and *Smart Money*, Reuter and Zitzewitz found a close interrelation between a company's ad volume and the likelihood of its products being recommended to investors. *Money*, for instance, listed 84 percent of all companies that had placed ads worth a million dollars or more in the previous year among their top 100 investment funds. Of the companies that had not advertised at all, only 7 percent made an appearance on the list.

In and of itself, this correlation does not suggest anything sinister—good funds may simply be written up in the media more often and therefore be in greater demand. Hence, the researchers investigated the quality of each fund, based on its historical track record, administrative fees charged and ratings. The economists developed a mathematical formula to determine which funds would be recommended when conforming to these quality criteria. The result: Of the 100 funds touted by *Money*, eight or nine were included only because their parent companies had placed lots of ads. *Kiplinger's* and *Smart Money* showed a similar trend.

In a second step, the researchers investigated whether funds investors following investment recommendations earned above-average returns—and found that "positive mentions have little ability to predict future returns." At least this is not because important ad clients receive preferential treatment, but because the publications apply the wrong criteria in selecting recommended funds. According to the study, they place too much emphasis on past performance while other vital factors like administrative fees are largely disregarded.

In the end, the only party to profit from investment tips is the company offering the funds. As the authors point out, positive press coverage of certain funds will result in considerable cash inflow over the next twelve months.

How a TV Station Helped George W. Bush Win the Election

Media can use their power not only to increase revenue, but also to elect the government they favor. Two economists from the United States and Sweden have scientifically analyzed the correlation between biased media reporting and election results. The results are quite striking: According to their study, President George W. Bush owes his 2000 victory to one-sided TV coverage. "Media can have a sizeable political impact," note authors Stefano Della Vigna (University of California, Berkeley) and Ethan Kaplan (Stockholm University).

The researchers specifically investigated how the emergence of Fox News influenced the behavior of U.S. citizens at the polls. Founded in 1996 by TV mogul Rupert Murdoch as a counterweight to CNN, Fox News was soon known for its unabashedly conservative news coverage. Media scientists in several studies have evidence that the broadcaster reporting is biased—Fox News invited many more experts from conservative institutions to its programs than other stations did.

A historical coincidence enabled the researchers to neatly calculate the effect of this bias on Americans' behavior at the polls: In its early years, Fox News could not be received in all regions of the country. In 2000, it could be viewed in only 20 percent of all cities. Thus, for some 9,200 cities in 28 states, the researchers were able to determine whether voting patterns diverged from regions that had no access to the station.

The answer was affirmative. The Murdoch station exerted massive influence on the electorate's behavior. In cities where Fox was viewed, the Republican share of votes rose between 0.4 and 0.7 percentage points, Della Vigna and Kaplan show. "The impact of Fox News is small but not negligible," the study asserts. "Assuming that Fox News did not affect turnout substantially, Fox News shifted approximately 200,000 votes from the Democratic candidate to the Republican candidate." In the state of Florida, which Bush took with a plurality of just 537 votes more than Democrat contender Al Gore, and which proved decisive for the election's outcome, Fox News may have driven more than 10,000 voters into the Republican corner.

To reaffirm that cause and effect did not become muddled in the analysis, Della Vigna and Kaplan also checked how voter behavior in the respective regions had evolved prior to the introduction of Fox News—for it would have been conceivable for cable networks to first introduce the station in regions with preponderantly conservative voting records. The possibility was analyzed exhaustively by Della Vigna and Kaplan—yet no indications were found that the station had initially concentrated on regions where Republicans were in the majority.

Another noteworthy finding was this: The less a city's variety in TV programming, the more pronounced was the Murdoch channel's significance for voter behavior. "When the Fox News message competes with a larger number of channels, its impact appears diminished," the study says. The rule of thumb was: With every additional ten channels in a city's TV landscape, the growth in Republican votes attributable to Fox was 0.2 percentage points lower.

Mind you, the Fox News effect is by no means restricted to the person of George W. Bush. As the economists show, the network's fairly slanted news reporting apparently influences viewers' fundamental political attitude. Even in Senate elections, when Fox generally does not cover local candidates in detail, Republicans have benefited from the station's presence. Non-voters, especially, seem to keep an open ear for its political messages—a large portion of the Fox effect is due to the increasing participation of conservatively predisposed people in the voting process.

When Wall Street Whistles, the IMF Jumps

The purpose of the International Monetary Fund (IMF) and the World Bank is to monitor and safeguard the operation of financial markets worldwide and to do development work. There is no mention in their charters of advocating the trading and other interests of large shareholders of the two institutions. Yet repeatedly, both institutions will come under attack from left and right. The left wing's accuses them of not representing the interests of developing and emerging countries in need— the organizations are mostly beholden to industrial nations. Frequently critics even maintain that in essence, the IMF only serves the interests of Wall Street and large U.S. corporations. The American right wing charges both institutions with the opposite: wasting American taxpayers' money on credits to incompetent governments.

Riccardo Faini and Enzo Grilli, two Italian economists who used to teach in Rome and Washington, have researched to what extent credit grants by the IMF and World Bank coincide with commercial interests of the main shareholders, the United States (17 percent), Europe (30 percent total), and Japan (7 percent). Faini and Grilli, who both died in 2007, knew the IMF and the World Bank intimately, having represented Italy as executive directors on the boards of the two institutions and having held leadership positions on their staff. In the decision-making committees of both institutions, votes are weighted according to capital quotas. However, since formal votes are rarely taken, the voting records of individual shareholders are hard to gauge.

Instead, Faini and Grilli compared the regional patterns of the largest capital contributors' trade relations with the regional patterns of credits granted, all for the period from 1990 through 2001. As the IMF is mainly called upon in the event of regional financial crises, as an additional variable to explain credit grants they introduced the criterion as to whether or not the region in question had suffered a credit crisis in that particular year. Figures were adjusted for the average rise in credit grants in cases of crisis, in order to prevent the randomness of crises from distorting analysis results.

It turned out that the trade and financial interests of the United States exerted the biggest influence on credit grants by the IMF and World Bank. In all five regions surveyed—Latin America, Asia, Africa, Eastern Europe and the Middle East—credit grants are intimately correlated to the share of American exports going into the region, and the relative size of claims the U.S. banking system has against these countries.

Unlike Wall Street, European banks cannot count on the IMF to help out with liquidity injections to debtor nations when loans go bad—at least not on a global level. Only in Central and East European transformation countries, where European banks are particularly involved, can a statistically meaningful influence on credit grants by the IMF and World Bank be found.

Europe's influence on the two institutions' credit policy seems to be motivated mainly by trade interests. All five recipient regions had an easier time obtaining credits when importing heavily from Europe. The statistical correlation, however, is much less pronounced than when U.S. interests come into play. Japan must content itself with tweaking the commercial policies of the IMF and World Bank where its banks' interests in the rest of Asia are concerned. In other regions, Japan's interests seem to be of no consequence for credit allocation.

Left-wing critics may well feel vindicated. The most interesting part is Europe's comparatively small influence. Although European countries hold a higher combined share in capital at the IMF and World Bank, their interests matter less. Here, Faini and Grilli contend that the Europeans' preoccupation with national concerns boomerangs on them, as they effectively neutralize each other.

References

Carlson, Mark and Galina Hale (2006): "Rating Agencies and Sovereign Debt Roll-Over," in *Topics in Macroeconomics,* Vol. 6, article 8.

Cooper, Michael J., Huseyin Gulen and Alexei V. Ovtchinnikov (2008): "Corporate Political Contributions and Stock Returns," working paper.

Degeorge, François, François Derrien and Kent Womack (2007): "Analyst Hype in IPOs. Explaining the Popularity of Book-building," in: *Review of Financial Studies,* Vol. 20, pp. 1021–1058.

Della Vigna Stefano and Ethan Kaplan (2007): "The Fox News Effect: Media Bias and Voting," in: *Quarterly Journal of Economics,* Vol. 122, pp. 1187–1234.

Faccio, Mara, Ronald W. Masulis and John McConnell (2006): "Political Connections and Corporate Bailouts," in: *The Journal of Finance,* Vol. 61, pp. 2597–2635.

Faccio, Mara and David Parsley (forthcoming): "Sudden Deaths: Taking Stock of Political Connections," *Journal of Financial and Quantitative Analysis.*

Faini, Riccardo and Enzo Grilli (2004): "Who runs the IFIs?" Centre for Economic Policy Research discussion paper no. 4666.

Leuz, Christian and Felix Oberholzer-Gee (2006): "Political Relationships, Global Financing, and Corporate Transparency: Evidence from Indonesia," in: *Journal of Financial Economics,* Vol. 81, pp. 411–439.

14

A Final Warning

"The only statistics you can trust are those you falsified yourself"—
who hasn't heard (or used) this phrase before? Churchill's cynical
words could similarly be applied to the econometric analyses that
provided the basis for most of the findings presented here: If there
are any people at all who resemble that theoretical creature *Homo
oeconomicus*, they are likely to be economists. Practitioners of the
science are judged by the quality of their research papers, and not
all results found are equally suitable for publication. A finding that
a given hypothesis cannot be verified statistically will hardly be
accepted in any economic journal. For those reasons, economists
have a strong incentive to produce statistically significant results.
And there are ways to make results look significant. For individuals
reading a final research paper these results are not easy to detect,
even for the referees at the scientific journals.

When scientists deliberately use those ways and means to
create publishable results, even though it turned out in the
course of their analyses that there is nothing that warrants evidence, it is considered unethical conduct and disdained by the
profession. But those are extreme cases. There also are some
methodological contrivances that can legitimately be tweaked
this way or that. Scientists cannot be blamed for trying to come up
with what works best and aligning their methods accordingly.

But economists want more than to just get published. More
often than not, they also wish to exert influence. Apolitical

people rarely choose to become economists—which is why many economists are not totally free of bias in pursuit of what they wish to demonstrate. Consciously or subconsciously, they will fiddle with the details of their methodology until the results suit their dogmas or value judgments. As such this is no malfeasance—after all, those setting forth certain hypotheses are still required to provide empirical evidence that those in opposition can verify or possibly refute.

Nonetheless, those immersing themselves in economic studies ought to realize: Advice from economists can be shot through with prejudice. A piece of empirical evidence supporting a given thesis should not be perceived as ironclad "proof" by the reader of an economic study. It is a strong indicator at best—the more conclusive the methodology and the less the contrivances to be tweaked in order to achieve meaningful results, the more persuasive the results will be. The same goes for the various studies discussed in this book. In particular, very recent papers still awaiting their publication in a respected academic journal should not be viewed as gospel by the reader. Even studies having passed the acid test of demanding and recognized professional publications are known to have been refuted at some later point.

We are introducing only the results of studies that we believe to reflect the current state of the art, as accepted by leading economists.

When Listening to Advice from Economists, Keep the Saltshaker Handy

At times, economists will even confront their own prejudices with scientific studies. A good example of that kind of critical navel-gazing is an investigation by four political scientists and economists from Israel and the United States. They delved into the question of whether economists, who by virtue of their profession have a profound impact on the debate about social and economic policies, enrich the discussion preponderantly with their own impartial expertise or with dearly held prejudices.

The essence of the team's findings is: Beware! The recommendation to always examine expert advice for inherent prejudices is particularly valid when dealing with economists: Their value system seems to diverge systematically from that of ordinary people.

The "egoism versus altruism" theme, however, does not seem to reflect those idiosyncrasies particularly well: While students of economics acted more selfishly than others in lab tests, other studies found that they do more volunteer work and return lost and found items more readily. Therefore, Neil Gandal, Sonia Roccas, Lilach Sagiv and Amy Wrzesniewski used a more differentiated psychological model, tested it by polling students of economics and other disciplines, and were thus able to resolve the apparent contradiction.

The team divided the egoism motif into three components: achievement, hedonism and power; within altruism they distinguished between universalism and benevolence. Benefactors like to help and support people close to them in one way or another. Universalists look after the welfare of those with whom they have little or no contact. According to the team's findings, students of economics are more consumption-oriented than those in other disciplines. Also, their striving for power and their preoccupation with professional achievement is more pronounced. What's more, they empathize less with anonymous fellow men. For people close to them, budding economists have just as much empathy and are as helpful as students of other subjects. "Economists make good friends or neighbors but are relatively less concerned with the welfare of people who are not part of their 'in-group,'" the study's authors summarize in their conclusion. Within the remainder of the value canon, the only significant difference was that tradition holds much less importance for economists than it does for other people.

The obvious question now is: Do economists become more self-ish because they constantly wrestle with the construct of *Homo oeconomicus?* The authors negate this. Rather, they argue, the phenomenon is a product of self-selection—young people with certain sets of values seem predisposed to study economics. They infer this from the fact that no significant differences in value judgments could be found between economics freshmen and students in graduate class. In other words, the difference to the average population was already evident in the first semester and did not get any stronger over the course of the studies.

The researchers tested their self-selection hypothesis by means of a control question: They asked freshmen about the particular values they associate with economists. Ambition, intelligence and success were the values mentioned most frequently. Those interested in studying economics seem to be very well aware of what breed of people they will be joining.

A politician advised by economists to institute reforms that promote liberty, individualism and private consumption, but that may be hard on certain groups of the population, should realize that the value judgments of his or her voters do not necessarily coincide with those of the advisers.

Soldiers of Fortune Riding the Statistics

Left-handed people suffer more frequently from high blood pressure and schizophrenia, but are less susceptible to arthritis and stomach ulcers. All this and more is set forth by three economics researchers at prestigious U.S. universities in the context of their study "Handedness and Earnings" and published in the renowned *Journal of Finance*. The subject of analysis were the income prospects of left-handers as compared to right-handers. The result: On the average, left-handers earn 15 percent more than comparable right-handers—at least (and only) when they are male and have a college degree.

The *Journal of Finance* enjoys an excellent reputation among economists and is considered to be selective and demanding. However, it is quite possible that the results of the study are owed to systematic data mining. In scientist circles, this is the term used for the theory-less analysis of data pools with the goal to uncover potentially interesting or useful statistical connections. But there is a problem with that kind of method: Statistical correlations of this kind are often coincidental and there is no causal relation.

Another telling example of data mining is presented by Walter Krämer, a professor of statistics in Dortmund, Germany, in his book *So lügt man mit Statistik* (How to Lie with Statistics): Together with his associate Ralf Runde he managed to provide evidence of a "divided by five, balance of one effect" for the German stock exchange: They found that during certain trading days the German stock market had significantly higher returns than on other days. These days were the first, the sixth, the eleventh, the sixteenth, the twenty-first, the twenty-sixth and the thirty-first day of each month. Those days have in common that when the day of the month is divided by five, there is always a balance of one left.

How did this result come about? The two statisticians tested a series of similar "rules," such as "divided by five, balance of two," "divided by five, balance of three" and so on. It would have been extremely bad luck if there had not emerged at least one significant result among them. By "significant" we mean: If the date was of no relevance for the development of stock prices, a respective deviation from the normal course would occur with a probability of no more than 1, 5, or 10 percent.

Data mining is the great divide among exponents of the science. Many software vendors offer complex programs for its use, advertising them as research tools for the expensive and cumbersome work of statisticians and econometrists. In academic circles, the programs have found buyers especially in the marketing sector. There, the theory-less treasure hunting of data is an esteemed method, for instance, for filtering out patterns of buying behavior from a firm's customer data.

For economists and scientists of many other disciplines, data mining is a disparaging term used to dismiss research results. Their reasoning goes as follows: When vetting a sufficient number of data blocks for possible correlations, you are bound to find coincidental correlations that could pass the acid test for statistical significance. These significance levels are only meaningful, however, if you had a hypothesis to begin with that you tested based on a strictly limited number of relevant series of data.

By contrast, when investigating a set of data comprising ten variables with the data mining approach, and in the absence of theoretical constraints, you will find 45 twin pairings you can test for statistical correlations. This is usually enough for two or three of these relations to pass the significance test by mere happenstance, according to the Australian economist and data mining critic John Quiggin. "If you look for a statistically relevant correlation qualifying for scientific publication, this strategy works wonders," he points out. There is an almost insuperable problem in debunking data mining approaches: When a scientist submits an empirical research paper, it is impossible to check how many streams of data he may have analyzed before he discovered the seemingly significant correlation through data mining.

But how do you detect data mining? With Krämer's "divided by five, balance of one effect," a theoretical explanation for the phenomenon is improbable, leaving enough room for suspicion. Yet how about the following study, which proves an effect of sports results on the stock market direction? Alex Edmans of the Sloan School of Management, Diego Garcia of the Tuck School of Business, Dartmouth, and Øyvind Norli of the Norwegian School of Management evaluated 1,100 international soccer matches since 1973 for 39 countries. What they found was that on the day following a defeat suffered by the national home team, prices on the exchange were 0.38 percent lower than could have been expected on average. For countries where soccer is not as popular, they proved similar but weaker effects in an analysis of 1,500 cricket, rugby, ice hockey and basketball matches.

Is this data mining, or did the researchers really unearth psychological mood effects on the exchanges? The expert advisers at the *Journal of Finance* seem to side with the latter. After all, the authors provided a rather plausible cause-and-effect hypothesis explaining the phenomenon: When in a good mood, traders and investors might be more inclined to buy—while backing off when sentiment plummets. Yet only defeats had a measurable effect on market direction; victories seemingly failed to push quotes to higher levels.

Before bothering with the plausibility of a finding, the critical reader ought to ask how many similar data sets the author may have had at his disposal, in order to select those rendering the desired result. In stock price studies, there will typically be a wealth of them.

To recognize potential data mining, you should ask yourself: Is it plausible the authors have started out with a hypothesis that was empirically verified, or is it just as likely that they have crafted or modified their hypothesis following the uncovering of a correlation? When someone writes a research paper explaining that male left-handers with a college degree earn more than right-handers of identical background, always remember that the author has probably also searched for correlations regarding the incomes of women, of other age groups, and generally of all possible combination of characteristics; if only one or two of these subsets showed significant correlations of income and left-handedness, the likelihood of an accidental correlation is very high.

Even economists considered experts in certain sub-disciplines and who are called upon to critique and review studies in top-flight economic journals are sometimes forced to admit defeat. A case in point is the controversy over whether the increase in obesity in the United States is causally linked to the concurrent decline in smoking. In an essay published by the leading *Journal of Health Economics*, MIT health economists Jonathan Gruber and Michael Frakes "refute" an analysis result by Shin-Yi Chou, Michael Grossman and Henry Saffer published in the same journal two years earlier. Gruber and Frakes retrace how a quite ordinary tweaking and retweaking of methodology can massively impact econometric results.

Chou and his coauthors had found that the spread of obesity is, indeed, an undesirable side effect of less smoking. Gruber and Frakes analyzed the same data using the same methods and arrived at the same results. This confirms the accuracy of the process. But with just the slightest changes of methodology the results fell apart.

Chou, Grossman and Saffer had compared the level and change in cigarette prices in individual U.S. states to the average weight of the states' residents. Ideally, this would enable researchers to isolate the impact of smoking on weight: If an extraordinary increase in cigarette prices concurs with the incidence of obesity in a statistically significant way, it is an indication of a fundamental causal relation.

In order to isolate the effect, however, scientists had to bring to bear an array of so-called control variables. For instance, they will have to adjust the data for the general tendency toward weight increase irrespective of smoking habits, or for the fact that there is more obesity in some states than in others. And precisely these methodical details have enormous significance for the outcome. A different approach offsetting the general tendency toward obesity is, in and by itself, sufficient to reduce the statistically captured effect of cigarette prices by half. Yet more dramatic are the effects when looking at tobacco taxes instead of cigarette prices: In that case, results are even reversed—suggesting that higher tobacco taxes will reduce, not increase, obesity.

The Economics of Erring

In their work, economists do not just do a lot of tweaking—sometimes they plainly fall victim to miscalculation. A notorious example is a paper by Harvard professor Martin Feldstein published in the respected *Journal of Political Economy* in 1974. Feldstein had found that Americans saved only half of what they used to because of U.S. social policies. One of the central tenets of Milton Friedman seemed verified: People will optimize consumption and savings rationally across their entire life cycle. At least for six years it did—until economists Dean Leimer and Selig Lesnoy attempted to reproduce Feldstein's results in detail. What they found was that the scientist had miscalculated. A programming error had heavily skewed his results upward. Feldstein admitted the mistake and apologized.

While independent experts will screen working papers prior to publication in academic journals, these "referees" cannot verify each number, especially since mathematical methods are highly complex and the devil is often in the details. "Reviewers are usually not expected to reproduce all regressions. They usually trust the authors," points out Bruce McCullough, professor in decision sciences at Drexel University in Philadelphia. Christopher L. Foote and Christopher F. Goetz, two economists at the Boston Federal Reserve, found another crucial error in a highly publicized paper. In a study that appeared in the *Quarterly Journal of Economics (QJE)* in 2001, the economists John Donohue and Steven Levitt came to the conclusion that the main reason for the decline in crime rates in the United States, a trend starting in the nineties, was the new legislation on abortions passed in 1973. Unwanted children, so the argument went, often grow up in difficult social environments and are likely to enter a life of crime when reaching adulthood. Foote and Goetz proved Levitt and Donohue's calculations to have deviated from the statistical methods portrayed as modus operandi in the text—the *QJE* referees had overlooked that. When calculating correctly they found "no compelling evidence that abortion has a selection effect on crime."

The only way to find those mistakes is "replication," as scientists call it—the effort on the part of other researchers to duplicate the results of a study by use of the same or comparable data. It should be stated, though, that economists only rarely buckle down to test their peers' studies inside and out. "Economists treat replication the way teenagers treat chastity—as an ideal to be professed but not to be practiced," writes economist Daniel Hamermesh of the University of Texas at Austin.

Stan Liebowitz, economics professor at the University of Dallas in Texas, is one of the few who will do the tedious work of replicating others' findings. Liebowitz delved into a study by economists Felix Oberholzer-Gee and Koleman Strumpf, two economists of the universities of Harvard and Kansas, on the effect of music exchanges on sales of music CDs. The astonishing finding had been that music exchanges are not to blame for the massive decline in sales of music labels; the study was published in the *Journal of Political Economy (JPE)*. The music industry, already haunting the exchanges and their customers with lawsuits over copyright violations, was in an uproar.

The two researchers' work had been based on internal statistics on music downloads, which they had obtained from music exchanges. Even before *JPE* went to press with the article, Liebowitz intervened with the responsible editor of the journal. In a letter he criticized the authors for not granting him an opportunity to verify the results, which had been published in a working paper beforehand, despite repeated requests on his part. Liebowitz asked the editor to exert his influence and make this verification possible. He also took issue with methodological weaknesses and contradictions in the work by Oberholzer-Gee and Strumpf. The letter was ignored, the study appeared with minor alterations.

Liebowitz wrote an extensive comment on the article, pointing out what he considered factual errors and misleading claims.

The same *JPE* editor who had ignored his first letter rejected the publication of Liebowitz's comment, even though an independent referee had sided with Liebowitz, concluding that the claims made by the authors were not supported by the evidence they had presented. The editor, however, based his rejection on the argument brought forward by the authors with a hefty dose of chutzpa. The authors and the editor claimed that Liebowitz's comment did not strike at the regression, which was at the core of the paper—a regression that is firmly protected by the refusal of the authors to share their data.

The episode is symptomatic of two problems existing on the economic journal scene. Most journals hardly bother to ascertain that published empirical works are verifiable and thereby meet the standards of science. In addition, the standards governing conflicts of interest are relatively lax compared to natural sciences. This is even true for top journals. Some changes are underway. In 1999, H. D. Vinod and Bruce McCullough attempted to replicate the results of all the articles in an issue of the *American Economic Review (AER)*. AER had a requirement at the time that authors had to provide data for replication purposes. Half of the authors refused to fulfill their commitment. They did not provide their data and codes upon request.

Other journals had an even worse record. When the two economists published their results in 2003, the current Federal Reserve chairman, Ben Bernanke, was the editor of *AER*. He reacted by establishing a mandatory data and code archive for *AER*. Other top journals, including the *Journal of Political Economy,* followed. Before a paper is published in such a journal, the author must now provide the journal with the data and the computer code. The journal then makes them available to third parties who want to check them.

Now it all depends on how and when editors will put the tightened rules into practice.

References

Chou, Shin-Yi, Michael Grossman and Henry Saffer (2004): "An Economic Analysis of Adult Obesity: Results from the Behavioral Risk Factor Surveillance System," in: *Journal of Health Economics*, Vol. 23, pp. 565–587.

Donohue, John J., III, and Steven D. Levitt (2001): "The Impact of Legalized Abortion on Crime," in: *Quarterly Journal of Economics*, Vol. 116, pp. 379–420.

Donohue, John J., III, and Steven D. Levitt (2008): "Measurement Error, Legalized Abortion, and the Decline in Crime: A Response to Foote and Goetz," in: *Quarterly Journal of Economics*, Vol. 123, February, pp. 425–440.

Edmans, Alex, Diego, Garcia and Øyvind Norli (2007): "Sports Sentiment6 and Stock Returns," *Journal of Finance*, Vol. 62, pp. 1967–1998.

Feldstein, Martin (1974): "Social Security, Induced Retirement and Aggregate Capital Accumulation," in: *Journal of Political Economy*, Vol. 82, pp. 905–926.

Feldstein, Martin (1982): "Social Security and Private Saving: Reply," in: *Journal of Political Economy* Vol. 90, pp. 630–642.

Foote, Christopher and Christopher Goetz (2008): "The Impact of Legalized Abortion on Crime: Comment," in: *Quarterly Journal of Economics*, Vol. 123, pp. 407–423.

Gandal, Neil, Sonia Roccas, Lilach Sagiv and Amy Wrzesniewski (2005): "Personal Value Priorities of Economists," in *Human Relations*, Vol. 58, pp. 1227–1252.

Gruber, Jonathan and Michael Frakes (2006): "Does Falling Smoking Lead to Rising Obesity?," in: *Journal of Health Economics*, Vol. 25, pp. 183–197.

Hamermesh, Daniel (2007): "Viewpoint: Replication in Economics," in: *Canadian Journal of Economics*, Vol. 40, pp 715–733.

Krämer, Walter and Gerd Gigerenzer (2005): "How to Confuse with Statistics," in: *Statistical Science* Vol. 20, pp 223–230.

Leimer, Dean, and Selig Lesnoy (1982) "Social Security and Private Saving: New Time-Series Evidence," in: *Journal of Political Economy*, Vol. 90, pp. 606–629.

Liebowitz, Stan J. (2007): "How Reliable is the Oberholzer-Gee and Strumpf Paper on File-Sharing?" Working paper.

Acknowledgments

Our thanks go to the scientists who have enriched mankind with the insights represented here. Special thanks are due to those who endured our persistent inquiries with the patience of saints. Our gratitude also goes to Frank Katzenmayer, who provided the original idea for the book, and Bernd Ziesemer, the *Handelsblatt* editor-in-chief. Without his encouragement, we would never have succumbed to the productive illusion that normal people could find the subject of economics actually quite exciting. Jutta Scherer (in cooperation with her colleague Klaus Beyer) did a superb job translating our writings under an impossibly tight deadline. Editor Laurie Harting and production editor Yasmin Mathew did everything humanly possible to make this an enjoyable book despite our shortcomings.

—*Norbert Häring* and *Olaf Storbeck,*
December 2008

About the Authors

Norbert Häring

grew up on a farm in the southern German region of Swabia, where people talk with a cute accent, which is as hard to understand as it is to get rid of. Were it not for that highly engaged grammar school teacher pushing him to seek a college education, he could have become a farmer, another example of how a low socio-economic background keeps you from having to work in artificially lit offices later in life, as described in chapter 3 of this book. He is an incorrigible skeptic, says his beloved American wife, Marianne. She is better educated and smarter and also makes more money, but gracefully conforms to the stereotype described in chapter 4, which involves doing more housework, anyway. He is incredibly proud of his children, Clio and Jeremy, who show every sign that they have higher IQs and abilities, as they should according to chapter 3—except maybe in playing backgammon. Norbert studied the neo-classics inside out and obtained a Ph.D. in economics, ingesting many valuable eternal truths, which have since been shown to be false. His academic claim to fame is the scientific proof that it is possible to publish thoroughly inconsequential results in a fairly well-respected journal. After stints as an economic analyst and a PR associate at *Commerzbank* and later as a journalist at *Boersen-Zeitung* and the *Financial Times Deutschland,* Norbert now writes from Frankfurt for the leading business daily *Handelsblatt* on economics, monetary policy and financial markets. On his initiative, prominent European economists joined to form the ECB Shadow Council. Since 2002, the council dispenses regular policy advice for the European Central Bank to consider and disregard.

Olaf Storbeck

is a child of the Ruhr Valley, the old and struggling industrial heart of western Germany. In 1974, when Olaf was born, the last coal mine closed down in his hometown. Olaf doesn't doubt the finding that watching too much TV does not make you happy, as described in chapter 2. Hence he and his wife, Katharina—who works as journalist herself—decided to get rid of their television set a few years ago. He also knows from painful personal experience that people tend to pay a lot of money not to go to the gym. Upon graduation from college, faced with the question: Should I study what's fun to me (history) or something holding greater promise of gainful employment—that is, economics? The Cologne School of Journalism made the choice easy for him. After passing the entrance exam, there was no doubt left: As mandated by the school, he was destined to study economics at the University of Cologne. Over the course of his studies he began to realize that economics is anything but a burdensome exercise that must be stoically endured. Cologne professor Susanne Wied-Nebbeling played a large part in this revelation. But Olaf still preferred journalism to science. He declined a research assistant job offer and joined the *Handelsblatt* daily in 2001. There, he wrote on business topics, later on the business cycle and economic policy. In 2005, he introduced a science section for *Handelsblatt* that is exclusively dedicated to the fields of economics and business management.

Index

advertising, 175–7, 181–2, 210–11
Africa, 24, 67–8, 71–2, 106–9, 175, 215
Aghion, Philippe, 102–3
Akerlof, George, 13–14
Allen, Franklin, 123–4
altruism, 3–4, 78, 219
Amazon, 172–3
American Economic Association (AEA), 13, 57
American Economic Review, 40, 143, 192, 204, 227
American Indians, 81–2
Amiti, Mary, 104
analysts, 113–23, 209–10; and conflicts of interest, 118–21 forecasts of, 121–3; and the herd instinct, 116–18
anthropometrics, 81–90. *See also* attractiveness; height
Ariely, Dan, 165–7
Ashcraft, Adam, 134–5
Asia, 82, 93–4, 104, 215
Assenmacher-Wesche, Katrin, 138–9
attractiveness, 18–19, 88–90
Australia, 49, 222
Austria, 79, 123

Bailey, Martha, 59–60
Bandiera, Oriana, 11
Barankay, Iwan, 11

Barker, David, 87
Barro, Robert, 74
Baur, Marieluise, 83
Bear Stearns, 130, 141
Becker, Gary, 22, 24–6, 60, 72
Becker, Sascha, 49–51
behavioral economics, xiv, 10, 13, 158–9
Benabou, Roland, 77–8
Bentham, Jeremy, 19
Bernanke, Ben, 227
Bewley, Truman, 39
Bhaskar, V., 190–2
Bible studies, 49–52
Biddle, Jeff, 88
birth control pill, 59–60
Blanchard, Olivier, 34–6
Bloom, Nicholas, 154–6
BMW, 153
Bradbury, J. C., 188
Brakman, Steven, 105–6
brand, 179–80
Brandts, Jordi, 161–3
Bretton Woods II, 144
Broda, Christian, 99–100
Brunnermeier, Markus, 130, 133–4, 141
Bush, George W., 75, 212–14

Cain, Daylian, 121
Calomiris, Charles W., 141–2
Camerer, Colin, 4–5

Canada, 82
Card, David, 40–3, 46
Carlson, Mark, 207
Case, Anne, 87–8
"catching up with the Joneses," 3,
    18–19, 25, 159, 193–4
Catholics, 50–1, 74–5
Cerra, Valerie, 143
Chatterjee, Santanu, 109
Chetty, Raj, 37–8
chief executive officers (CEOs), 147,
    150–3, 163–7
children, 8–9, 46–9, 81, 86–8
China, 96–7, 100–2, 105, 144
Chou, Shin-Yi, 224
Cinnirella, Francesco, 84
Clark, Andrew, 18
coaches, 194–6
Cohen, Jonathan, 5
commutes, 27–8, 30
comparative advantage, 97–100
competition, 3, 5, 65–8, 100–5, 201
computers, xv, 94, 105
contrarian investing, 123
communication, 161–3
Cooper, David, 161–3
Cooper, Michael, 202–3
cooperation, 1–4, 8
coordination failures, 161
corruption, 71–2, 206
credit cards, 6–7
creditworthiness, 207–8
cricket, 190–2
crime, 46, 78, 225–6
culture, 71–80; and corruption,
    71–2; and prosperity, 75–6. *See
    also* religion

da Gama, Vasco, 93
data mining, 221–2
De Grauwe, Paul, 95–6
Deaton, Angus, 24, 26–7
Debaere, Peter, 97–8

decision making, 5–6, 13–15
Degeorge, François, 209
Dell'Ariccia, Giovanni, 132
Della Vigna, Stefano, 173–5,
    212–13
Denmark, 36, 149–50
Derrien, François, 209
Dichev, Ilia, 126–7
Dickens, William, 49
Donohue, John, 225–6
Dooley, Michael, 144–5
dotcom bubble, 118, 137–8
Draca, Mirko, 43
Easterlin, Richard, 17–19, 26
Easterlin Paradox, 17–19, 26
eBay, 169–73
economics. *See* behavioral
    economics; economists;
    experimental economics;
    Homo oeconomicus;
    macroeconomics; neoclassical
    economics; neuro-economics
economies of scale, 98–9
economists, ix–xi, xv–xvi, 1–2, 13,
    17–18, 35, 38–41, 47–8, 56–7,
    72–3, 79, 217–27; and errors,
    225–7; and influence, 217–18;
    and politicians, 35, 220. *See
    also* data mining; statistics
Edmans, Alex, 222–3
Edwards, Albert, 116
Egypt, 71–2
employees, 11–12, 38–9, 45, 62,
    89–90, 149–50, 158–62; and
    mergers, 149–50; motivating,
    158–60; performance, 11–12
employers, 11–12, 38–9, 58, 89–90,
    158–62. *See also* managers
Estrada, Javier, 125
Europe, 23, 28–9, 33–6, 38, 43,
    56–9, 73, 75–8, 82–4, 93–8,
    140, 155–6, 214–16; and drugs,

95–6; employment, and women, 56–8; health care system, 83; and height, 82–4; and the IMF, 214–16; managers, 155–6; spice trade, 93–4; work hours, 33, 56
evolution, 24–7
experimental economics, xii-xiv, 10

Faccio, Mara, 204–7
Faini, Riccardo, 214–16
fairness, 2–3, 11, 45, 77, 180
Falk, Armin, 3, 9, 11–12, 44–6
Fama, Eugene, 111, 117
fast food industry, 40–3, 83, 147–8
Federal Reserve System, 130, 134, 137–44, 207, 227
Fehr, Ernst, 1, 4–5, 44–6
Feldstein, Martin, 225
Ferguson, Thomas, 203
Fernández, Raquel, 73
financial markets, 78–80, 111–27, 129–45 fluctuations of, 125–6 stock returns, 126–7. *See also* analysts; contrarian investing; market efficiency; price bubbles; rating agencies; Sharpe ratio; subprime mortgage crisis
Firestone, 11–12
Fisman, Raymond, 71–2
Flynn, James, 49
Fogli, Alessandra, 73
Foote, Christopher L., 225–6
Folkerts-Landau, David, 144–5
football, 188–90
foreign aid, 108–9
Fox News, 212–14
Frakes, Michael, 224
framing effects, 175–7
France, 33, 36, 41–2, 155–6
Frank, André Gunder, 93
Freeman, Richard, 56, 58, 60–1
Friedman, Milton, 14, 141
Friedman, Thomas L., 105, 130

Frey, Bruno, 29–30, 193
Fudenberg, Drew, 5–6

Gabaix, Xavier, 163–5
Galor, Oded, 51–2
game theory, xii-xiv, 190–3
Gandal, Neil, 219
Garber, Peter, 144–5
Garcia, Diego, 222–3
Garicano, Luis, 196–7
gender roles, 60–1, 64, 67–8
Gerlach, Stefan, 138–9
German Council of Economic Advisors, 41–2
Germany, 33, 39–42, 50, 56, 59, 72, 79, 84–5, 103–4, 129, 155–6, 179, 194, 196, 198–9, 203–4
Gibbs, Michael, 149–50
Giuliano, Paola, 109
globalization, 78, 93–109; and competition, 102–5; and drugs, 95–6; and shrimp, 96–7
Gneezy, Uri, 7–8, 65–8
Goetz, Christopher F., 225–6
Golder, Peter, 177–9
Goldin, Claudia, 57–8
Google, 208–10
Great Britain, 28, 52, 87, 96, 155–6, 191–2, 199
Greenspan, Alan, 137–40, 142
Grilli, Enzo, 214–16
Grossman, Michael, 224
Gruber, Jonathan, 224
Grund, Christian, 195–6
Guiso, Luigi, 74–5, 78–80, 113–14
Gulen, Huseyin, 202–3
Gürtler, Oliver, 195–6

Haifang, Huang, 31
Hale, Galina, 207
Hamermesh, Daniel, 88, 226

happiness, 17–30; and commutes, 27–8, 30; and evolution, 24–7; and income, 17–18, 22, 27–8, 30; and the television, 29; and U-index, 26–7
Harris, Lawrence, 112–13
heart surgeons, 156–8
Heckman, James, 46–8
height, 81–3, 86–8
Hein, Oliver, 122
Helliwell, John, 31
Hemenway, David, 18–19
hidden online advertising, 181–2
Hilary, Giles, 115
Hirsch, Boris, 62
Hitler, Adolf, 203–5
Homburg, Christian, 179–80
Homo oeconomicus, xiv, 2–3, 6–9, 12, 72, 111, 175, 217, 220; and children, 8–9. *See also* "ultimatum game"
Hoyzer, Robert, 198
Huckman, Robert, 156–8
human capital, 51–2, 58, 158
hunter-gatherers, 25–6

Ierulli, Kathryn, 149–50
Igan, Deniz, 132
immigration, 73, 82
incentives, 7–8, 10–12, 36–7, 72, 158–9, 162–7, 187–8, 193–4, 196–9; side effects of, 193–4, 196–7
income, 17–20, 22, 27–8, 35–6, 39, 62, 82–3, 86–90, 163–7, 193–4; and attractiveness, 88–90; and CEOs, 163–7; and happiness, 17–18; and height, 82–3, 86–8; and utility, 19–20
India, 24, 67–8, 93–4, 96, 144, 165–6
Indonesia, 104, 204
Industrial Revolution, 48–52, 94

inflation, 14, 40, 124
initial public offering (IPO), 208–10
Institute of International Finance, 140
intelligence, 48–9, 87–8
interest rates, 122, 132, 137–9, 145
International Monetary Fund (IMF), 34, 129, 131–3, 137, 140, 143, 214–16
Iran, 24
Iraq, 75
Israel, 7, 51–2, 65–7
Italy, 75, 79, 113–14

Japan, 97, 101–3, 214–15
Jappelli, Tullio, 113–14
Jegadeesh, Narasimhan, 116–18
Journal of Political Economy, 37, 189, 225–7

Kahneman, Daniel, 20–1, 26
Kaplan, Ethan, 212–13
Kaya, Ilker, 109
Kenya, 24, 108–9
Kern, Markus, 194
Keys, Benjamin, 133
Keynes, John Maynard, 13, 49, 123
Kiff, John, 131, 140
Kim, Woojin, 116–18
Klaassen, Franc, 187
Kocher, Martin, 8–9, 198
Köhler, Horst, 129
Komlos, John, 81, 83–4
Konings, Jozef, 104
Kosfeld, Michael, 12
Krämer, Walter, 221
Krueger, Alan, 11, 40–3, 46
Krugman, Paul, 98–9, 165

labor markets, 10, 33–52, 56, 60–2, 89, 188; and beauty, 89; and women, 56, 60–2. *See also* minimum wage; unemployment
Laeven, Luc, 132

Laibson, David, 5
Landier, Augustin, 163–5
Latin America, 82, 215
Layard, Richard, 22–3, 27
Leamer, Edward, 144
Leimer, Dean, 225
Lee, Hahn, 170–1
Leonhard, Kenneth, 67–8
Lesnoy, Selig, 225
Leuz, Christian, 204–5
Levine, David, 5–6
Levitt, Steven, 225–6
Liebowitz, Stan, 226–7
List, John, 67–8
literacy, 50–2
Loewenstein, George, 4–5, 121,
    165–7

Machin, Stephen, 43
macroeconomics, 13–14, 74, 80,
    123, 142
Magnus, Jan, 187
Malmendier, Ulrike, 118–19, 151,
    170–1, 173–5
managers, 147–67; and
    communication, 161–3; and
    external knowledge, 147–9;
    good managers, 154–6; and
    mistakes, 152–4; and
    motivation, 158–60; and
    overconfidence, 147, 150–2. *See
    also* chief executive officers;
    outsourcing
market capitalization, 164, 203
market efficiency, 111–13, 117
marketing, 169, 175–82. *See also*
    advertising; brand
Marx, Karl, 52
Mas, Alexandre, 11
Mason, Joseph, 135
mathematics, xiv-xv, 77
Mayzlin, Dina, 181–2
McCleary, Rachel, 74

McCullough, Bruce, 225
media, 210–14
Menon, Tanya, 147–8
Menzly, Lior, 115
mergers, 149–51
Metcalf, David, 43
Mian, Atif, 132
Miguel, Edward, 71–2
Mill, John Stuart, 19
Mills, Paul, 131, 140
minimum wage, 39–46; defense of,
    39–44; side-effects of, 44–6
Mishkin, Frederic, 138, 140, 142–4
Mitra, Debanjan, 177–9
mixed strategy, 192
Moav, Omer, 51–2
Mobius, Markus, 89–90
Moore, Don, 121
moral hazard, 37, 141–2
Morris, Stephen, 123–4
Morton, Fiona Scott, 183–4
motivation, 7–8, 10, 13, 15, 47,
    158–63
Mukherjee, Tammoy, 133
Murdoch, Rupert, 212–14
Muslims, 74–5

Nazi Party (NSDAP), 203
neoclassical economics, 10, 13–14,
    29, 37
Netherlands, 79, 82–3, 187
Neumark, David, 41, 44
neuro-economics, xiv, 1, 4–7, 158–60
Niederle, Muriel, 65–7
Norli, Øyvind, 222–3
Nunn, Nathan, 106–8

O'Connor, Sandra Day, 55–6, 58
O'Rourke, Kevin, 93–5
Oberholzer-Gee, Felix, 204–5, 226
obesity, 85, 224
Obstfeld, Maurice, 98
Ockenfels, Axel, 170–3

Organization for Economic
    Co-operation and Development
    (OECD), 40, 102
Oswald, Andrew, 28
outsourcing, 156–8
Ovtchinnikov, Alexei, 202–3
oxytocin, 4–5

Palacios-Huerta, Ignacio, 196–7
Parsley, David, 205–7
Paxson, Christina, 87–8
Pfeffer, Jeffrey, 147–8
Pisano, Gary, 156–8
Pischetsrieder, Bernd, 153
political patronage, 201–7
Portugal, 34–5, 94
Prelec, Drazen, 4–5
Prescott, Edward, 34
price bubbles, 123–4, 137–8. See
    also dotcom bubble; subprime
    mortgage crisis
price search engines, 183–4
Prince, Chuck, 134
principal-agent relationship, 197–9
Protestants, 50–1, 74–5
psychology, xiv, 1, 7–8, 20–1, 27–8,
    45–9, 57, 66, 148–9, 151, 160,
    175–7, 223
punishment, 3–4

quality, 177–9
Quiggin, John, 222

Rasul, Imran, 11
rating agencies, 134–7, 207–8
rationality, 2–3, 5, 13, 29, 111,
    117, 175–8
Rayo, Luis, 24–6
Reagan, Ronald, 55
reciprocal behavior, 3, 9–12
referees, 197–9
regulation, 139–42
Reinhart, Carmen, 143–4

relative compensation systems, 10–11
religion, 74–5. See also Catholics;
    Protestants; Muslims
Reuter, Jonathan, 210–12
rewards, 3–4, 77, 158–63. See also
    incentives
Ricardo, David, 96–8
Rickman, Neil, 198–9
Rissanen, Aila, 85
Roccas, Sonia, 219
Rogoff, Kenneth, 140, 143–4
Romer, David, 189–90
Rosenblat, Tanya, 89
Rosner, Joshua, 135
Roth, Alvin, 171–3
Runde, Ralf, 221
Russia, 96, 204
Rustichini, Aldo, 7–8, 65–7

Saffer, Henry, 224
Sagiv, Lilach, 219
Sala-i-Martin, Xavier, 106
Sapienza, Paola, 74–5, 78–80
Saxena, Sweta Chaman, 143
Schank, Thorsten, 62
Schettkat, Ronald, 56, 58
Schnabel, Claus, 62
Schott, Peter, 100–2
Schuermann, Til, 134–5
Schwartz, Anna, 141
Securities and Exchange
    Commission (SEC), 112
securitization, 130–6
self-discipline, 26, 173–5
selfishness, 1–4, 8, 10, 13, 29, 153,
    198, 201, 219–20
Sen, Amartya, 22–4, 26
Seru, Amit, 133
Shanthikumar, Devin, 118–19
Sharpe ratio, 113–14
Shiller, Robert, 144
Shin, Hyun Song, 123–4
Silva-Risso, Jorge, 183–4

slavery, 106–8
Sliwka, Dirk, 152–3
Smeets, Valerie, 149–50
Smith, Adam, 19, 201
smoking, 86, 224
soccer, 193–4, 196–9
social interaction, 1, 2, 8–9
social security, 37, 56, 62, 77
Solnick, Sara, 18–19
Sørensen, Thorkild, 85
Storti, Claudia Costa, 95–6
Spain, 34–5, 196–8
Spiwoks, Markus, 122
sports, 187–99, 222–3. See also
    coaches; cricket; football;
    referees; soccer; tennis
statistics, 217–25
status, 18, 23, 147–8
Steckel, Richard, 83–4
Stigler, George, 72
stigma theory, 66
Strumpf, Koleman, 226
Stutzer, Alois, 30
Süßmuth, Bernd, 194
subprime mortgage crisis, 129–45.
    See also Federal Reserve
    System; rating agencies;
    regulation; securitization
Sufi, Amir, 132
Sunder, Marco, 84–5
supply and demand, 40, 43, 95–6,
    208
Sutter, Matthias, 8–9, 198
Sweden, 79
Switzerland, 29, 44, 72

Tabellini, Guido, 75–6
Tanzania, 67–8
Tate, Geoffrey, 151–2
Taylor, John, 137
tennis, 192–3
Thailand, 97–8
Tirole, Jean, 77–8

trade, 93–109; restrictions, 97–8.
    See also comparative advantage
transportation, 93–5, 105–6
trust, 1, 4–5, 8–9, 12, 31, 36, 74–5,
    78–80
Turner, Henry, 203

"ultimatum game," 2–3
unemployment, 10, 14, 28, 33–8,
    40, 46–9, 132, 142; benefits,
    36; and kindergarten, 46–9
United Kingdom, 22, 43,
    102–3, 155
United Nations, 71–2, 95
United States, 17, 24, 28, 33, 36–7,
    39–43, 46–8, 56–9, 73, 76–9,
    82–5, 95–101, 104–5, 116,
    129–45, 152, 155–6, 164–5,
    177–9, 181, 188, 201–3, 206,
    212–16, 224; and China, 100–1;
    and drugs, 95–6; employment,
    and women, 56–9; happiness, 17;
    heath care system, 24, 83; and
    height, 82–3; and the IMF,
    214–16; labor markets,
    39–40; managers in, 155–6;
    optimism in, 76–8; and
    unemployment, 36; wages, 39;
    work hours, 33, 56. See also
    football; Fox News; subprime
    mortgage crisis
utility, 17, 19–20

van Marrewijk, Charles, 105–6
van Reenen, John, 43, 154–6
Varian, Hal R., 169
Vig, Vikrant, 133
von Mises, Ludwig, 123
Voth, Hans-Joachim, 203
wage cuts, 38–9
wages, 10–11, 14, 34, 38–46,
    89–90. See also minimum
    wage; wage cuts

Walker, Mark, 192–3
Wascher, William, 41, 44
Weber, Max, 50, 74–5
Weel, Bas ter, 194–5
weight, and lifespan, 84–6
Weinstein, David, 99–100
Welch, Ivo, 116
Whalen, Christopher, 139
Williamson, Jeffrey, 93–5
winner's curse, 169–71
Witt, Robert, 198–9
Wittgenstein, Ludwig, 25
Woessmann, Ludger, 49–51
women, 55–68, 73, 75, 86, 89–90;
    and competition, 65–8;
    emancipation of, 57–60; and
income, 61–2; and negotiation,
    62–5; and weight, 86. *See also*
    gender roles
Wooders, John, 192–3
Womack, Kent, 209
work hours, 23, 33–4
World Bank, 214–16
World Soccer Association (FIFA), 196
World Trade Organization, 104
World War II, 58, 142–3
Wrzesniewski, Amy, 219

Zehnder, Christian, 44–6
Zettelmeyer, Florian, 183–4
Zingales, Luigi, 74–5, 78–80
Zitzewitz, Eric, 210–12